THE GREAT BRITISH
BAKE OFF
BIG BOOK OF BAKING

THE GREAT BRITISH BAKE OFF
BIG BOOK OF BAKING

LINDA COLLISTER

INCLUDES RECIPES BY

MARY BERRY & PAUL HOLLYWOOD

BBC
BOOKS

THIS BOOK IS PUBLISHED TO ACCOMPANY THE TELEVISION SERIES ENTITLED THE GREAT
BRITISH BAKE OFF, FIRST BROADCAST ON BBC ONE IN 2014.

LOVE
productions

Executive Producer: Anna Beattie
Series Producer: Samantha Beddoes
Series Director: Andy Devonshire
Producers: Chloe Avery, Jake Senior, Hannah Griffiths, Helen Cawley, Mark Drake
Home Economists: Becca Watson, Georgia May, Faenia Moore
Commercial Director: Rupert Frisby
BBC Commissioning Exec: Emma Willis

1 3 5 7 9 10 8 6 4 2

Published in 2014 by BBC Books, an imprint of Ebury Publishing.
A Random House Group Company.

Text and recipes © Love Productions 2014
Photography and design © Woodlands Books Ltd 2014

The Random House Group Limited Reg. No. 954009

Addresses for companies within the Random House Group can be found at
www.randomhouse.co.uk

A CIP catalogue record for this book is available from the British Library.

ISBN 978 1 849 90483 4

The Random House Group Limited supports the Forest Stewardship Council® (FSC®), the leading
international forest certification organisation. All our titles that are printed on Greenpeace
approved FSC® certified paper carry the FSC® logo. Our paper procurement policy can be found
at
www.randomhouse.co.uk/environment

Editorial Director: Lizzy Gray
Project Editor: Louise McKeever
Copy-editor: Norma MacMillan
Design: Allies Design, Susanna Cook & Maeve Bargman
Photography: Kristin Perers and Mark Bourdillon pages 125, 319
Food Stylists: Annie Hudson and Annie Rigg
Cover Food Stylist: Lizzie Kamenetkzy
Props Stylist: Jo Harris
Production: Helen Everson and Beccy Jones

Colour origination by Altaimage, London.
Printed and bound in Germany by Mohn Media GmbH.

To buy books by your favourite authors and register for offers, visit
www.randomhouse.co.uk

CONTENTS

INTRODUCTION

MEETING THIS YEAR'S BAKERS IS
HEART WARMING: THEY ARE ALL TRUE
AMATEURS – THEY BAKE FOR THE SHEER
LOVE OF IT. WHETHER THE CONTESTANTS
HAVE PICKED UP THEIR BAKING SKILLS
FROM GRANDPARENTS, PARENTS, FROM
SCHOOL OR ARE COMPLETELY SELF-
TAUGHT, ALL OUR BAKERS KNOW THAT
ANYONE CAN LEARN SOME SIMPLE
BAKING SKILLS AND ENJOY DELICIOUS
HOME-MADE MEALS AND TREATS.

Apart from the pleasure of watching the faces of loved ones light up as you share your bakes, there are many other joys to home cooking: kneading and shaping bread dough is thoroughly relaxing after a day at work and decorating a cake or icing biscuits is very satisfying – plus you get a great loaf or tasty afternoon snacks.

Baking turns the produce from another favourite hobby, gardening, into gloriously healthy and appealing meals: imagine how good it would be to have a bowl of vegetable soup with Jordan's Rye and Spelt Rolls or to fill the Ciabatta Rolls from Paul's Technical Challenge with homegrown salad?

If you are fairly new to baking there is plenty of advice and lots of ideas to get you started, and you won't need expensive ingredients or equipment. Experts Paul Hollywood and Mary Berry pass on their wealth of knowledge – and many wonderful recipes. Have a go at Paul's Savoury Biscuits or Mary's classic Cherry Cake. Many of the recipes come with step-by-step pictures to guide you to success.

On the other hand, if you already enjoy the challenges of baking and are keen to master some new techniques, and find out how to use new ingredients, you can bake along with Mary and Paul as they show you how it's done in the masterclasses. Mary has some impressive cakes: her Showstopper Doboz Torte, made from 12 cake layers, will thrill seasoned bakers; and the Swedish favourite, Prinsesstarta is bound to wow baking clubs. Our bakers produced some humdingers too: such as Nancy's stunning Summer Pudding Alaska and Iain's flavourful Moroccan Plait.

Be inspired by this year's batch of lovely bakers; watch their progress and see their confidence grow from week one to the final as they tackle those tricky challenges.

The Great British Bake Off: Big Book of Baking includes much-loved favourites, some with a new twist, and plenty of brand-new baking ideas to try out in the kitchen. So if you're after something to surprise and delight for a once-in-a-lifetime occasion, would like a mouth-watering savoury bake for dinner or simply want a great slice of home-made cake for a mid-afternoon tea break, now's the perfect time to grab a mixing bowl, pick up a spoon and get baking!

A BAKER'S GUIDE

Here are explanations for the common terms and techniques that appear in this book.

WHAT DOES IT MEAN?

FOLD: This is a way to delicately combine 2 (or more) ingredients so you don't knock out all the air you've carefully beaten or whisked into a mixture – for example, adding sifted flour to a creamed mixture of butter, eggs and sugar for a cake. A large metal spoon or a plastic spatula is best for folding. Turn the spoon so one side cuts down through the mixture. When you touch the bottom of the bowl, turn the spoon upwards and draw it up through the mixture to the top, then flip the spoon over so the mixture flops on to the surface. Give the bowl a quarter turn (so you start folding from a different place) and repeat. Keep lightly cutting, lifting and flopping over until you cannot see any streaks of unmixed ingredients. Use the least number of folding movements possible.

RUB IN: This is how you combine butter and flour when making pastry and simple cake mixtures. Use the fingertips and thumbs of both hands – try to keep your palms clean (your fingertips are cooler). Pick up a little of the butter and flour mixture, lift your hands up to the top of the bowl and gently rub your fingers and thumbs together so the mixture is combined as it falls back down into the bowl. Continue doing this until the mixture has a crumb-like consistency. The rubbing-in will add air, which will make the mixture lighter.

SIFT: This means shaking dry ingredients such as flour, a raising agent or icing sugar through a sieve into a bowl. Sifting will remove any lumps, as well as adding air, and it helps to combine ingredients – important for raising agents added to flour to be sure they are evenly dispersed (you can also do this in a food processor by 'pulsing' the flour with the raising agents a few times).

WORK: This is a way of saying to mix, stir, blend or combine ingredients using a spoon, plastic spatula or your hands until they have come together (or look smooth, or soft, or thickened), depending on the recipe instructions.

HOW DO YOU DO THIS?

PREPARING TINS
Note: in the equipment information in the recipes, an asterisk has been added to refer to the instructions here.

GREASE AND BASE-LINE A SPRINGCLIP TIN, A DEEP ROUND OR SQUARE TIN, A SANDWICH TIN OR A TRAYBAKE/BROWNIE/ RECTANGULAR CAKE TIN: Lightly and thoroughly brush the base and sides of the tin (including the rim) with melted butter. Set the tin on a sheet of baking paper and draw around it, then cut out the circle (or square or rectangle). Turn the baking paper over so that the pencil or pen marks are underneath, and press it on to the base of the tin.

GREASE AND LINE A SPRINGCLIP TIN OR A ROUND DEEP CAKE TIN: Brush the base and sides with melted butter, then cut out 2 rounds of baking or greaseproof paper very slightly smaller than the base of the tin (measure as for base-lining above, then cut inside the drawn line). Also cut out a double-thickness strip of baking or greaseproof paper long enough to go around the tin and stand about 5cm above it. Make a 2.5cm fold along one edge of this strip, then snip diagonally up to the fold at 1cm intervals (it will look like a thick fringe). Press one paper round on to the base of the tin, then place the strip around the inside of the tin so the snipped edge lies flat on the base and the paper is pressed smoothly to the side of the tin (no creases). Brush the paper on the base and the snipped edge of the side strip with a little more melted butter, then press the second round of paper on top. Lightly brush the paper on the base and sides with melted butter to hold it all in place.

GREASE AND LINE A LOAF TIN WITH A LONG STRIP OF PAPER: Lightly brush the base, sides and rim of the tin with melted butter. Cut a strip of baking or greaseproof paper the width of the tin and long enough to cover the base and 2 short sides. Press the paper into the greased tin to line the base and short sides. The paper will help you to lift the loaf out of the tin after baking.

COOKING WITH CHOCOLATE

MELT CHOCOLATE: Chop or break up the chocolate into even-sized pieces so it will melt at the same rate. Put it into a heatproof bowl and set this over a pan of steaming hot but not boiling water – don't let the base of the bowl touch the water. As the chocolate starts to soften, stir it gently so it melts evenly. It is ready to use as melted chocolate as soon as it is liquid and smooth, around 30°C. Take care not to leave it over the heat any longer: if the chocolate overheats and reaches 50°C it will 'seize up' – become grainy and hard – and be unusable.

TEMPER CHOCOLATE: This process of melting and cooling chocolate makes it shiny and very smooth, and will give a professional finish when you are covering a cake or dessert, or when you are making decorations such as chocolate curls. You'll need a cooking thermometer or a special digital chocolate and caramel thermometer. First melt the chocolate (see above), then put in the thermometer. Slightly increase the heat under the pan of water so the temperature of the chocolate rises. Keep stirring so the chocolate heats evenly. As soon as the temperature reaches 45°C (no higher), remove the bowl from the pan and set it in a larger bowl of cold but not icy water. to quickly cool the chocolate (take care not to let any water get into the chocolate bowl). Gently stir until the temperature falls to 27°C. Set the bowl over the pan of steaming hot water again and reheat the chocolate, stirring, until it reaches 29–30°C. When the chocolate gets up to temperature, remove the bowl from the pan. The tempered chocolate is now ready to use.

COOKING WITH EGGS

WHISK EGG WHITES: Separate your eggs carefully – any trace of yolk (or speck of grease in the bowl) will stop the whites from being beaten to their full volume – and use the whites at room temperature. Put them into a large, spotlessly clean and grease-free bowl. Whisk (on low speed if using an electric mixer) for about 30 seconds until frothy. If you add a pinch of cream of tartar or dash of vinegar or lemon juice at this point, the slight acidity will help the structure of the whites to stiffen. Then increase the speed and continue

whisking – the whites will become a mass of tiny bubbles, with a very smooth and fine texture. Soft peak is when you lift the whisk and the peak of whites on it slightly droops down. The next stage, after more whisking, is stiff peak when the peak stands upright. You should be able to turn the bowl upside down without the whites falling out.

WHISK TO THE 'RIBBON STAGE': For whisked sponges, the eggs and sugar must be whisked thoroughly to build up a thick mass of tiny air bubbles that forms the structure of the cake. Use a large bowl – after 4 or 5 minutes of whisking on high speed the initial volume of eggs and sugar will increase 5-fold. A large free-standing electric mixer is the easiest and quickest way to whisk eggs and sugar to the ribbon, but you can also use a hand-held electric mixer or, if you're not making a large quantity, a rotary whisk. The ribbon stage is reached when the mixture becomes very thick: when you lift the whisk out of the bowl, the mixture on it will fall back on to the surface of the mixture in the bowl to make a distinct thick, ribbon-like trail.

COOKING WITH CREAM

WHIP CREAM: Make sure the cream is well chilled before you start (and in warm weather pop the bowl and whisk into the fridge to chill too). This will prevent the butterfat in the cream from separating out and the mixture curdling as you whip. You can use an electric mixer, rotary whisk or hand wire whisk. If you are going to fold the cream into another mixture, whip the cream to soft peak stage (see Whisk Egg Whites, left). For piping, continue whipping the cream to a slightly firmer peak.

MAKING A PASTRY CASE

LINE A FLAN TIN OR PIE PLATE: Roll out the pastry dough on a lightly floured worktop to a circle about 8cm larger than your tin. Roll up the pastry around the rolling pin and lift it over the tin, then unroll the pastry gently so it drapes into the tin. Flour your fingers and gently press the pastry on to the base and up the side of the tin, smoothing out any pockets of air. Leave the excess pastry hanging over the rim of the tin, or roll the pin over the top of the tin to cut off the excess (if there are any holes in the pastry case, use this leftover dough to patch them).

With your thumbs, ease the pastry up the side of the tin, just slightly higher than the rim, to allow for shrinkage during baking. Curve your forefinger inside this new rim and gently press the pastry over your finger so it curves slightly inwards – this will make it easier to unmould after baking. Prick the base of the pastry case well with a fork, then chill for 20 minutes. If you need to keep the pastry case in the fridge for any longer, loosely cover with clingfilm to prevent the pastry from drying out.

BAKE A PASTRY CASE BLIND: Crumple up a sheet of baking or greaseproof paper (this makes the paper easier to fit), then flatten it out. Line the pastry case with the paper and fill with ceramic baking beans or dried beans. Place in the heated oven and bake for 12–15 minutes until the pastry is firm. Carefully remove the paper and beans, then return the tin to the oven and bake for a further 5–7 minutes until the pastry is thoroughly cooked and starting to colour (this is vital to avoid the dreaded 'soggy bottom'). *Pastry containing sugar needs to be watched carefully as it can burn on the edges before the base is cooked through.* If this happens reduce the oven temperature slightly, or cover the rim with a long strip of foil.

'KNOCK UP' A PUFF PASTRY EDGE: Use the back of a small knife blade to make small horizontal cuts all round.

FLUTE OR SCALLOP A PASTRY EDGE: Place 2 fingers on the pastry to press it down and draw a small knife between them.

BAKING CAKES
FINGERTIP TEST: For delicate sponge cakes the most reliable test to check if the cake is done is to gently press the top of the sponge, in the centre, with your finger – the cake is ready if the sponge springs back into place. If a slight dent is left, the mixture is still soft, so bake for a couple of minutes more and test again. When done, a sponge will also have started to shrink from the side of the tin.

SKEWER TEST: For richer, heavier cakes, fruit cakes and dense chocolate cakes, the way to test if the cake is done is to stick a wooden cocktail stick or fine skewer into the centre of the cake. If the stick or skewer comes out clean rather than damp with cake mixture, the cake has finished baking. Note though that some recipes, such as for Brownies, say the cocktail stick should come out slightly sticky; this is to avoid over-cooking a cake that is supposed to be moist and fudgy.

COOL A SPONGE ON A WIRE RACK: To avoid a wire rack leaving marks on the top of a sponge, cover a clean board with a clean, dry tea towel. Invert the sponge (in its tin) on to the tea towel, then lift off the tin and remove the lining paper. Set the wire rack on top and turn the whole thing over. Carefully remove the board and towel. Leave the sponge to cool, right side up, on the wire rack.

CUT A SPONGE INTO 2 LAYERS: First, make a small vertical nick or cut in the side of the sponge with the tip of a small sharp knife (this will help you align the layers when sandwiching). Gently but firmly press down on the top of the sponge with the flat of your hand and, using a long serrated knife (like a bread knife), carefully saw the sponge horizontally in half to make 2 even layers.

MAKING YEASTED BREAD
MIX THE DOUGH: Many bread doughs raised with yeast specify lukewarm liquid (milk, water, etc) in the recipe. *It's important that the liquid is not too hot or it could kill the yeast.* After warming the liquid, check the temperature by dipping your little finger into it: it should feel comfy. For lukewarm water you can mix half boiling water with half cold water from the tap.

HYDRATE THE FLOUR: If you leave the mixed dough in its bowl for 5 minutes (uncovered) before you start to knead, you'll find it an easier process because the flour will have had time to absorb the liquid properly – a particularly important step for wholemeal and rye flours, which are slow to hydrate. You can judge whether or not the dough needs a touch more flour or water at this point.

KNEAD THE DOUGH: Working a dough develops the gluten (in the flour's protein) and turns it from a messy ball into neat bundles of strands that are capable of stretching around the bubbles of carbon dioxide gas (produced by the growing yeast). The dough will then rise slowly, thanks to the yeast and gluten, and set in the oven. You can knead by hand or in a free-standing electric mixer fitted with a dough hook.

KNEAD BY HAND: First lightly dust the worktop with flour, or grease with a teaspoon of oil, to prevent the dough from sticking. Turn the dough out on to the worktop. Stretch the ball of dough away from you by holding down one end with your hand and using the other hand to pull and stretch out the dough as if it were an elastic band. Gather the dough back into a ball again and give it a quarter turn (so you start from a different section of the dough), then repeat the stretching and gathering-back movements. As you knead you'll notice the dough gradually changes in the way it looks and feels – it will start to feel pliable and then stretchy and very elastic, and be silky smooth. Nearly all doughs need 10 minutes of thorough kneading by hand.

KNEAD IN AN ELECTRIC MIXER: Fix the dough hook. Set the mixer on the lowest possible speed and knead for about 5 minutes. While it's almost impossible to over-knead by hand (your arms will give out first), take care when using a mixer as you can stretch the gluten beyond repair, which means the dough won't rise well at all.

KNEAD A RYE FLOUR DOUGH: If you are having a hard time kneading a dough made with rye flour, give the dough (and your arms) a break: cover the dough with the upturned bowl and have a rest for 5–10 minutes, then continue. Rye flour has very little gluten, which means it doesn't really become stretchy like a wheat flour dough does.

TEST IF THE DOUGH HAS BEEN KNEADED ENOUGH: Take a small piece and stretch it between your fingers to make a thin, translucent sheet. If it won't stretch out or it tears easily, continue to knead a while longer.

BAKE A LOAF WITH A GOOD CRUST: Make sure the oven is thoroughly heated so the dough quickly puffs (called 'oven-spring') and then sets, bakes evenly and forms a good crust. If you are worried about the oven temperature dramatically dropping as you load the bread in the oven, heat it slightly higher than the recipe says, then turn it down to the specified temperature once the oven door is shut again.

BAKE A LOAF WITH A CRISP CRUST: Creating a burst of steam in the oven at the start of baking will help give your loaf a crisp crust – the steam keeps the surface moist, helping the bread rise easily; once the surface has set, the moisture evaporates, leaving a crisp finish. To do this, put an empty roasting tin on the floor of the oven when you turn it on to heat it. Then, immediately after you've put the loaf in to bake, pour cold water – or throw a handful of ice cubes – into the hot tin. Quickly close the oven door to trap the resulting steam inside.

BAKE A LOAF WITH A CRISP BOTTOM: When you turn on the oven, put a baking sheet or baking stone in to heat up. Then carefully transfer your loaf (in a tin or on a sheet of baking paper) on to the hot baking sheet or stone for baking.

TEST BREAD TO SEE IF IT IS DONE: Carefully remove the bread from the oven and turn out, upside down, on to one hand (thick oven gloves are needed here). Tap the underside of the loaf with your knuckles. If the bread sounds hollow, like a drum, then the loaf is cooked through, but if you just get a dull 'thud', put the bread back into the oven – straight on to the oven shelf. Bake for a few more minutes, then test again. A rule of thumb: a slightly over-baked loaf will taste far better than one that is undercooked.

COOL BAKED BREAD: Cool on a wire rack, not in the tin or on a baking sheet, so the steam from the loaf cannot condense during cooling and turn the crust soggy.

COOK'S NOTES

SKILL LEVELS: The level of skill needed for each recipe is clearly indicated in the top corner of the recipe page. The number of spoons equals the level of difficulty – 1 spoon means the recipe is easy, 2 is slightly more difficult and 3 is tricky.

OVEN TEMPERATURES: Recipes give temperatures for a conventional oven. If you have a fan-assisted oven, set the temperature 20°C lower than specified. Don't forget that ovens vary – from the front to the back of the oven, as well as between top and bottom shelves – so an oven thermometer is very useful. Get to know your oven, and where the 'hot spots' are. Always allow time to preheat the oven, and be sure your oven gloves are dry.

EGGS: Some recipes contain raw or partially cooked eggs. Pregnant women, the elderly, babies and toddlers, and people who are unwell should avoid these recipes.

SALT: If a recipe calls for a small, or hard to weigh, amount, remember that ½ teaspoon fine salt weighs 2.5g, and ¼ teaspoon weighs 1.25g. If you are using sea salt it is best to crush the flakes into a fine powder before adding to your recipe.

SPOON MEASURES: All teaspoons and tablespoons are measured level unless otherwise stated in the recipe.

PECAN SHORTIES • GRASMERE GINGER
SHORTBREAD • DIGESTIVES • ENWEZOR'S PUMPKIN
& SUNFLOWER BISCUITS • GOLDEN CARROT
TRAYBAKE • DOUBLE CHOCOLATE CRUNCH
COOKIES • PEANUT BUTTER SANDWICHES •
CHOCOLATE CHUNK BARS • PRALINE BISCOTTI •
CHOCOLATE PECAN MACARONS • LEMON
BISCOTTI• NORMAN'S FARTHING BISCUITS •
OAT & HONEY FLAPJACK COOKIES •
CHOCOLATE FUDGE BROWNIES • DOUBLE
GINGER CRACKLES • WELSH CAKES • SCONES •
MAPLE & LEMON DROP SCONES • MARY'S
FLORENTINES • PAUL'S SAVOURY BISCUITS

BISCUITS
& TRAYBAKES

PECAN SHORTIES

The best shortbread is made to the classic recipe of one part sugar to two of butter and three of flour. Icing sugar gives a crisper texture than caster sugar (which makes them sandy and crumbly or 'short'). Toasted nuts and melted chocolate make these shorties extra special.

MAKES TWENTY

75g pecan halves
250g plain flour
175g unsalted butter, softened
85g icing sugar, sifted
½ teaspoon vanilla extract

To finish
100g dark chocolate (about 70% cocoa solids), chopped

2 baking sheets, lined with baking paper

1 Heat your oven to 180°C/350°F/gas 4. Tip the nuts into a small tin and toast in the heated oven for 5–7 minutes until lightly coloured. Leave to cool, then chop or break up the nuts fairly coarsely. Mix with the flour in a bowl. Set aside.

2 Put the soft butter into another mixing bowl (or the bowl of a free-standing electric mixer fitted with the whisk attachment). Beat with a wooden spoon (or the mixer) until the butter is as smooth and creamy as mayonnaise.

3 Beat in the icing sugar a tablespoon at a time (use the lowest speed of the mixer). Once all the sugar has been worked in, add the vanilla and beat well for a couple of minutes until the mixture becomes almost white in colour, and light and fluffy in texture (about a minute in the mixer). Add the flour and nut mixture and stir in with a wooden spoon or plastic spatula to make a firm dough.

4 Divide the dough into 20 even-sized pieces. Lightly flour your hands and roll each piece into a neat ball. Set the balls on the lined baking sheets, spacing them well apart to allow for spreading. Gently squash each ball with your fingers to make a disc about 5.5cm across and 1cm thick.

5 Bake in the heated oven for 14–16 minutes until pale gold in colour with slightly darker edges, rotating the baking sheets halfway through so the shortbreads bake evenly. Set the sheets on a heatproof surface. Leave the shortbreads to firm up for 5 minutes before transferring them to a wire rack to cool completely. Leave the lined sheets on the worktop.

6 Once the biscuits are cold, gently melt the chocolate in a heatproof bowl set over a pan of steaming hot water. Remove the bowl from the pan and stir the chocolate until smooth.

7 Hold one shortbread horizontally by the sides and gently dip the base into the melted chocolate so that the chocolate comes halfway up the sides of the biscuit. Lay the shortie chocolate side up on a lined baking sheet. Repeat with the rest of the shorties, then leave to set. Once the chocolate is firm and hard, store in an airtight container for about 3 days.

GRASMERE GINGER SHORTBREAD

Popular in Cumbria, these shortbread fingers have a coarse sandy and slightly crunchy texture thanks to the inclusion of oatmeal and wholemeal flour. Stem ginger adds warmth and a slight stickiness to the mixture. For a richer, fancier treat you can add a ginger cream filling (see below).

CUTS INTO FOURTEEN FINGERS

150g plain flour
150g plain wholemeal flour
  (wheat or spelt)
50g medium oatmeal
1 teaspoon ground ginger
$\frac{1}{2}$ teaspoon bicarbonate of soda
125g light brown muscovado sugar
1 lump stem ginger (from a jar), drained
  of syrup and coarsely chopped
125g slightly salted butter, chilled and
  diced

1 x 20cm square cake tin OR brownie
  tin, greased with butter

1 Heat your oven to 180°C/350°F/gas 4. Tip both flours, the oatmeal, ground ginger, bicarbonate of soda, sugar and stem ginger into the bowl of a food processor. 'Pulse' a few times to combine everything thoroughly – the mixture should look like coarse crumbs. Add the lumps of butter and process until the mixture looks like sandy crumbs.

2 Remove 4 tablespoons of the crumbs and put into a small bowl. Tip the rest of the crumbs into the prepared tin. Give the tin a shake to settle the mixture, then press it on to the base with the back of a spoon to make an even layer.

3 Sprinkle the reserved crumbs over the top. Bake in the heated oven for 25–28 minutes until a light golden colour with darker edges.

4 Set the tin on a wire rack. Run a round-bladed knife around the inside of the tin to loosen the shortbread. Gently cut it down the centre, then cut across to make 14 fingers. Leave to cool and firm up in the tin before removing carefully. Store in an airtight container for about 5 days.

GINGER SHORTBREAD WITH GINGER CREAM FILLING

Beat 50g slightly salted butter with 1 tablespoon of ginger syrup (from the jar), then beat in 100g sifted icing sugar and 1 lump stem ginger, finely chopped. Taste and add a couple of drops of lemon juice if you think the icing needs it to enhance the flavour of the stem ginger. Spread the icing on the flat underside of 7 fingers and top with the other fingers, crumb side out. Store in an airtight container in a cool spot but not the fridge.

DIGESTIVES

Home-made digestives have a coarser texture and more satisfying crunch than a pack from the supermarket. You also know what's gone into them! You can finish the biscuits with a coating of melted chocolate or make a savoury version to eat with cheese, dips and pâtés.

150g plain wholemeal flour
   (spelt or wheat)
150g medium oatmeal
1 tablespoon bran
$\frac{1}{4}$ teaspoon crushed sea salt
1 teaspoon baking powder
75g dark muscovado sugar
   (sieved if lumpy)
150g unsalted butter, chilled and diced
1–2 tablespoons milk

1 x 7.5cm plain round cutter; 1–2 baking
   sheets, lightly greased with butter

1 Put the flour, oatmeal, bran, salt, baking powder and sugar into the bowl of a food processor. 'Pulse' several times until everything is thoroughly combined.

2 Add the chunks of butter and run the machine until the mixture looks like fine crumbs. With the machine running, add enough milk through the feed tube to bring the mixture together into a firm but not dry dough. (You can also make the biscuit mixture by combining all the dry ingredients in a mixing bowl, then rubbing in the butter and finally stirring in the milk with a round-bladed knife.)

3 Lift the dough out of the processor bowl, flatten into a thick disc and wrap in clingfilm. Chill for 30 minutes until firm.

4 Set the disc of dough between 2 sheets of clingfilm or baking paper and roll out 4mm thick. Stamp out rounds with the plain cutter and set slightly apart on the greased baking sheets. Gather up the trimmings and work them together, then re-roll and cut out more rounds.

5 Prick each round several times with a fork, then chill in the fridge for about 10 minutes. Meanwhile, heat your oven to 190°C/375°F/gas 5.

6 Bake the biscuits for 10–12 minutes until golden and slightly darker around the edges. To make sure the biscuits cook evenly, rotate the sheet or sheets after 5 minutes. Remove the sheet or sheets from the oven and set on a heatproof surface. Leave the biscuits to cool and firm up for 5 minutes, then transfer them to a wire rack. When cold store in an airtight container for about a week.

SAVOURY DIGESTIVES
Make up the basic recipe but reduce the sugar to 50g. Add an extra $\frac{1}{4}$ teaspoon sea salt plus $\frac{1}{2}$ teaspoon garam masala, $\frac{1}{4}$ teaspoon crushed dried chilli and a pinch of cumin seeds. Roll out in the same way and cut out 5cm rounds. Chill, then bake for about 8 minutes. Makes about 35.

ENWEZOR

Where do you live?
Southsea in Portsmouth.

What do you get up to when you are not baking?
With 4 small children, life is full, busy and fun as my wife and I rush around trying to keep on top of things. Outside bringing up a family, I'm pretty sporty with cycling and running being my favourite pastimes although I also do a fair amount of yoga, swimming and circuits. I also love having friends round for dinner and I nearly always cook something new because I love the challenge and the opportunity to learn something different. I'm also an avid reader and hope to one day write a book.

How would you define yourself as a baker?
I've been baking for the last 10 years or so but much more seriously in the last 2-3 years driven largely by setting up a baking group. I like to try my hand at everything. I don't stick to any one style, which I think means I'm not an expert in any one thing. However, I do find myself drawn to the more difficult and technical challenges!

How did you get into baking?
I'm a self-taught baker. I think it was probably my love of pies that got me into baking. The taste of some quality shortcrust pastry surrounding a nice steak and ale filling for me is to die for!

What are your favourite 3 items of kitchen equipment?
My dough cutter.
My bench scraper.
My favourite pink spatula!

ENWEZOR'S
PUMPKIN & SUNFLOWER BISCUITS

▼▼▼

Thin, crunchy, round crackers bursting with seeds are served with a chutney of red onions slowly cooked with roasted caraway seeds. Perfect with a good extra mature Cheddar.

MAKES ABOUT TWENTY-FOUR
PLUS A SMALL JAR OF CHUTNEY

For the biscuits

70g rye flour
70g plain wholemeal flour
120g plain white flour
50g pumpkin seeds
50g sunflower seeds
small bunch of chives, finely chopped
   (about 5g)
1 teaspoon English mustard powder
1 teaspoon fine salt
1$\frac{1}{2}$ teaspoons baking powder
30g sun-dried tomato purée
3 tablespoons olive oil
180ml cold water

For the chutney

4 large red onions, thinly sliced
50g caster sugar
$\frac{1}{2}$ teaspoon caraway seeds, toasted
   and ground
50ml red wine vinegar
50ml red wine
1 teaspoon good blackcurrant squash,
   or to taste

1-2 baking sheets, lined with baking
   paper; a 7cm plain round cutter

▼▼▼▼▼▼▼▼▼▼▼▼▼▼▼▼▼▼

1 To make the dough, put the 3 flours into a mixing bowl and add the next 6 ingredients. Mix well. Make a well in the mixture and add the tomato purée, oil and half the water. Mix these ingredients together, then gradually work in the dry ingredients, using your hand, adding more water as needed to make a soft but not sticky dough (you may not need all the water).

2 Turn out the dough onto a lightly floured worktop and knead for 5 minutes until it feels firmer and very supple. Shape into a ball and cover it with the upturned bowl. Leave to relax for 15 minutes while you heat the oven to 230°C/450°F/gas 8.

3 Divide the dough in half. Keep one portion covered by the upturned bowl while you roll out the other portion to a very thin rectangle about 30 x 35cm. Cover the dough rectangle with the sheet of baking paper you are using to line the baking sheet, then roll up the dough (with the paper inside) around the rolling pin. Lift the pin over the baking sheet, then gently unroll the dough – with the paper – on to the baking sheet so the paper is underneath the dough. If necessary, trim off any dough hanging over the edges of the baking sheet.

4 Bake in the heated oven for about 7 minutes until the top of the dough is golden. Remove the baking sheet from the oven and set it on a heatproof surface. Using a large palette knife to help you, flip the dough over, then return to the oven to bake the second side until lightly coloured, about 6 minutes.

5 Slide the sheet of dough on to a large board and quickly stamp out rounds using the cutter. Alternatively, cut the sheet into squares or rectangles using a large, sharp knife. Return the cut biscuits to the lined baking sheet and bake for a further 5 minutes until crisp and golden. Leave to cool on a wire rack while you bake the second batch of biscuits in the same way.

6 While they are cooling, make the chutney. Put the onions, sugar and ground caraway into a medium-sized heavy-based pan. Cover tightly and cook the onions over medium heat, stirring occasionally, for 15 minutes until very soft and tender. Add the vinegar and wine and cook uncovered over medium heat for 10 minutes until very thick. Taste and add squash as needed to flavour the chutney. Leave to cool, then spoon into a bowl or jar. Serve with the biscuits and good strong cheese.

GOLDEN CARROT TRAYBAKE

A change from the usual carrot cake: here the sponge is lighter in colour and texture, and it's flavoured with fruit, both dried and fresh (look for fresh ready-prepared pineapple in the chiller shelves of larger supermarkets), rather than lots of spices. The traybake is finished with a quick orange-flavoured cheesecake icing, but it is also very good if left plain.

MAKES ONE LARGE CAKE

3 medium carrots (about 180g in total), peeled and coarsely grated
100g fresh pineapple slices or pieces, drained
40g soft-dried apricots
50g sultanas OR golden jumbo raisins
grated zest and juice of 1 large navel orange
150g unsalted butter, softened
270g caster sugar
2 medium free-range eggs, at room temperature, beaten to mix
275g plain flour
1 1/2 teaspoons bicarbonate of soda
1/2 teaspoon ground cinnamon
50g chopped toasted hazelnuts (optional)

To finish
250g mascarpone
150g icing sugar
50g chopped toasted hazelnuts (optional)

1 traybake tin, baking tin OR brownie tin, 20 x 25cm x 5cm, greased and base-lined*

1 Heat your oven to 180°C/350°F/gas 4. Weigh 125g grated carrots and put into a bowl (keep any leftover carrots for a salad). Cut the pineapple and apricots into 1cm pieces and add to the carrots along with the sultanas.

2 Add half the orange zest and 3 tablespoons of the juice to the carrot mixture (save the rest of the orange zest and juice for the icing). Give the carrot mixture a good stir to combine thoroughly, then set aside for now.

3 Put the soft butter into a mixing bowl with the sugar and beat thoroughly with a wooden spoon or electric mixer until fluffy and paler in colour. Gradually add the eggs, beating well after each addition, then continue to beat for a minute until the mixture is very pale and light in texture.

4 Sift the flour, bicarbonate of soda and cinnamon into the bowl and fold in with a large metal spoon or plastic spatula. When you can no longer see any streaks of flour, add the carrot mixture and the nuts (if using) and stir in until thoroughly combined. Transfer the heavy and sticky mixture to the prepared tin and spread evenly.

5 Bake in the heated oven for 30–35 minutes until the cake is golden brown and a wooden cocktail stick inserted into the centre comes out clean. Remove from the oven and set the tin on a wire rack. Run a round-bladed knife around the inside of the tin to loosen the cake, then leave to cool.

6 To make the icing, put the mascarpone into a mixing bowl. Sift the icing sugar into the bowl and add the reserved orange zest. Mix thoroughly with a wooden spoon. If the mixture is bit too stiff to spread easily, work in some of the reserved orange juice a teaspoon at a time. Cover the bowl and chill for about 30 minutes until the cake is completely cold.

7 Spread the icing over the cake and scatter the nuts on top (if using). Leave uncovered in a cool spot, not the fridge, until the icing has firmed up enough to cut the cake into slices or squares. Store in an airtight container in a cool spot and eat within 2 days.

GOLDEN CARROT TRAYBAKE CONTINUED...

GOLDEN WEDDING CAKE
Make 2 Golden Carrot Traybake cakes and
sandwich them with the icing. Decorate with more
icing, or cover with Buttercream (see page 134) or
ready-rolled white or gold-coloured fondant icing.

DOUBLE CHOCOLATE CRUNCH COOKIES

These cookies owe their crunchy texture to cornflakes, which also make them look craggy and rough. They have a chewy-soft centre plus a small extra hit of chocolate added at the end of baking. Take the eggs out of the fridge at least an hour before you start – if they're too cold, the mixture will start to set when you add the chocolate, making it hard to work in the cornflakes.

MAKES TWENTY-FOUR

150g dark chocolate (about 70% cocoa solids)

30g unsalted butter, cut into pieces

2 medium free-range eggs, at room temperature

130g caster sugar

$\frac{1}{2}$ teaspoon vanilla extract

85g plain flour

$\frac{1}{4}$ teaspoon baking powder

50g cornflakes

24 large or giant chocolate buttons (milk, dark or white chocolate)

2 baking sheets, lined with baking paper

1 Break or chop up the chocolate into small, even-sized pieces and put into a heatproof bowl. Add the butter, then set the bowl over a pan of steaming hot but not boiling water and melt gently. Remove the bowl from the pan and stir until the mixture is smooth. Allow to cool until barely warm, stirring occasionally so the mixture maintains an even temperature.

2 Meanwhile, put the eggs, sugar and vanilla into a mixing bowl and whisk with an electric mixer for about 2 minutes until very thick and frothy. Stir in the chocolate mixture using a plastic spatula or large metal spoon. When thoroughly combined, sift the flour and baking powder into the bowl and stir in. When you can no longer see any streaks of flour, gently stir in the cornflakes. Cover the bowl and chill for 1 hour.

3 Towards the end of the chilling time, heat your oven to 170°C/325°F/gas 3.

4 Scoop up a rounded tablespoon of the cookie mixture and, using a teaspoon, push it on to a lined baking sheet. Repeat with the rest of the mixture, spacing the heaps well apart to allow for spreading. Gently flatten each heap with your fingers to make a rough, craggy cookie about 6cm across.

5 Bake in the heated oven for about 12 minutes until the cookies look cracked and almost cooked. Remove the sheets from the oven and set on a heatproof surface. Quickly press a chocolate button into the centre of each cookie. Return them to the oven and bake for a further 2 minutes.

6 Transfer the sheets to the heatproof surface again and leave for 10 minutes to allow the cookies to firm up a bit, then transfer them to a wire rack to cool completely. Store in an airtight container for about 5 days.

PEANUT BUTTER SANDWICHES

Probably the quickest and easiest cookie recipe ever, this is made with storecupboard ingredients. For the best results you need a peanut butter made with 100 per cent peanuts – no palm oil, salt or sugar added (this also happens to be gluten- and dairy-free). You could also sandwich the cookies with your favourite chocolate spread instead of jam, or even ganache (see recipe for Chocolate Pecan Macarons on page 35).

MAKES TEN PAIRS

280g crunchy peanut butter
150g light brown muscovado sugar
1 medium free-range egg, at room
   temperature
$^1\!/_2$ teaspoon vanilla extract
1 tablespoon polenta
about 4 tablespoons raspberry
   or strawberry jam

2 baking sheets, lined with baking
   paper

1 Heat your oven to 180°C/350°F/gas 4. Put the peanut butter and sugar into a mixing bowl and beat well with a wooden spoon to combine thoroughly.

2 Put the egg and vanilla into a small bowl and beat with a fork just to mix, then beat into the peanut butter mixture in 3 batches. Sprinkle the polenta over the mixture and mix it in to make a stiff dough.

3 Shape the dough into 20 balls using your hands and set well apart on the lined baking sheets. Gently flatten with the back of a fork so the cookies are attractively ridged with crinkly edges, and measure about 6.5cm across.

4 Bake in the heated oven for 12–14 minutes until golden with slightly darker edges. Set the sheets on a heatproof surface and leave the cookies to cool and firm up for 10 minutes, then carefully transfer them to a wire rack.

5 When completely cold, sandwich the cookies in pairs with the jam. Store in an airtight container for about 3 days.

CHOCOLATE CHUNK BARS

The moist, not-too-rich sponge mixture for these bars is made with melted butter – there's no creaming or beating needed. It slices neatly without making a lot of crumbs, so is ideal for picnics. Use your own favourite flavourings: chopped dark, milk or white chocolate, toasted chopped nuts or raspberries, blueberries or dessert blackberries. To add decoration, finish with piped chocolate in a different colour.

CUTS INTO TWENTY BARS

200g unsalted butter
275g self-raising flour
200g caster sugar
2 medium free-range eggs,
    at room temperature
½ teaspoon vanilla extract
300ml buttermilk, at room
    temperature
100g dark chocolate (about 70%
    cocoa solids), roughly chopped
100g raspberries
1–2 tablespoons demerara or large
    crystal sugar OR chopped nuts,
    for sprinkling
icing sugar, for dusting (optional)

1 traybake tin, brownie tin OR cake
    tin, 25 x 20 x 5cm, greased and
    base-lined*

1 Heat your oven to 180°C/350°F/gas 4. Gently melt the butter in a small pan, or in the microwave. Leave to cool until just barely warm.

2 While the butter is cooling, sift the flour and caster sugar into a mixing bowl and make a well in the centre. Add the eggs and vanilla to the buttermilk and beat with a fork until combined. Pour the buttermilk mixture and the melted butter into the well in the flour and mix everything together with a wooden spoon until just combined – you are going to add more to the bowl so don't overmix at this stage.

3 Add the pieces of chocolate and the raspberries and mix in gently with a plastic spatula or large metal spoon.

4 Transfer the mixture to the prepared tin and spread evenly. Sprinkle the demerara sugar or nuts evenly over the top, then bake in the heated oven for 45–50 minutes until the cake is golden and a wooden cocktail stick inserted into the centre comes out clean.

5 Set the tin on a wire rack and run a round-bladed knife around the inside of the tin to loosen the sponge, then leave to cool. When cold, dust it with sifted icing sugar, if you like, and cut into bars. These are best eaten the same or next day.

ADDING A PIPED CHOCOLATE DECORATION
Melt 50g chocolate (dark, milk or white), then spoon into a disposable piping bag, or small plastic bag, and snip off the tip. Pipe zigzag lines or swirls over the top of the sponge. Or just drip or drizzle the chocolate over the sponge using a teaspoon. Leave until set before cutting into bars.

PRALINE BISCOTTI

Adding nuts to biscotti provides a crunchy texture as well as extra flavour, but turning the nuts into praline first is really something else. Cooking hazelnuts (still in their brown skins) with sugar until it becomes a chestnut caramel is a bit tricky – you need to be careful the mixture doesn't burn – but the result is quite wonderful. The bittersweet caramel and crunchy nuts make these biscotti a special treat.

For the hazelnut praline
100g caster sugar (white rather than
  golden works best)
100g unblanched hazelnuts

For the biscotti dough
150g unsalted butter, softened
200g caster sugar
1 medium free-range egg plus 1 yolk,
  at room temperature
$\frac{1}{2}$ teaspoon vanilla extract
375g plain flour
2 teaspoons baking powder

1 baking sheet, greased with oil;
  baking paper

1 Start by making the praline. Put the caster sugar and nuts into a medium heavy-based pan. Set over low heat and let the sugar melt gently, occasionally shaking the pan and stirring gently with a metal spoon. As soon as the sugar has melted turn up the heat to medium and let the syrup bubble away until it turns a chestnut brown – you can stir gently now and then with the metal spoon so the nuts brown evenly. Tip the mixture on to the oiled baking sheet and spread out evenly with the metal spoon. Leave until completely cold and set.

2 Break up the praline into chunks. Put them into a food processor and grind to make coarse crumbs with a few larger lumps (you can also chop up the praline with a large knife or bash it up – in a plastic bag – with a rolling pin). Set aside until needed (you can make the praline a day in advance; keep tightly covered).

3 Heat your oven to 180°C/350°F/gas 4. Put the soft butter into a large mixing bowl (or the bowl of a free-standing electric mixer fitted with the whisk attachment) and beat well with a wooden spoon (or the mixer) until very creamy. Add the sugar and beat until light and fluffy, scraping down the sides of the bowl from time to time.

4 In a small bowl, beat the egg and the yolk with the vanilla, just to mix, then gradually add to the butter mixture, beating well after each addition.

5 Sift the flour and baking powder into the bowl and mix in with a plastic spatula or wooden spoon. As soon as all the flour has been incorporated, add the praline and work in until evenly distributed. Put your hands into the bowl and bring the dough together into a ball.

6 Divide the dough in half. Line the clean baking sheet with baking paper. Lift one portion of dough on to one side of the sheet. Lightly dust your hands with flour, then mould and shape the dough into a flat brick shape about 30 x 7.5cm and 1.5cm thick. Repeat with the second portion of dough, setting this block slightly apart from the first (to allow for expansion).

PRALINE BISCOTTI CONTINUED...

7 Bake in the heated oven for about 30 minutes until light brown and firm. Remove the sheet from the oven and set it on a heatproof surface; turn the oven down to 300°C/150°F/gas 2. Leave the biscotti blocks to cool for 10 minutes, then slide them, still on the baking paper, on to a chopping board. With a serrated knife cut the blocks across, on a slight diagonal, into slices about 1.5cm thick – it will be easier if you use a gentle sawing motion.

8 Line the baking sheet with a fresh piece of baking paper. Set the slices cut-side down on the sheet. Return the biscotti to the oven and bake for about 20 minutes until crisp and golden brown. Transfer to a wire rack and leave until cold. Store in an airtight container for about a week.

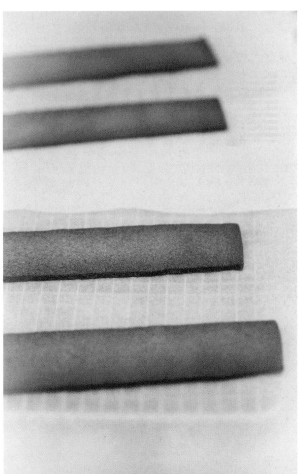

CHOCOLATE PECAN MACARONS

The finest of French macarons are made with almonds ground almost to a powder. These macarons, which use ground pecans and plenty of cocoa, may not look quite so chic but they have the most wonderful flavour that becomes more intense as the macarons age. The filling is a contrast of creamy white and bitter chocolate ganaches. For a very glam finish, lightly dust the sandwiched macarons with edible gold dust.

For the macarons

100g pecans
75g icing sugar
2 large free-range egg whites,
    at room temperature
good pinch of salt
75g caster sugar
25g cocoa powder

For the ganaches

50g good-quality white chocolate,
    finely chopped
50g dark chocolate (about 70% cocoa
    solids), finely chopped
100ml whipping cream

1 baking sheet, lined with baking paper
    (see recipe); a piping bag; a 1.5cm
    plain tube; a star tube (OR a duo
    piping bag fitted with the star tube)

1 Draw 18 x 5cm circles on the sheet of baking paper (use a 5cm cutter as a guide), then turn the paper over and lay it on the baking sheet. Tip the pecans and icing sugar into the bowl of a food processor and grind to a fine, sandy powder. Set aside for now.

2 Put the egg whites and salt into a spotlessly clean and grease-free mixing bowl, or the bowl of a free-standing electric mixer. Whisk until the whites stand in soft peaks that slightly flop at the tip when you lift out the whisk.

3 Whisk in the caster sugar a tablespoon at a time, on full speed, then continue to whisk until the mixture stands in stiff peaks (no flopping) when the whisk is lifted.

4 Sift the cocoa powder into the bowl and add the pecan mixture. Gently but thoroughly fold everything together with a large metal spoon or plastic spatula until there are no streaks: the mixture will feel slightly stiffer than the usual almond macaron mixture.

5 Transfer the mixture to the piping bag fitted with the plain tube. Pipe small mounds of the mixture just inside each circle drawn on the baking paper (you can also use a teaspoon of mixture to make each macaron). Dip your finger in cold water, then gently flatten the peaks. Bang the sheet on the worktop to knock out any air pockets. Leave the macarons, on the sheet on the worktop, for 30 minutes to allow a skin to form (the macarons will look slightly matt). Meanwhile, heat your oven to 180°C/350°F/gas 4.

6 Bake in the heated oven for 15–20 minutes until the macarons feel firm when gently pressed on top – the inside centre will still be soft. Don't overcook the macarons as they will firm up as they cool, and you want the centres to remain slightly soft. Carefully slide the macarons, on the sheet of baking paper, on to a wire rack and leave to cool.

7 Meanwhile, make up the 2 ganaches. Put the white chocolate into a heatproof bowl and the dark chocolate into

CHOCOLATE PECAN MACARONS CONTINUED...

another heatproof bowl. Heat the cream in a small saucepan until steaming hot but not quite boiling, then pour half over each type of chocolate. Leave for a minute before stirring each gently until smooth and creamy. Leave until thick and firm enough to pipe.

8 Spoon the white ganache into the washed and dried piping bag fitted with the star tube. Pipe a ring of ganache on to the flat underside of half of the macarons, leaving the middle empty. Spoon or pipe (using the cleaned piping bag fitted with the plain tube) the dark ganache into the centre of each ring. If you are using a duo piping bag fit the star tube, spoon one ganache into each side of the bag (be sure they are both the same consistency - if one is too firm it won't work), then pipe a dual swirl to cover the flat underside of half the macarons.

9 Sandwich with the remaining macarons (flat side to flat side) to make pairs. Store in an airtight container in a cool spot (not the fridge) and eat within 4 days.

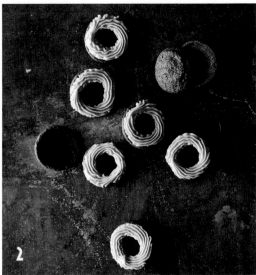

LEMON BISCOTTI

These very light and delicately flavoured biscotti are perfect at the end of a meal, served with berries and sorbets or fruit ice creams. The 'twice-baked' slices can be kept for a week, but once you've added the icing they should be eaten within five days.

85g unsalted butter, softened
125g caster sugar
finely grated zest of 1 large
    unwaxed lemon
1/4 teaspoon almond essence
2 medium free-range eggs,
    beaten to mix
250g plain flour
3/4 teaspoon baking powder
2 tablespoons lemon juice
25g flaked almonds, plus extra
    for sprinkling

For the lemon glaze
50g icing sugar, sifted
2 teaspoons lemon juice

1 baking sheet, lined with baking paper;
    a disposable piping bag OR small
    plastic bag (optional)

1 Heat your oven to 180°C/350°F/gas 4. Beat the butter in a mixing bowl with a wooden spoon or electric mixer until very creamy and soft. Add the sugar, lemon zest and almond essence and beat until fluffy – scrape down the sides of the bowl from time to time so everything is incorporated.

2 Gradually beat in the eggs a tablespoon at a time. Sift the flour and baking powder into the bowl, add the lemon juice and stir. As soon as the flour is worked in, get your hands into the bowl and press the mixture together.

3 Scatter half the almonds evenly on the lined baking sheet to cover a rectangle about 30 x 9cm. Flour your hands and shape the dough into a rough log, then lift it on to the nuts on the sheet. Gently pat out the log to make a neat and even brick shape 30 x 9cm and 1.5cm thick. Scatter the rest of the nuts over and gently press on to the dough.

4 Bake in the heated oven for 30–35 minutes until light golden in colour and firm to the touch. Remove the baking sheet from the oven and set it on a heatproof surface. Lower the oven temperature to 170°C/325°F/gas 3.

5 Leave the biscotti block to cool for 5 minutes on the baking sheet, then carefully transfer it to a chopping board (the easiest way to do this is to slide it, still on the lining paper, on to the board). Set a fresh sheet of paper on the baking sheet.

6 Using a serrated knife, carefully cut (using a sawing action) across the biscotti on a slight diagonal into slices about 1.5cm thick. Set the slices cut-side up on the baking sheet. Return to the oven and bake for 20–25 minutes until crisp and dry and turning a light golden colour. Leave to cool on the baking sheet for 5 minutes, then transfer to a wire rack.

7 When the biscotti are cold, make the icing glaze by mixing the icing sugar with the lemon juice in a medium bowl; the mixture should be the right consistency to be piped or drizzled. To pipe, spoon the icing glaze into the piping or plastic bag and snip off the tip, then pipe the icing in a zigzag pattern over the biscotti. Alternatively, dip a fork into the icing and drizzle it over the biscotti. Scatter some extra nuts on top and leave to set. Store in an airtight container.

NORMAN

Where do you live?
Buckie, but I am still a Portknockie man at heart.

What do you get up to when you are not baking?
Presently retired. My hobbies include: baking, cooking, slab pottery, music (clarinet), long walks with the dog, caravanning, as well as making and drinking beer in the shed.

How would you define yourself as a baker?
I'm a classic home baker who has been baking for many, many years. I mainly bake bread, scones, sticky buns and pies.

Why do you enjoy baking?
It keeps me off the street corners.

Who do you tend to bake for?
Me and her indoors, and sometimes the dog gets a bit.

What are your favourite 3 items of kitchen equipment?
The bottle opener.
The corkscrew.
A low-fat fryer.

SIGNATURE BAKE

NORMAN'S
FARTHING BISCUITS

Large, slightly crumbly and light, these biscuits – along with home-made butter – make an excellent accompaniment for a plate of cheeses. They are also ideal for serving with fish pâtés and spreads.

MAKES ABOUT TWENTY-TWO

For the biscuits
225g plain flour
225g self-raising flour
1 teaspoon fine salt
1 teaspoon caster sugar
85g lightly salted butter, chilled
   and diced
85g lard, chilled and diced
about 90ml icy-cold water, to bind

For the butter
300ml double cream, chilled
25g sea salt crystals, or to taste

1 x 8.75cm plain round cutter; a
wire-mesh pizza baking sheet OR
1–2 baking sheets, lightly greased
with butter

1 Sift both flours, the salt and sugar into a large mixing bowl. Add the pieces of cold butter and lard and rub into the flour with the tips of your fingers until the mixture looks like fine crumbs. Using a round-bladed knife or a palette knife, stir in enough icy-cold water to bind the ingredients into a dough.

2 Use your hands to work the dough in the bowl so it comes together in a neat, firm ball. Slightly flatten it to a thick disc, then wrap it in clingfilm and leave in the fridge to relax for 15 minutes (don't leave the dough too much longer or it will become too hard to roll out).

3 Meanwhile, heat your oven to 180°C/350°F/gas 4. Unwrap the dough and roll it out on a very lightly floured worktop to slightly thinner than the thickness of a pound coin. Stamp out rounds using the cutter. Gather up the trimmings into a ball, then re-roll and stamp out more rounds.

4 Using a biscuit-pricker or a fork, prick each biscuit round all over, leaving a 5mm border unpricked around the edge. Set the rounds slightly apart on the baking sheet (you may have to bake in batches).

5 Bake in the heated oven for 15–16 minutes until the biscuits are firm and cooked through but not coloured – they must be pale. Transfer to a wire rack to cool. (If baking in batches, quickly cool the baking sheet under the cold tap, dry and lightly grease with butter – don't grease a mesh baking sheet – then bake more biscuits.)

6 To make the butter, whip the cream in a large bowl with an electric mixer or a rotary whisk until it separates into yellow lumps and watery buttermilk. Drain in a sieve (discard the buttermilk), then gently rinse the lumps of butter in a bowl of very cold water, squeezing out the remaining buttermilk. Repeat until the water runs clear. Add salt to taste to the final bowl of cold water and swish the butter around in it. Lift the butter out into a dish, cover and keep in the fridge until ready to serve with the biscuits.

BISCUITS & TRAYBAKES

OAT & HONEY FLAPJACK COOKIES

Halfway between a sticky flapjack and a crunchy oat biscuit, these robust cookies have a chewy centre and crisp edge. You can add whatever you like to the oat mix: dried fruit – raisins, cranberries, sour cherries, sultanas and even chopped dates – plus whole or chopped macadamias, hazelnuts, pecans or walnuts, or even chunks of chocolate.

MAKES ABOUT TWENTY-TWO

120g unsalted butter, softened
140g light brown muscovado sugar
2 tablespoons well-flavoured honey
1 medium free-range egg, at room
   temperature, beaten to mix
100g plain wholemeal flour
   (wheat or spelt)
½ teaspoon baking powder
1 teaspoon ground cinnamon
200g porridge oats
100g dried fruit and nuts (see above)

1–2 baking sheets, lined with
   baking paper

1 Heat your oven to 200°C/400°F/gas 6. Put the soft butter, sugar and honey into a mixing bowl and beat well with a wooden spoon or electric mixer for about 2 minutes until fluffy and slightly lighter in colour.

2 Scrape down the sides of the bowl, then beat in the egg in 3 batches. Sift the flour, baking powder and cinnamon into the bowl, adding any bran left in the sieve. Add the oats and the fruit and nuts and mix in thoroughly with a wooden spoon, making sure the fruit and nuts are evenly distributed.

3 Using a rounded tablespoon of mixture for each cookie, spoon on to the lined baking sheet, setting the cookies well apart to allow for spreading. Gently press out using the back of the tablespoon so the cookies are about 1.25cm thick – they should be rather craggy rather than neat and tidy.

4 Bake in the heated oven for about 12 minutes until golden with light brown edges. Remove the sheet from the oven and set on a heatproof surface. Leave the cookies to cool and firm up for about 10 minutes, then carefully transfer them to a wire rack and leave until cold. Store in an airtight container for about 5 days.

CHOCOLATE FUDGE BROWNIES

Very dark, dense and intensely fudgy, these chocolate brownies are made the easy way – all in one pan with just a wooden spoon. You can add your own contrast of texture, such as nuts, dried fruit or more chocolate. Very good with a scoop of vanilla ice cream.

MAKES SIXTEEN

100g pecan halves, soft-dried
  morello/sour cherries OR white
  chocolate chips
175g unsalted butter
65g cocoa powder
340g caster sugar
2 medium free-range eggs,
  at room temperature
1 teaspoon vanilla extract
100g plain flour
salt

1 x 20cm square brownie tin OR
  cake tin, greased and base-lined*

1 Heat your oven to 180°C/350°F/gas 4. The nuts will have a deeper flavour if they are toasted, so if you are using them, rather than the cherries or chocolate chips, put them in a small tin or baking dish and toast in the heated oven for 5 minutes. Leave to cool, then chop roughly. Set aside.

2 Put the butter into a saucepan that is large enough to hold all the ingredients. Set over low heat and melt the butter gently, stirring every now and then.

3 Take the pan off the heat and set it on a heatproof surface. Sift the cocoa into the pan and stir into the butter with a wooden spoon. When the mixture is smooth stir in the sugar.

4 Beat the eggs with the vanilla using a fork, just until combined, then stir into the cocoa mixture. Sift the flour and a couple of pinches of salt into the bowl and stir in. When thoroughly combined, and you can no longer see any streaks of flour, stir in the chopped nuts, cherries or chocolate chips.

5 Transfer the mixture to the prepared tin and spread evenly. Bake in the heated oven for about 30 minutes until a wooden cocktail stick inserted into the brownie cake halfway between the side of the tin and the centre comes out just clean; the centre will still be a bit soft and moist. (The mixture will keep on cooking for a few minutes after it comes out of the oven, and you don't want the brownies to be dry or cake-like.)

6 Set the tin on a wire rack. Run a round-bladed knife around the inside of the tin to loosen the brownie cake, then leave to cool. When cold, cut into 16 squares. Store in an airtight container for up to 5 days.

DOUBLE GINGER CRACKLES

Properly gingery biscuits, well flavoured with freshly grated ginger
plus ground ginger and black treacle, are easy and quick to mix and bake.
You can use caster sugar (white or golden) or cinnamon sugar. (Buy this in tubs
at the supermarket or make it yourself – see below.)

MAKES TWENTY-FIVE

4cm piece fresh root ginger
115g unsalted butter, diced
85g black treacle
350g self-raising flour
pinch of salt
1 teaspoon bicarbonate of soda
1 tablespoon ground ginger
200g caster sugar OR cinnamon sugar
1 medium free-range egg, at room
  temperature, beaten to mix
40g demerara sugar OR cinnamon
  sugar, for sprinkling

1–2 baking sheets, lined with
  baking paper

1 Heat your oven to 170°C/325°F/gas 3. Peel the ginger, then grate it finely into a bowl. Measure 2 slightly rounded teaspoons into a small pan. Add the butter and black treacle to the pan and melt gently over low heat. Stir with a wooden spoon until smooth, then set the pan aside on a heatproof surface to cool until just barely warm.

2 While you are waiting, sift the flour, salt, bicarbonate of soda and ground ginger into a mixing bowl. Add the caster or cinnamon sugar and mix well. Make a well in the centre.

3 Pour the egg and the melted mixture into the well and mix everything together with the wooden spoon. Then get your hands into the bowl and press and work the ingredients together to make a dough.

4 With your hands roll the mixture into 25 walnut-sized balls and arrange them well apart on the lined baking sheets. Slightly flatten the balls with your fingers, then sprinkle with demerara or cinnamon sugar.

5 Bake in the heated oven for 14–16 minutes until the biscuits are slightly darker around the edge (14 minutes will give you a softer, slightly chewy biscuit, and 16 minutes a crisper one). Set the baking sheets on a heatproof surface and leave the biscuits to cool and firm up for about 5 minutes, then carefully transfer them to a wire rack. When cold, store in an airtight container for about 5 days.

TO MAKE CINNAMON SUGAR
Shake 250g golden caster sugar with 1 teaspoon ground cinnamon and a cinnamon stick in a lidded container. Leave to infuse for a couple of days before using.

WELSH CAKES

Warm, slightly spicy and sweet, these little treats are very quick indeed – there's no oven to heat up as they are cooked on top of the stove, or over the fire, on a heavy griddle or in a frying pan.

225g self-raising flour
$\frac{1}{2}$ teaspoon ground mixed spice
80g caster sugar, plus extra for
 sprinkling
100g slightly salted butter, chilled
 and diced
25g currants OR sultanas, or
 a mixture
1 free-range egg yolk
about 4 tablespoons milk

1 x 5cm fluted round cutter; a griddle
 OR heavy-based frying pan

1 Sift the flour, mixed spice and sugar into a mixing bowl. Add the pieces of butter and toss them around in the flour so they are lightly coated. Using the tips of your fingers, rub the butter into the flour until the mixture looks like fine crumbs. Add the currants or sultanas and stir in with your hand.

2 Mix the egg yolk with 3 tablespoons of the milk and pour into the bowl. Stir in with a round-bladed knife to make a rather soft but not sticky dough. If the mixture feels dry and is hard to bring together, add more milk a teaspoon at a time.

3 Turn out the dough on to a lightly floured worktop. Lightly dust a rolling pin with flour, then roll out the dough to about 1cm thick. Dip the cutter in flour and stamp out rounds. Gather up the trimmings, re-roll and stamp out more rounds.

4 Heat the griddle or frying pan – grease it lightly only if necessary as the Welsh cakes shouldn't be fried in fat. Cook the little cakes, in batches, for about 2 minutes on each side until they are puffed up and a good golden brown and feel firm when gently pressed. Remove from the pan with a palette knife, dust with caster sugar and eat warm immediately.

SCONES

The lightest scones are quickly made with the least possible handling
and then baked immediately. Buttermilk adds a lovely taste as well as
an excellent texture, but you can also use milk, or a tablespoon of natural yoghurt
(with no sugar or flavourings) made up to 100ml with milk.

MAKES EIGHT OR NINE

250g self-raising flour
good pinch of salt
50g caster sugar
50g unsalted butter, chilled and diced
1 medium free-range egg
about 100ml buttermilk

1 x 6cm round cutter (plain or fluted);
  a baking sheet, greased with butter

1 Heat your oven to 220°C/425°F/gas 7. Sift the flour, salt and sugar into a mixing bowl. Add the butter and toss the pieces in the flour just to separate and coat them. Rub the butter into the flour using just the tips of your fingers, lifting your hands up to the rim of the bowl so the crumbs and flakes of the mixture fall through your fingers back into the bowl – this adds to the lightness of your scones. Continue rubbing in until the mixture looks like fine crumbs – give the bowl a shake to check there are no lumps of butter visible.

2 Beat the egg with the buttermilk, just until thoroughly combined. Stir the egg mix into the crumbs using a round-bladed knife to make a fairly soft, but not wet or sticky, dough. If there are dry crumbs at the bottom of the bowl or the dough feels dry and is difficult to bring together, add a little more buttermilk (or milk) a teaspoon at a time. The dough should look a bit rough and shaggy. Don't overwork it – a light touch is vital.

3 Turn the dough out on to a lightly floured worktop and knead just for a few seconds to bring the dough together so it looks slightly smoother. Lightly flour your fingers, then press and pat out the dough to about 3cm thick. Dip the cutter in flour and stamp out rounds. Press the trimmings together and stamp out more rounds.

4 Set the rounds slightly apart on the prepared baking sheet. Dust lightly with flour, then bake in the heated oven for about 12 minutes until a good golden brown. Transfer to a wire rack and cool slightly. Eat warm from the oven – or the next day, toasted and spread with butter.

FRUITY SCONES
Stir in 50g sultanas or raisins before you add the egg mixture.

MAPLE & LEMON DROP SCONES

Drop scones – or Scotch pancakes as they are also known – are best eaten warm from the pan, but any leftover scones can be toasted the next day.

MAKES ABOUT SIXTEEN

110g plain flour
$^3/_4$ teaspoon bicarbonate of soda
$1^1/_2$ teaspoons cream of tartar
1 tablespoon caster sugar
finely grated zest of 1 small
  (or $^1/_2$ medium) unwaxed lemon
1 medium free-range egg, beaten
  to mix
140ml milk
2 tablespoons maple syrup
butter or oil for the griddle

1 griddle OR heavy-based frying pan

1 Sift the flour, bicarbonate of soda, cream of tartar and sugar into a mixing bowl. Add the lemon zest and mix in.

2 Make a well in the mixture and add the egg, milk and maple syrup. Mix to a lump-free batter using a wire hand whisk; stop whisking as soon as the batter looks smooth – if over-whisked the scones could be tough.

3 Heat the griddle or frying pan over medium heat. Grease it very lightly by rubbing with a ball of kitchen paper and a knob of butter or splash of oil. To check the pan is the right temperature drop a teaspoon of the scone batter into the centre; the batter should hold its shape and the underside turn golden in 2 minutes. Adjust the heat if necessary.

4 Cook the scones in batches, using a tablespoon of batter for each one. Cook for about 2 minutes until the top surface has started to set and the underside is golden. Turn the scones over with a palette knife and cook for another 2 minutes until the other side is golden. Re-grease the pan as needed between scones.

5 Keep the cooked scones warm in a clean, dry cloth and eat as soon as possible, with butter or maple syrup.

MARY'S FLORENTINES

MAKES EIGHTEEN

50g unsalted butter
50g demerara sugar
50g golden syrup
50g plain flour
25g dried cranberries, finely chopped
50g candied peel, finely chopped
25g blanched almonds, finely chopped
25g walnut pieces, finely chopped
200g dark chocolate
   (70% cocoa solids)

3 baking sheets, lined with baking
   paper OR silicone sheets;
   thermometer

1 Heat your oven to 180°C/350°F/gas 4. Measure the butter, sugar and syrup into a pan and heat gently until the butter has melted. Remove from the heat.

2 Add the flour, cranberries, candied peel and nuts to the pan and stir well to mix.

3 Using a teaspoon of mixture for each Florentine, spoon 6 dollops on to each of the prepared baking sheets, leaving plenty of room for the biscuits to spread.

4 Bake in the heated oven for 8-10 minutes until golden brown. Leave the Florentines to cool and firm up before lifting them on to a wire rack with a palette knife. If they have become too hard to remove, pop them back into the oven for a few moments so they soften.

5 Break 100g of the chocolate into a heatproof bowl and set over a pan of simmering water. Heat, stirring frequently, until the chocolate reaches a melting temperature of 53°C. Meanwhile, finely chop the remaining chocolate.

6 Carefully remove the bowl from the pan. Add the finely chopped chocolate and stir gently until smooth. Keep stirring until the chocolate has cooled to 26°C.

7 Spread a little melted chocolate over the flat base of each Florentine. Cool slightly before marking a zigzag in the chocolate with a fork. Leave to set, chocolate side up, on the wire rack or baking paper. Store in an airtight container.

PAUL'S SAVOURY BISCUITS

2 medium free-range eggs
375g plain flour
1 teaspoon salt
125g unsalted butter, softened
40ml water

For the flavourings

2 tablespoons poppy seeds
40g Parmesan cheese, freshly grated
1 tablespoon sun-dried tomato paste
1 tablespoon sesame seeds

1 x 7cm round cutter; 2 large baking
sheets, dusted with flour; stand mixer
with dough hook

1 Lightly beat one of the eggs in a bowl. Add the flour,
salt, butter and water and, using a mixer, mix well for
5 minutes to make a dough.

2 Divide the dough in half. In a mixer and working one half at
a time, add the poppy seeds to one half of the dough and the
cheese and tomato paste to the other.

3 Using a rolling pin, roll out each piece of dough on a lightly
floured worktop to about 3mm thick. Place on a baking sheet
or tray, cover with clingfilm and chill for 30 minutes.

4 Heat your oven to 200°C/400°F/gas 6. Using the round
cutter, cut out 18 discs from each sheet of dough. Place the
discs on the floured baking sheets.

5 Beat the remaining egg and brush over the discs. Sprinkle
the sesame seeds on to the Parmesan and tomato discs.

6 Bake in the heated oven for 10–15 minutes until golden
brown. Transfer to a wire rack to cool. Serve warm or cold.

THE PERFECT SOFT WHITE SANDWICH BREAD •
POPPYSEED WHITE BLOOMER • CHEDDAR &
MUSTARD LOAF • MULTIGRAIN LOAF • IAIN'S
MOROCCAN PLAIT WITH BESSARA DIP •
FIG & TOASTED HAZELNUT WHOLEMEAL BREAD •
PLAITED RICH SAFFRON LOAF • PIGS
IN A BLANKET • IRISH BRACK • PIZZETTE •
JORDAN'S RYE & SPELT ROLLS • CINNAMON &
RAISIN JUMBLE LOAF • CHEAT'S SOURDOUGH •
STICKY HONEY CINNAMON BUNS • CRUNCHY
CRAGGY LOAF • STUFFED FOCACCIA • BANANA
BREAD • HOT CROSS BUN LOAF • PAUL'S
CHOCOLATE & CHERRY LOAF • PAUL'S CIABATTA •
PAUL'S POVITICA • PAUL'S ROQUEFORT &
WALNUT-FILLED LOAF • PAUL'S CHOCOLATE &
RASPBERRY DOUGHNUTS

BREADS

THE PERFECT SOFT WHITE SANDWICH BREAD

This bread slices well, without too many crumbs, and has a soft, light and moist texture and plenty of flavour. It makes wonderful toast too and keeps well for several days. The same dough can be shaped into oval baps with a thin, floury crust, just right for splitting and filling.

MAKES ONE MEDIUM LOAF

500g strong white bread flour
1 x 7g sachet fast-action dried yeast
7g sea salt, crushed
30g unsalted butter, melted but not hot
1 teaspoon golden syrup
about 325ml lukewarm milk
dab of unsalted butter, to finish

1 x 900g loaf tin, about 26 x 12.5 x 7.5cm, greased with butter

1 Put the flour, yeast and salt into a large mixing bowl (or the bowl of a free-standing electric mixer fitted with the dough hook) and mix well. Make a well in the centre. Add the melted butter and golden syrup to the well, then pour in the lukewarm milk. Mix everything together with your hand (or the mixer on the lowest speed) to make a soft dough.

2 If there are dry crumbs in the base of the bowl, or the dough feels dry and too firm to bring together, add more milk a tablespoon at a time. If the dough is sticky or feels wet, or clings to the sides of the bowl, then work in a little more flour. Leave the dough uncovered in the bowl to rest for 5 minutes to allow the flour to become fully hydrated (see the Baker's Guide page 10 for more information).

3 Turn out the dough on to a very lightly floured worktop and knead thoroughly for 10 minutes (or 5 minutes in the mixer on the lowest speed) until slightly firmer, silky smooth and very pliable. Return the dough to the bowl and cover with a snap-on lid or clingfilm. Leave to rise at normal room temperature for about 1 hour until doubled in size.

4 Punch down the risen dough to deflate it before turning it out on to a very lightly floured worktop. Knead the dough a couple of times, then flour your fingers and firmly press out to an evenly thick rectangle about 26 x 30cm. Roll up the dough fairly tightly from one short end, like a Swiss roll, pinching the dough together each time you roll it. Pinch the seam firmly together, then tuck the ends under and set the loaf in the prepared tin.

5 Gently press your hand down flat on top of the dough to push it into the corners and to flatten the surface – you want the loaf to have a neat, fairly brick-like shape when it's baked instead of the normal domed top.

6 Slip the tin into a large plastic bag, inflate slightly so the plastic won't stick to the dough as it rises and secure the ends. Leave the loaf to rise at normal room temperature for about 1 hour until doubled in size. Towards the end of the rising time, heat your oven to 220°C/425°F/gas 7.

7 Uncover the tin and bake the loaf for 15 minutes, then reduce the temperature to 180°C/350°F/gas 4. Bake for a further 20 minutes until the loaf is golden brown and sounds hollow when tapped on the underside (see the Baker's Guide page 11 for more information).

8 Set the turned-out loaf on a wire rack. Hold a dab of butter in a scrap of kitchen paper and gently rub over the top of the loaf (this will keep the crust soft). Leave until cold before slicing.

FLOURY BAPS

Make the dough as above and leave it to rise. After punching down, weigh the dough and divide into 8 equal portions. Lightly flour the worktop and your rolling pin, then roll out each piece to a neat oval about 12 x 7.5cm. Set the baps well apart on a baking sheet lined with baking paper. Brush them lightly with milk and dust the tops lightly with flour. Leave to rise uncovered at normal room temperature for 30 minutes only – the dough should not quite double in size. Just before baking (at the same temperature as above), dust the baps again with flour, then gently press your thumb into the centre of each (this will keep them flat during baking). Bake for about 15 minutes until golden brown. Transfer to a wire rack and leave to cool covered with a clean dry tea towel (for a soft crust). Makes 8.

POPPYSEED WHITE BLOOMER

From one 1.5kg bag of flour you can make a batch of bread for the week: a large loaf with a thin, crisp crust that slices neatly for sandwiches and toast, plus rolls for soup (or a second loaf to freeze). The dough is made in two bursts of action: the first mixture is left to ferment for several hours, which gives the bread extra flavour and helps it keep longer. Then a second dough is made and combined with the first one, and the bread is baked.

MAKES ONE LARGE LOAF AND
TWELVE ROLLS

1.5kg strong white bread flour
2 x 7g sachets fast-action dried yeast
about 900ml lukewarm water
25g sea salt, crushed
poppyseeds, for sprinkling

2 baking sheets, lined with
    baking paper

1 Put 1kg of the flour into a large bowl (or the bowl of a free-standing electric mixer fitted with the dough hook). Add 1 sachet of yeast and mix thoroughly. Add 600ml lukewarm water and mix by hand (or with the mixer on lowest speed) to make a soft but not sticky dough. If the dough feels wet and sticky, work in more flour a tablespoon at a time; if it's too dry, add more water a tablespoon at a time.

2 Turn out the dough on to a very lightly floured worktop and knead thoroughly for about 10 minutes (or 5 minutes in the mixer on the slowest speed) until the dough feels slightly firmer, and is very smooth and elastic.

3 Return the dough to the bowl and cover it tightly with a snap-on lid or clingfilm. Leave for at least 4 hours but no more than 6 hours at normal room temperature (or overnight in the fridge). The dough will puff up then slightly collapse.

4 When you're ready to finish the breads, mix 450g of the remaining flour with the other sachet of yeast and the salt in another mixing bowl. Add 300ml lukewarm water and mix to a fairly firm dough. Add this dough to the first batch of dough and knead together for 5 minutes on a lightly floured worktop (3–4 minutes in the mixer on slowest speed) until thoroughly combined and the resulting dough feels smooth and pliable but fairly firm (it will need to hold its shape as it is not baked in a tin). Cover the dough lightly with a sheet of clingfilm and leave on the worktop to rest for 15 minutes.

5 Divide the dough in half. Cover one portion again and set aside. Pat out the other portion to a large rectangle 3cm thick and about 30cm long. Fold in both short ends by about 4cm, then roll up the dough fairly tightly from one long side (like a Swiss roll), pinching it together every time you roll it over. Make sure the final seam is sealed well by pinching. Tuck the ends under slightly to make a fat roll, then set seam-side down on the lined baking sheet. This may sound fiddly, but it will result in an even-textured crumb without random air pockets.

6 Slip the baking sheet into a large plastic bag, slightly inflate it so the plastic won't stick to the dough as it rises and secure the end. Leave to rise at normal room temperature for 45-60 minutes until almost doubled in size (allow a bit longer if the first dough was in the fridge overnight).

7 Now weigh the second portion and divide it into 12 equal pieces. Shape each into a neat ball and arrange well apart on the other lined baking sheet. Leave to rise as for the loaf – the rolls will take 30-45 minutes to almost double in size.

8 Towards the end of the rising time, heat your oven to 220°C/425°F/gas 7. Put a roasting tin into the bottom of the oven to heat up.

9 When the loaf is ready to bake, uncover it and quickly brush the surface with lukewarm water. Sprinkle with poppyseeds. Slash the top with a sharp, serrated knife – 13 slashes are traditional. Working quickly, slide the baking sheet into the oven, then pour cold water into the hot roasting tin to create a good burst of steam and immediately close the oven door. Bake for 35-40 minutes until the loaf is a good golden brown and sounds hollow when tapped on the underside (see the Baker's Guide page 11 for more information).

10 When the rolls are ready for baking, uncover them, brush with water and sprinkle with seeds, then cut a cross in the top of each. Bake for 20-25 minutes until a good golden brown.

11 Transfer the cooked loaf and rolls to a wire rack and leave to cool.

CHEDDAR & MUSTARD LOAF

The perfect bread for ham sandwiches or to go with vegetable soup, this smells very enticing as it bakes. Use a strong Cheddar, with a good dollop of Dijon mustard to give a savoury kick. The same dough can be shaped into appealing plaited rolls that freeze well.

MAKES ONE LARGE LOAF OR EIGHT ROLLS

150g extra strong or mature
   Cheddar cheese, coarsely grated
500g strong white bread flour
5g sea salt, crushed
1 x 7g sachet fast-action dried yeast
2½ tablespoons Dijon mustard
300ml lukewarm milk

To finish
milk, for brushing
25g extra strong or mature Cheddar
   cheese, coarsely grated

1 x 900g loaf tin, about 26 x 12.5 x
   7.5cm, well greased with butter

1 Put the 150g grated cheese into a small bowl, add a tablespoon of the weighed flour and mix well (the flour will prevent the cheese from forming clumps in the dough). Set aside until needed.

2 Put the rest of the flour into a large mixing bowl (or the bowl of a free-standing electric mixer fitted with the dough hook). Add the salt and yeast and mix thoroughly. Make a well in the centre and add the mustard and milk, then work everything together with your hand (or the mixer on the lowest speed) to make a slightly firm dough. If it feels very soft, or sticks to your fingers or the sides of the bowl, work in a little more flour; if there are dry crumbs in the bottom of the bowl and it's hard to bring the dough together, or it feels stiff and dry, work in a little more milk (or water) a tablespoon at a time.

3 Turn out the dough on to a lightly floured worktop and knead for 5 minutes (3 minutes in the mixer on lowest speed). Cover the dough lightly with a sheet of clingfilm and leave it to rest for 5 minutes. Uncover the dough, scatter the cheese over and knead until it has been thoroughly incorporated - about 4-5 minutes (2-3 minutes in the mixer).

4 Return the dough to the bowl and cover with a snap-on lid or clingfilm. Leave to rise at normal room temperature for about 1 hour until doubled in size.

5 Punch down the risen dough to deflate it before turning it out on to a lightly floured worktop. Press out the dough to a rectangle about 26 x 30cm, then roll up from one short end, like a Swiss roll, pinching the dough together each time you roll. Pinch the seam together, then tuck the ends under. Set the roll, seam side down, in the prepared tin.

6 Slip the tin into a large plastic bag, slightly inflate it so the plastic won't stick to the dough when it is risen and secure the ends. Leave the dough to rise at normal room temperature for about 1 hour until almost doubled in size. Towards the end of the rising time, heat your oven to 190°C/375°F/gas 5.

7 Uncover the loaf and gently brush milk over the top. Scatter the grated cheese evenly over the surface – take care not to let the cheese fall too close to the rim of the tin as this could stop the 'oven-spring' (the almost instant extra rise of the dough when it meets the heat of the oven, before it starts to set).

8 Bake the loaf in the heated oven for 35–40 minutes until a good golden colour. To test if the bread is thoroughly baked, turn it out and tap the underside – it should sound hollow (see the Baker's Guide page 11 for more information).

9 Cool on a wire rack before slicing. This is excellent toasted – think about making toasted sandwiches and welsh rarebits too.

CHEDDAR & MUSTARD ROLLS

Weigh the dough, then divide it into 8 equal portions. With floured fingers, press each piece of dough into an 8 x 12cm rectangle. Cut each rectangle into 3 long strips, keeping the strips attached at one end by about 1cm; plait the strips and tuck the ends under. Set the rolls well apart on a baking sheet lined with baking paper, then leave to rise and finish as in steps 6 and 7 above. Bake in the heated oven for about 25 minutes until a good golden brown. Makes 8 rolls.

MULTIGRAIN LOAF

There's plenty of texture and flavour in this bread, but the mix of flours ensures it's not heavy or dense. Soaking the seed mixture helps to prevent the loaf from crumbling as you slice it, so don't skip this stage.

MAKES ONE LARGE LOAF

30g wheatgerm
30g porridge oats
30g linseeds (flaxseeds)
30g sesame seeds
30g sunflower seeds
10g sea salt
about 400ml lukewarm water
75g stoneground wholemeal bread
  flour (wheat or spelt)
50g stoneground rye flour
375g strong white bread flour
1 x 7g sachet fast-action dried yeast

1 x 900g loaf tin, about 26 x 12.5 x
  7.5cm, greased with butter

1 Put the wheatgerm, oats, linseeds, sesame and sunflower seeds, and salt into a bowl. Add 100ml of the lukewarm water and stir well, then leave to soak for an hour.

2 Mix together the 3 flours and the yeast in a large mixing bowl (or in a free-standing electric mixer fitted with the dough hook). With your hand (or the mixer on lowest speed) work in enough of the remaining lukewarm water to make a dough that's slightly firm rather than sticky or soft, but not dry or hard. Leave for 5 minutes to allow the flours to become fully hydrated (see the Baker's Guide page 10 for more information).

3 Turn out the dough on to a lightly floured worktop and knead thoroughly for 10 minutes (or 5 minutes in the mixer on lowest speed) until the dough feels quite elastic and pliable.

4 Add the soaked mixture to the kneaded dough and work in, kneading the dough gently until the seeds are evenly distributed. Return the dough to the bowl and cover with a snap-on lid or clingfilm. Leave to rise at normal room temperature for about 1 hour until doubled in size.

5 Punch down the risen dough to deflate before turning it out on to a lightly floured worktop. Shape it into a loaf to fit your tin: flatten the dough to a rectangular shape as wide as your tin is long and 2.5cm thick. Roll up the dough from one short end – like a Swiss roll – pinching the dough as you roll. Pinch the seam firmly, then tuck the ends under and lift the roll into the prepared tin seam side down.

6 Slip the tin into a large plastic bag, slightly inflate it so the plastic won't stick to the dough as it rises and secure the ends. Leave to rise at normal room temperature for about an hour until the loaf has almost doubled in size. Towards the end of the rising time, heat your oven to 230°C/450°F/gas 8.

7 Uncover the loaf and slash the top, straight down the centre, using a sharp knife. Bake in the heated oven for 15 minutes, then reduce the temperature to 200°C/400°F/gas 6 and bake for a further 15–20 minutes until the loaf is a good golden brown and sounds hollow when tapped on the underside (see the Baker's Guide page 11 for more information).

8 Leave the turned-out loaf to cool on a wire rack.

BREADS

67

IAIN

Where do you live?
London.

What do you get up to when you are not baking?
I enjoy visiting coffee shops or cafés at the weekends to enjoy their home bakes. I am also a keen photographer. But my biggest passion has to be travelling – my girlfriend and I love to experience new places.

How would you define yourself as a baker?
I consider myself an adventurous baker as I like to use new ingredients that I have discovered on my travels and that are in season. Having baked for about 20 years, since the age of ten – baking cake with my mum and bread with my dad – I have become a meticulous baker, and like to clean up after each task.

Why do you enjoy baking?
I think I enjoy baking because it is so different from my day job, and I like to eat cakes and pastries and there is nothing better than making them yourself.

What is your favourite thing to bake?
CAKE!

What are your favourite 3 items of kitchen equipment?
The food mixer I got for my birthday a few years ago.
A vintage flour shaker.
My cast-iron mortar and pestle.

MOROCCAN PLAIT WITH BESSARA DIP

Impressive to look at, this savoury four-strand plait ring is filled with black olives, goat's cheese and a spicy onion mixture, and served with a warm bean dip (see overleaf).

MAKES ONE LARGE LOAF PLUS DIP

For the dough

800g very strong white bread flour
4 teaspoons fast-action dried yeast
  (measured from 2 x 7g sachets)
450ml lukewarm water
2 teaspoons fine salt
3 tablespoons olive oil, plus extra
  for working
beaten egg, to glaze

For the filling

10 saffron threads
1 tablespoon very hot water
1 tablespoon olive oil
1 large white onion, finely chopped
2 tablespoons tomato purée
1 teaspoon harissa paste
150g small pitted black olives, drained
125g full-fat goat's cheese, crumbled
  or finely diced

1 To make the dough, mix 400g of the flour with 2 teaspoons of the dried yeast in a large mixing bowl. Work in the water with your hand to make a smooth, thick batter. Cover the bowl with clingfilm and leave on the worktop (at normal room temperature) for 30 minutes until puffed and bubbly.

2 Mix 200g of the remaining flour with the remaining 2 teaspoons of yeast and the salt. Add this mixture to the bowl of batter along with the oil and work in. Then add enough of the remaining flour to make a soft but not sticky dough.

3 Lightly oil the worktop and your fingers, then turn out the dough and knead thoroughly for 10 minutes until very smooth and elastic. Clean the mixing bowl, grease it lightly with olive oil and put the dough back into it. Cover the bowl with clingfilm and leave in a warm spot for about 1 hour until doubled in size.

4 While the dough is rising make the filling. Soak the saffron in the hot water in a small bowl. Heat the oil in a non-stick frying pan, add the chopped onion and fry until softened and starting to colour. Remove the pan from the heat and stir in the tomato purée, harissa and saffron mixture to make a paste. Leave to cool until needed.

5 Punch down the risen dough to deflate it, then turn it out on to the lightly floured worktop. Divide into 4 equal portions. Cover 3 portions with clingfilm. Roll out the last portion to a 50 x 10cm rectangle that is about 4mm thick.

6 Carefully spread a quarter of the onion paste over the dough, leaving a 2.5cm border of dough clear along one long side. Scatter a quarter of the olives and a quarter of the cheese over the onion paste. Starting from the long edge opposite the dough border, roll up the dough, fairly tightly, like a Swiss roll. Pinch the seam securely together to prevent the filling from leaking out. With your floured hands, very gently roll the sausage to and fro to stretch it out to 80cm. Set this thinner sausage aside on the worktop. Shape the remaining 3 portions of dough in the same way.

For the dip

1 x 400g jar/can fava or broad beans,
    drained
juice of 1 medium lemon
4 tablespoons olive oil
1 teaspoon ground cumin
1 teaspoon sweet smoked paprika
salt and black pepper
chopped mint, to garnish

1 x 15cm metal ring OR cake tin, well
    greased with oil; a large baking sheet,
    lined with baking paper

▼▼▼▼▼▼▼▼▼▼▼▼▼▼▼

7 Now make the 4-strand plait. Lay the 4 sausages side by side on the worktop and pinch them together at one end. Plait following the method and photographs on pages 78-79.

8 Set the oiled ring (or upturned cake tin) in the middle of the lined baking sheet. Handling the plait gently, loosely wrap it around the ring and pinch the ends together to form a neat wreath. Cover loosely with clingfilm and leave on the worktop, at normal room temperature, for about 45 minutes until almost doubled in size.

9 Towards the end of the rising time, heat your oven to 220°C/425°F/gas 7. Uncover the wreath and carefully brush with beaten egg to glaze (take care not to 'glue' the dough to the metal ring).

10 Bake in the heated oven for 20 minutes, then turn down the temperature to 200°C/400°F/gas 6 and bake for a further 20-25 minutes until the loaf is a good golden brown. To test if the loaf is cooked, carefully remove it from the baking sheet and metal ring, then tap the underside of the loaf – if it sounds hollow then it's cooked. If not, return the wreath to the baking sheet (no need for the metal ring now) and bake for a further 5 minutes, then test again. Transfer the loaf to a wire rack and leave to cool.

11 While the bread is baking or cooling, make the dip. Put the beans in a food processor and add half the lemon juice, all the oil and spices, and 4 tablespoons water. Blitz to make a creamy soup-like consistency (add a little more water if needed), then taste and add more lemon juice if you like and some seasoning. Transfer to a small pan. When the bread is ready to serve, heat the dip gently.

12 Pour the dip into a warmed tiny tagine or serving dish. Set the loaf on a board with the dip in the centre of the wreath. Garnish with mint and serve.

FIG & TOASTED HAZELNUT WHOLEMEAL BREAD

A good-looking, great-tasting, not too heavy loaf that's good just spread with butter, or served with cheese or cold meats. Try toasted slices with hummus or pâté, plus salad for lunch.

MAKES TWO MEDIUM LOAVES

100g blanched (skinned) hazelnuts
350g stoneground wholemeal
  bread flour
350g strong white bread flour
1 x 7g sachet fast-action dried yeast
10g sea salt, crushed
about 500ml lukewarm water
1–2 teaspoons rapeseed or olive
  oil, for kneading
150g soft-dried figs

2 baking sheets, lined with
  baking paper

1 Heat your oven to 180°C/350°F/gas 4. Tip the nuts into a small baking dish or tin and toast in the oven for 6–8 minutes until a light golden brown (keep an eye on the nuts as they can burn easily). Leave to cool, then chop roughly.

2 Meanwhile, start the dough. Put both flours, the yeast and salt into a large bowl (or the bowl of a free-standing electric mixer fitted with the dough hook). Mix well. Gradually work in enough lukewarm water to make a soft but not sticky dough (flours vary so you may need a bit more or less than 500ml). Leave the dough in the bowl, uncovered, for 5 minutes so the flours can become fully hydrated (see the Baker's Guide page 10 for more information).

3 Rub a teaspoon of oil on to your hands, then punch down the dough to deflate it. Turn it out on to a lightly oiled worktop. Knead the dough for 10 minutes until smooth and stretchy (or 5 minutes in the mixer on slowest speed).

4 With kitchen scissors, snip the woody stalks from the figs, then cut large figs into 8 chunks, smaller ones into 6 chunks. Scatter the figs and toasted nuts over the dough and knead for a couple of minutes until evenly distributed.

5 Divide the dough in half. Shape each piece into an oval about 22 x 12cm – these loaves don't have to be perfectly neat; in fact, they'll look better if they are not. Set each on a lined baking sheet. Slip the sheets into large plastic bags, slightly inflate so the plastic won't stick to the dough as it rises and secure the ends. Leave the loaves to rise at normal room temperature for 50–60 minutes until almost doubled in size. Towards the end of the rising time, heat your oven to 220°C/425°F/gas 7.

6 Uncover the loaves and bake in the heated oven for 15 minutes. Reduce the oven temperature to 190°C/375°F/gas 5 and bake for a further 20 minutes until the bread sounds hollow when the underside is tapped (see the Baker's Guide page 11 for more information). Transfer to a wire rack to cool.

PLAITED RICH SAFFRON LOAF

A magnificent loaf, perfect for a feast: a rich, glossy chestnut crust and soft, bright golden crumb with the unique taste and scent of saffron, that most luxurious of spices. For a really deep flavour, before soaking the saffron toast it in a moderate oven for 8–10 minutes until it is slightly darker in colour. Take the chance to learn how to make a four-strand plait – it'll be worth the effort!

$^3/_4$ teaspoon saffron threads
150ml hot water
700g strong white bread flour
35g unsalted butter, diced
1 x 7g sachet fast-action dried yeast
10g sea salt, crushed
1 teaspoon runny honey
1 medium free-range egg, at room temperature, beaten to mix
300ml milk, at room temperature
1 medium free-range egg, beaten with a pinch of salt, to glaze

1 baking sheet, lined with baking paper

1 Crumble the saffron into a small heatproof dish, pour over the hot water and leave to soak for at least an hour, or up to 6 hours if you can (the longer the better).

2 When you're ready to make the dough put the flour into a large bowl (or the bowl of a free-standing electric mixer fitted with the dough hook). Add the butter and rub in using just the tips of your fingers until the pieces of butter disappear. Stir in the yeast followed by the salt, then make a well in the centre of the mixture.

3 Pour the saffron liquid into the well and add the honey, egg and 250ml of the milk. Gradually work the flour into the liquids in the well using your hand (or the mixer on lowest speed) to make a dough that feels slightly firm rather than slightly soft; add more of the milk as you need. The texture is important – a dough that is stiff and dry or too firm will be as hard to plait as one that's slightly sticky or very soft.

4 Turn out the dough on to a lightly floured worktop and knead thoroughly for 10 minutes (or 5 minutes in the mixer on the lowest speed) until the dough is very stretchy and pliable and will keep its shape; knead in a little more flour if necessary. Return the dough to the bowl and cover with a snap-on lid or clingfilm. Leave to rise at normal room temperature for about 1$^1/_2$ hours until doubled in size.

5 Punch down the dough to deflate it, then turn it out on to the worktop. Weigh the dough and divide it into 3 or 4 equal portions, depending on which plait you are going to make.

6 To make a 3-strand plait: use your hands to roll each portion of dough to and fro on the unfloured worktop to make a 40cm-long rope of even thickness. Set the 3 ropes on the lined baking sheet and pinch them together at one end. (Don't worry if they are longer than the sheet at this point.) Plait the ropes together fairly loosely, without stretching the dough, to give a neat shape, then tuck the ends under.

7 To make a 4-strand plait: use your hands to roll each portion of dough to and fro on the unfloured worktop to make a 33cm-long rope of even thickness. Set the ropes on the lined baking sheet and pinch them together at one end. (Don't worry if they are longer than the sheet at this point.) Turn the baking sheet so the ropes are lying vertically in front of you, side by side and slightly apart, with the join at the top. Now run the far-left strand under the 2 middle ones, then take it back over the last one it went under. Then run the far-right strand under the twisted 2 in the middle, then back over the last strand it went under. Repeat until all the dough is plaited. Pinch the open ends together at the bottom of the plait and tuck them under to make a neat shape.

8 Slip the baking sheet into a large plastic bag, slightly inflate it so the plastic won't stick to the dough as it rises and secure the end. Leave the plait to rise at normal room temperature for 45–50 minutes until almost doubled in size – it's important that the plait keeps its shape so don't leave it in a warm spot or over-prove the dough. Towards the end of the rising time, heat your oven to 230°C/450°F/gas 8.

9 Uncover the loaf and carefully brush a thin layer of beaten egg over it to glaze. Leave it for a minute, then brush with a second fine layer – you'll get a glossier, more even result this way. Bake the plait in the heated oven for 15 minutes. Reduce the oven temperature to 200°C/400°F/gas 6 and bake for a further 20–25 minutes until the plait is a rich golden brown, smells deeply aromatic and sounds hollow when tapped on the underside (see the Baker's Guide page 11 for more information). Cool on a wire rack.

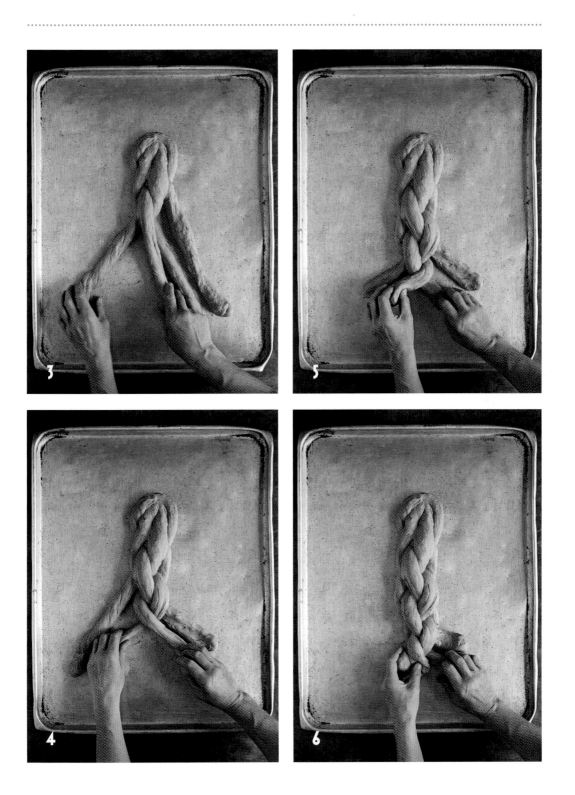

PIGS IN A BLANKET

Good sausages, with herbs or plenty of spice to flavour, are really delicious baked in a spiral of pretzel dough. You need medium to large sausages, rather than chipolatas here.

For the pretzel dough
250g strong white bread flour
1 teaspoon fast-action dried yeast
   (from a 7g sachet)
1 teaspoon caster sugar
½ teaspoon crushed sea salt
about 175ml lukewarm milk

For the filling
8 top-quality sausages (pork, beef,
   chicken – whatever is your favourite)
about 1 tablespoon your favourite
   mustard, for brushing
beaten free-range egg, to glaze
sesame seeds, for sprinkling

1 baking sheet, lined with baking paper

1 First make the pretzel dough. Put the flour, yeast, sugar and salt into a large bowl (or the bowl of a free-standing electric mixer fitted with the dough hook) and mix well. Add the lukewarm milk and mix everything together with your hand (or the mixer on the lowest speed) to make a fairly soft dough.

2 If there are dry crumbs in the bowl, or the dough feels dry or firm, work in more milk a tablespoon at a time. If the dough is very sticky and clings to the sides of the bowl or your fingers, work in a little more flour. Leave the dough uncovered in the bowl to rest for 5 minutes to allow the flour to become fully hydrated (see the Baker's Guide page 10 for more information).

3 Turn out the dough on to a very lightly floured worktop and knead for 10 minutes (or 5 minutes in the mixer on the lowest speed) until it feels slightly firmer and is very smooth and pliable. Return to the bowl, cover tightly with a snap-on lid or clingfilm and leave for 30 minutes until the dough looks puffy.

4 Punch down the dough, just to deflate it, then turn it out on to an unfloured worktop (the slight friction from the unfloured surface will make the dough easier to shape). Weigh the dough and divide it into 8. Shape each portion into a ball, then leave uncovered on the worktop to rest for 5 minutes.

5 With your hands roll each ball to and fro on the worktop to make a 30cm-long rope of even thickness.

6 Lightly brush each sausage with mustard, just enough to make it sticky, then wrap a rope of dough around it, in a spiral. Arrange spaced well apart on the lined baking sheet, with the ends of each rope of dough tucked underneath.

7 Leave to rise, uncovered, on the worktop for 15 minutes until the dough looks puffy. Meanwhile, heat your oven to 220°C/425°F/gas 7.

8 Lightly brush the dough with beaten egg to glaze and sprinkle with sesame seeds. Bake in the heated oven for 18–20 minutes until the dough is a good golden brown and the sausages are piping hot and cooked through (check by piercing the centre with the tip of small sharp knife).

9 Eat warm or cool, with extra mustard. Store any leftovers in a sealed container in the fridge for up to 24 hours.

IRISH BRACK

A dark and richly flavoured bread – thanks to strong tea – this is not too sweet to eat with some punchy cheese, or simply spread with good butter (try the kind flavoured with crystals of sea salt). You can use your favourite dried fruit mix – with or without mixed peel – but note that you do need to soak the fruit overnight.

2 tea bags (a strong breakfast blend or Assam)
300ml boiling water
350g dried mixed fruit
150g dark brown muscovado sugar
250g plain flour
$^1/_4$ teaspoon salt
1 teaspoon ground mixed spice
2 teaspoons baking powder
75g unsalted butter, chilled and diced
1 medium free-range egg, beaten to mix

1 x 450g loaf tin, about 19 x 12.5 x 7.5cm, greased with butter and lined with a long strip of baking paper*

1 Put the tea bags into a medium-sized heatproof bowl. Pour on the boiling water, then add the dried mixed fruit and sugar and stir well. Cover the bowl loosely with a clean, dry tea towel and leave on the worktop to soak overnight.

2 Next day, heat your oven to 170°C/325°F/gas 3. Remove the tea bags from the fruit mixture (give the bags a squeeze over the bowl before discarding).

3 Sift the flour, salt, mixed spice and baking powder into a large mixing bowl. Add the pieces of butter to the bowl and rub in until the mixture looks like fine crumbs. Add the beaten egg and the fruit/sugar/tea mixture and mix thoroughly with a wooden spoon.

4 Transfer the heavy, sticky mass to the prepared tin and spread evenly. Bake in the heated oven for 1-1$^1/_4$ hours until well risen and dark golden brown, and a wooden cocktail stick inserted into the centre of the loaf comes out clean.

5 Leave to cool in the tin for 15 minutes, then run a round-bladed knife around the inside of the tin to loosen the loaf and carefully lift it out (using the ends of the paper strip) on to a wire rack. Wait until completely cold before slicing. The loaf will be even better if you wrap it in foil and leave it to mature for 1-2 days before slicing.

PIZZETTE

These mini pizzas are great for entertaining as much of the work can be done well ahead. Instead of the usual tomato, mozzarella and olive topping, here red onions are slowly cooked until caramelised, then baked on the pizzette with a sharp blue Italian cheese.

MAKES TWENTY-FIVE MINI PIZZAS

For the dough

500g strong white bread flour
1 x 7g sachet fast-action dried yeast
5g sea salt, crushed
1/2 teaspoon dried herbes de Provence
1 tablespoon olive oil, plus extra
  for kneading
about 300ml lukewarm water

For the topping

3 tablespoons olive oil
5 medium to large red onions,
  finely sliced
sprig of fresh thyme OR a few fresh
  oregano leaves, chopped
1 tablespoon white wine
300g Gorgonzola piccante
salt and black pepper

2 baking sheets; baking paper

1 Start with the dough. Put the flour, yeast, salt, a few grinds of black pepper and the dried herbs into a large mixing bowl (or a free-standing electric mixer fitted with the dough hook). Mix thoroughly, then make a well in the centre and add the oil and water. Mix everything together with your hand (or the mixer on the slowest speed) to make a soft but not sticky dough. If there are dry crumbs at the bottom of the bowl, or the dough feels stiff and dry, work in more water a tablespoon at a time. If the dough is very sticky, and clings to the side of the bowl or your hands, work in a little more flour.

2 Rub your hands and the worktop with a few drops of olive oil so the dough won't stick, then turn out the dough and knead it thoroughly for about 10 minutes (or 5 minutes in the mixer on lowest speed) until very pliable and silky smooth.

3 Return the dough to the bowl and cover with a snap-on lid or clingfilm. Leave to rise on the worktop for about 1 hour until doubled in size (or leave in the fridge overnight).

4 Meanwhile, make the topping. Heat the oil in a medium-sized heavy-based pan. Add the onions and herbs and stir well. Cut a disc of greaseproof or baking paper to fit inside the pan and dampen it under the cold tap, then press the paper on top of the onions. Cover tightly with the lid and turn down the heat so the onions can cook gently in their own steam for 35 minutes until very tender, giving them an occasional stir.

5 Uncover the onions and stir gently over medium high heat until all the watery liquid has evaporated and the onions are slightly caramelised and darker in colour. Take care not to let them catch around the side of the pan. Add the wine (this livens up the rich topping) with a little salt and pepper and boil until the wine disappears. Leave to cool before removing the thyme sprig. Set aside until you're ready to bake the pizzas.

6 Heat your oven to its highest setting (check first to be sure it's clean or it may set off the smoke alarm). Punch down the risen dough before turning out on to a lightly oiled worktop. Weigh the dough and divide into 25 portions. Roll each into a neat ball, then oil your fingers and press out each ball to a disc about 7.5cm across. (If you prefer, you can roll out all of the dough and then stamp out discs with a round cutter.) Arrange the discs on sheets of baking paper that have been cut to fit your 2 baking sheets.

7 Put the (unlined) baking sheets into the oven to heat while you finish the pizzette. Spread the onions over the dough discs, right to the edge. Crumble or break the cheese into small lumps – sugar-cube-size if possible – and arrange in the centre of the dough discs. Remove the hot baking sheets from the oven, set them on a heatproof surface and carefully slide or lift the baking paper on to them.

8 Bake in the very hot oven for 6–10 minutes until the pizzette are puffed and golden brown around the edges (watch carefully to prevent them from over-browning). Leave to cool for a couple of minutes before serving.

JORDAN

Where do you live?
Nottingham.

What do you get up to when you are not baking?
I spend my days at work in front of a screen, so when I get home, I prefer to stay away from computers! When I'm not baking you can find me trying to DJ, playing board games, reading comics and painting.

How would you define yourself as a baker?
I have only been baking for three years now, but I am an adventurous and technical baker. I enjoy the process of baking and the rules that must be followed to get a good bake.

How did you get into baking?
My girlfriend used to decorate cakes and I was always more the chef of the house but, about three years ago, we both joined a local baking club. Once I discovered that the baking club awarded a 'best cake' each month it was like a red rag to a bull! At first the girlfriend and I would take it in turns, but that soon stopped as I became crazed by buttercreams and custards! I have taught myself everything I know from the internet and various books. I'm a firm believer that anyone can learn anything if they want to.

What is your favourite thing to bake?
I have two very different baking loves. My traditional love is iced buns and cinnamon rolls and my modern day favourites are sweets of all kinds!

What are your favourite 3 items of kitchen equipment?
The oven – What can you bake without one of these?!
A stand mixer – Vital for meringues and sugar work.
A sugar thermometer – You can't temper chocolate or make sweets without one!

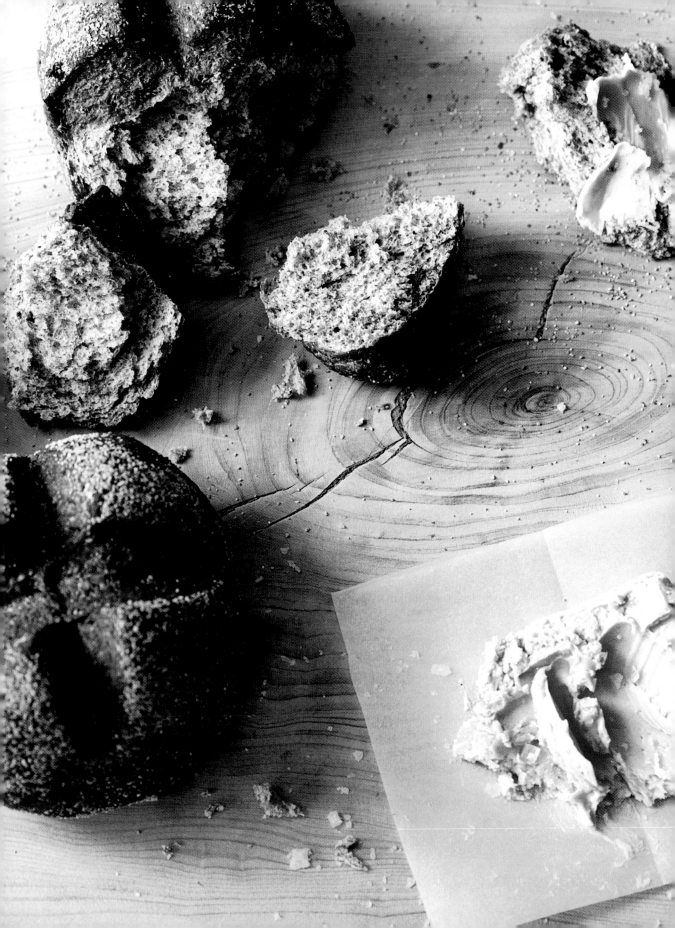

SIGNATURE BAKE

JORDAN'S
RYE & SPELT ROLLS

▼▼▼▼▼▼▼▼▼▼▼▼▼▼▼▼▼▼▼▼▼▼▼▼▼▼▼▼▼▼▼▼▼

There's plenty of flavour in these good-looking rolls. Combining spelt and white bread flours with rye flour gives the crumb a chewy but not heavy texture.

MAKES TWELVE LARGE ROLLS
PLUS HOME-MADE BUTTER

For the dough
500g medium rye bread flour
250g spelt bread flour
250g strong white bread flour
2 tablespoons vital wheat gluten
(optional)
15g fine sea salt
20g fast-action dried yeast
(from 3 x 7g sachets)
4 tablespoons runny clear honey
finely grated zest of 1 large
unwaxed lemon
15g poppyseeds
4 tablespoons olive oil, plus extra
for working
about 650ml lukewarm water
cornmeal or polenta, for dusting

For the butter
300ml double cream
fine sea salt

1-2 baking sheets; a roasting tin

▼▼▼▼▼▼▼▼▼▼▼▼▼▼▼

1 Put the 3 flours (and gluten, if using) into a large mixing bowl. Mix the salt into the flour on one side of the bowl and the yeast into the flour on the other side. Make a well in the centre and add the honey, lemon zest, poppyseeds and oil. Start to bring together with your hands, slowly adding enough water to make a rough-looking, slightly soft dough.

2 Lightly oil the worktop and your hands, then knead the dough for 10-15 minutes until it feels firmer and looks smooth and shiny. Pull and stretch out a little of the dough; if you can see through it and it doesn't tear then it's ready.

3 Clean and oil the bowl. Add the dough, cover with clingfilm and let rise in a warm place for 1 hour until doubled in size.

4 Punch down the risen dough, then turn out on to the oiled worktop and knead for 20 seconds or so, to make sure there are no pockets of air. Weigh the dough and divide it into 12 equal portions. Shape each into a neat ball and rub with a little cornmeal to give the rolls a light dusting. Also dust the baking sheet(s) with cornmeal, then arrange the rolls on it, set well apart to allow for expansion. Slip the sheet into a large plastic bag, fasten the end and leave to rise at normal room temperature for about 50 minutes until doubled in size.

5 Towards the end of the time, heat your oven to 220°C/425°F/ gas 7. Put an empty roasting tin in the bottom to heat up.

6 Uncover the rolls and cut a deep cross into the tops using a knife. Place in the oven. Pour cold water into the hot roasting tin to create steam, then quickly close the oven door. Bake for 25 minutes until the rolls are golden and sound hollow when tapped on the underside. Transfer to a wire rack to cool.

7 Meanwhile, make the butter. Put the cream into a large jar and screw the lid on tightly. Shake vigorously until the cream separates into lumpy curds of butter and watery buttermilk (this will take time!). Drain in a sieve set over a jug. Discard the watery buttermilk. Rinse the lump of butter left in the sieve in a bowl of cold water (swish it about with your hand; repeat with fresh water until the water is clear). Squeeze out excess water, then work in the salt with a round-bladed knife. Press into a dish, cover and keep in the fridge until needed.

BREADS

CINNAMON & RAISIN JUMBLE LOAF

A fun way to make bread, this sweet raisin dough is rolled up with brown sugar and cinnamon, then cut up and put into a loaf tin in a jumble. The result is that each slice of the baked bread looks different. Spread with butter or cream cheese, or toast the slices.

MAKES ONE LARGE LOAF

For the raisin dough
500g strong white bread flour
1 x 7g sachet fast-action dried yeast
7g sea salt, crushed
2 teaspoons caster sugar
250ml milk
50g unsalted butter, diced
1 medium free-range egg, at room
   temperature
75g raisins

For the filling
65g light brown muscovado sugar
1 teaspoon strong white bread flour
   OR plain flour
1 tablespoon ground cinnamon
milk, for brushing

1 x 900g loaf tin, about 26 x 12.5 x
   7.5cm, greased with butter and lined
   with a long strip of baking paper*

1 To make the dough, put the flour, yeast, salt and sugar into a large mixing bowl (or the bowl of a free-standing electric mixer fitted with the dough hook). Mix thoroughly.

2 Gently warm the milk with the butter until the butter has melted. Remove from the heat and cool until lukewarm – your little finger should feel quite comfy dipped in the mixture. Add the egg and beat with a fork just to combine.

3 Add the milky liquid to the flour mixture and work everything together with your hand (or the mixer on lowest speed) to make a very soft but not sticky dough. If there are dry crumbs in the bowl or the dough seems dry and stiff, and hard to bring together, add more milk (or water) a tablespoon at a time; if the dough sticks to your fingers or the side of the bowl, work in a little more flour.

4 Turn out the dough on to a worktop lightly dusted with flour and knead thoroughly for about 8 minutes (about 4 minutes with the mixer on lowest speed) until the dough is silky smooth and feels very pliable and stretchy. Scatter the raisins over the dough and gently knead in for about 2 minutes (slightly less if using the mixer) until evenly distributed.

5 Return the dough to the bowl and cover with a snap-on lid or clingfilm. Leave to rise at normal room temperature for about 1 hour until doubled in size.

6 Punch down the dough to deflate it before turning out on to a lightly floured worktop. Flour your fingers and, without kneading, gently pat out the dough to a rectangle roughly 2cm thick. Cover it lightly with a sheet of clingfilm and leave it to rest for 5 minutes – this will make it easier to roll out.

7 Meanwhile, for the filling, mix together the sugar, flour and cinnamon in a small bowl.

8 Flour a rolling pin, then roll out the dough to a neat rectangle 30 x 40cm. Brush the dough with milk, then sprinkle the filling evenly over the damp surface, leaving a 1cm border clear at one long side. Roll up the dough, like a Swiss roll, from the other long side, then pinch the seam firmly together to seal.

9 With a large sharp knife, slice the roll of dough across into 14 rounds. Set the slices cut side up and cut them in half to make half-moon shapes.

10 Arrange a layer of dough pieces in the lined tin, dough-side down. The rest of the dough pieces can be set on top in a higgledy-piggledy jumble – make sure the pieces are touching but don't press them in. Don't flatten or neaten the top; let it look a bit lumpy.

11 Slip the tin into a large plastic bag, slightly inflate it so the plastic won't stick to the dough as it rises and secure the ends. Leave the dough to rise at normal room temperature for about 1 hour until doubled in size. Towards the end of the rising time, heat your oven to 180°C/350°F/gas 4.

12 Uncover the loaf and brush the bumpy top very gently with milk. Bake in the heated oven for about 35 minutes until the loaf is a good golden brown. To test if it is thoroughly cooked, run a round-bladed knife around the inside of the tin to loosen the bread, then lift it out using the ends of the paper strip. Peel off the paper and tap the underside of the loaf – it should sound hollow. If it doesn't, put the paper back in place and the loaf back in the tin and bake for a further 5 minutes, then test again.

13 Cool on a wire rack before cutting into slices.

CHEAT'S SOURDOUGH

'True' sourdough is when a flour and water mixture is left so natural yeasts can be captured from the air and the flour, and then developed over many days, during which the mixture is 'fed' regularly with fresh flour and water. This recipe uses a much quicker method with a small amount of yeast – the long fermentation time yields a bread with a good chewy, slightly irregular crumb and crust that will keep fresh for even longer.

MAKES TWO MEDIUM LOAVES

50g rye flour OR wholemeal bread
    flour (wheat or spelt) OR strong
    white bread flour
800g strong white bread flour
1 teaspoon fast-action dried yeast
    (from a 7g sachet)
600ml water, at room temperature
15g sea salt, crushed

2 baking sheets (or 1 large sheet),
    lined with baking paper; a roasting tin

1 Put the 50g rye flour (or wholemeal or white flour) into a medium-sized mixing bowl. Add 300g of the 800g strong white bread flour and the yeast and mix thoroughly with your hand. Pour in 350ml room-temperature water and mix well with your hand to make a thick, sticky mixture.

2 Cover the bowl with a dampened tea towel and leave on the worktop (at normal room temperature) for 24 hours.

3 Uncover the bowl – the mixture will look bubbly and slightly grey. Add 250ml room-temperature water and stir in with your hand to make a smooth and runny batter. Tip this mixture into a bigger bowl.

4 Add half of the remaining 500g strong white bread flour to the bowl and beat/work in with your hand until fully incorporated. Sprinkle the salt over the mixture and work in, then gradually work in enough of the remaining flour to make a soft but not sticky dough.

5 Turn out the dough on to a lightly floured worktop and knead thoroughly for about 10 minutes until very elastic (you can also knead the dough on lowest speed in a free-standing electric mixer fitted with the dough hook).

6 Return the dough to the bowl and cover with a snap-on lid or clingfilm. Leave to rise until doubled in size – about 3 hours, depending on how lively your dough was to begin with and the room temperature.

7 Punch down the risen dough to deflate it before turning it out on to a lightly floured worktop. Divide the dough in half and leave it to rest, uncovered, for 5 minutes. Gently knead each piece for a minute, then shape into a neat round loaf. Set the loaves on the lined baking sheets (if using 1 sheet, set the loaves well apart).

8 Dust the top of each loaf with a little flour, then cover them loosely with a dry tea towel and leave to rise on the worktop for 1–1½ hours until doubled in size. Towards the end of the rising time, heat your oven to 220°C/425°F/gas 7; put an empty roasting tin in the bottom of the oven to heat up.

9 When the loaves are ready for baking, slash the top of each with a sharp knife. Put the baking sheet(s) into the oven. Add a handful of ice cubes or a mugful of cold water to the hot roasting tin to create a burst of steam, then quickly close the oven door. Bake for about 30 minutes until golden on top and they sound hollow when the underside is tapped (see the Baker's Guide page 11 for more information). Leave to cool on a wire rack.

STICKY HONEY CINNAMON BUNS

If you are a fan of Chelsea Buns try these – the soft sweet dough is similar
(the original recipe for Chelseas uses a lot of honey) but the filling is
gloriously sticky and nutty. A well-flavoured honey is essential.
You can replace the walnuts with almonds, pecans or macadamias.

MAKES TWELVE

For the sweet dough
450g strong white bread flour
1 x 7g sachet fast-action dried yeast
7g sea salt, crushed
1 medium free-range egg, at room
   temperature
2 tablespoons set honey
about 250ml lukewarm milk

For the sticky filling and topping
140g set honey
140g unsalted butter, softened
1 tablespoon ground cinnamon
140g light brown muscovado sugar
about 50ml whipping or single cream
100g walnut pieces

1 roasting tin OR baking tin (not
   loose-based), about 22 x 30 x 5cm,
   greased with butter

1 To make the dough, put the flour, yeast and salt into a large mixing bowl (or the bowl of a free-standing electric mixer fitted with the dough hook) and mix together. Make a well in the centre.

2 Mix the egg with the honey and 225ml of the lukewarm milk. When thoroughly combined pour into the well in the flour and mix everything together by hand (or with the mixer on the lowest speed) to make a very soft but not sticky dough that leaves the side of the bowl clean – add more milk as needed to make a dough that isn't hard or dry.

3 Turn out the dough on to a lightly floured worktop and knead thoroughly for 10 minutes (or 5 minutes in the mixer on lowest speed) until the dough feels silky smooth and very stretchy.

4 Return the dough to the bowl and cover with a snap-on lid or clingfilm. Leave to rise at normal room temperature for about 1$\frac{1}{2}$ hours until doubled in size.

5 Punch down the risen dough to deflate it before turning it out on to a lightly floured worktop. Press or roll it out to a 25 x 30cm rectangle of even thickness. Cover lightly with a sheet of clingfilm and leave to rest while you make the filling/topping mix.

6 Put the honey, soft butter, cinnamon and sugar into a mixing bowl and beat well with a wooden spoon until smooth and slightly fluffy. Stir in just enough cream to make the mixture slightly sloppy (don't worry if it looks as if it is about to curdle).

7 Uncover the dough and spread over about a third of the cinnamon mixture. Scatter half the nuts evenly over the dough, then roll up from one long side – the roll will feel (and look) a bit sticky at this point. Pinch the seam so the dough roll doesn't unravel, then cut across into 12 even-sized pieces with a very sharp knife.

8 Spoon the rest of the sticky cinnamon mixture into the prepared tin and spread evenly. Set the rolls cut side up on top so they are barely touching. Slip the tin into a large plastic bag, slightly inflate it so the plastic won't stick to the dough as it rises and secure the ends. Leave to rise as before for about 45 minutes until doubled in size. Towards the end of the rising time, heat your oven to 180°C/350°F/gas 4.

9 Uncover the tin and bake in the heated oven for about 25 minutes until the buns are golden and the filling is bubbling up around them. Set the tin on a heatproof surface and leave to cool for a couple of minutes until the bubbling subsides.

10 Carefully run a round-bladed knife around the inside of the tin to loosen the buns. Place an upturned large rimmed baking sheet on top of the tin and very carefully turn them over while holding them tightly together – the caramel is still very hot. The buns will fall out on to the baking sheet. Lift off the tin and scrape any caramel left in the tin on to the buns.

11 Scatter the remaining nuts over the top, then leave the buns to cool before pulling them apart. These are best eaten the same or the next day.

CRUNCHY CRAGGY LOAF

Unlike a yeasted dough made with strong bread flour, the dough here should be mixed with a light touch, until the ingredients just come together, to avoid a tough, heavy result. If you prefer a slightly softer crust, as soon as the loaf comes out of the oven, rub the top with a dab of butter on a scrap of greaseproof paper.

MAKES ONE MEDIUM LOAF

300g plain stoneground wholemeal flour (spelt or wheat)
100g plain white flour
1 teaspoon bicarbonate of soda
1 teaspoon salt
25g unsalted butter, chilled and diced
50g porridge oats
50g medium oatmeal, plus extra for dusting
1½ tablespoons black treacle
375ml buttermilk

1 baking sheet, lined with baking paper

1 Heat your oven to 220°C/425°F/gas 7. Put both flours into a mixing bowl, add the bicarbonate of soda and salt, and mix everything together well with your hand. Add the butter and rub in with the tips of your fingers until the pieces of butter disappear. Stir in the oats and oatmeal with your hand.

2 Add the treacle to the buttermilk and mix thoroughly (this will prevent streaks in the cooked bread). Pour into the flour mixture and quickly mix everything together: you can use a wooden spoon, a round-bladed knife or a plastic spatula, although your hands do a fine job. Don't overwork the dough or the bread will be tough – stop mixing once you have a slightly sticky and rather shaggy-looking dough. If there are dry crumbs and it's hard to bring the dough together, add more buttermilk (or milk or water) a tablespoon at a time. If the dough sticks to your fingers or the side of the bowl, work in a little more flour.

3 Tip the dough out on to a very lightly floured worktop and knead it 3 or 4 times just to shape it into a slightly craggy ball. Set the ball on the lined baking sheet and dust it with oatmeal, then cut a deep cross into the top.

4 Bake in the heated oven for about 35 minutes until the loaf is browned and sounds hollow when you tap the underside (see the Baker's Guide page 11 for more information). Cool on a wire rack and eat the same or the next day, or toasted.

SWEET FRUITED SODA BREAD

Start making the dough as above. Once you've rubbed in the butter stir in the oats, but omit the oatmeal and add 50g demerara sugar, 1 teaspoon ground ginger and 150g raisins or sultanas (or a mixture). Mix thoroughly before adding the treacle/buttermilk mixture. Shape as above, but sprinkle the ball of dough with demerara sugar instead of oatmeal. Bake as above. No need for jam – just cut thick slices from the warm loaf and spread with butter.

STUFFED FOCACCIA

Enjoy this rosemary-scented focaccia warm from the oven. It has a layered filling of small tender spinach leaves, salami and pecorino (a hard Italian cheese), but you could use roasted sweet peppers, firm mozzarella, crumbled goat's cheese, sun-dried tomatoes, a few anchovy fillets or olives instead. Don't be tempted to add more olive oil to the dough as you'll risk it becoming heavy and soggy.

MAKES ONE LARGE BREAD

For the focaccia dough
500g strong white bread flour
1 x 7g sachet fast-action dried yeast
7g sea salt, crushed
1 slightly rounded teaspoon finely
  chopped fresh rosemary
3 tablespoons olive oil, plus extra for
  kneading and brushing
about 300ml lukewarm water

For the filling
75g fresh young spinach leaves
100g pecorino cheese, thinly sliced
100g thinly sliced salami OR ham
  OR prosciutto
1 medium-hot red chilli, finely chopped,
  or to taste
black pepper

1 roasting tin OR baking tin (not
  loose-based), about 20 x 30cm,
  brushed with olive oil

1 To make the focaccia dough put the flour, dried yeast, salt and rosemary into a large mixing bowl (or the bowl of a free-standing electric mixer fitted with the dough hook). Mix thoroughly. Add the oil and water and mix with your hand (or the mixer on lowest speed) to make a very soft dough. If there are dry crumbs in the bottom of the bowl, or the dough feels stiff and dry or is difficult to bring together, work in more lukewarm water a tablespoon at a time. If the dough feels wet or sticky and clings to the sides of the bowl, or your fingers, work in a little more flour.

2 Rub a little olive oil on to the worktop and your fingers, to prevent the dough from sticking, then turn out the dough and knead it very thoroughly for 10 minutes (or 5 minutes in the mixer on lowest speed) until slightly firmer and very elastic.

3 Return the dough to the bowl and cover tightly with clingfilm or a snap-on lid. Leave to rise at normal room temperature for about 1 hour until the dough has doubled in size.

4 While the dough is rising, thoroughly wash and dry the spinach leaves (a salad spinner works best); trim any rind from the cheese; and remove the skin from the salami.

5 Punch down the risen dough to deflate it, then turn out on to a lightly oiled worktop. Don't knead it, just divide it in half. Gently pat and press out 1 piece to a rectangle to fit your tin. Place in the tin and gently push out to touch the sides – don't worry if the dough springs back.

6 Cover the dough with the salami, arranged in an even layer, leaving a 1cm border of dough clear around the edges. Lightly season with pepper, then cover the salami with the cheese slices. Scatter chilli evenly on top, then finish with the spinach.

7 Press and pat out the remaining dough to a rectangle to fit the tin. Set on top of the filling. Gently press out any pockets of air, then pinch the dough seams together all around the edges to seal in the filling. Make a few air holes with the tip of a small sharp knife. Slip the tin into a large plastic bag, slightly inflate it so the plastic won't stick to the dough as it rises and seal the end. Leave to rise at normal room temperature for about 45 minutes until almost doubled in size. Towards the end of the rising time, heat your oven to 220°C/425°F/gas 7.

8 Uncover the tin and gently brush the top of the focaccia with a little olive oil. Bake in the heated oven for 20–25 minutes until crisp and golden brown. Carefully turn the focaccia out of the tin on to a wire rack and leave to cool (if cooled in the tin, the bread would turn soggy as the steam condenses). Cut into large squares and eat warm or at room temperature. Store any leftovers in the fridge.

BANANA BREAD

Here's a great way to use up those bananas with skins that have almost entirely turned brown. They'll make an excellent bread that's good with cream cheese or eaten plain. The addition of a little crème fraîche lightens the crumb. To turn the bread into a cake to enjoy with coffee, add a quick, crunchy streusel topping that is often used on fancy muffins.

MAKES ONE MEDIUM LOAF

75g walnut pieces
125g unsalted butter, softened
150g light brown muscovado sugar
2 medium free-range eggs, at room
   temperature, beaten to mix
250g plain flour
2 teaspoons baking powder
$1/4$ teaspoon ground cinnamon
good pinch of salt
250g peeled ripe bananas
   (about 2 large or 3 smaller bananas)
2 tablespoons crème fraîche OR
   soured cream

1 x 900g loaf tin, about 26 x 12.5 x
   7.5cm, greased with butter and lined
   with a long strip of baking paper*

1 Heat your oven to 180°C/350°F/gas 4. Tip the walnut pieces into a small baking dish or tin and toast in the heated oven for 5–7 minutes until lightly coloured (toasting deepens the flavour). Remove from the oven and leave to cool while you make the banana mixture. Leave the oven on.

2 Put the butter and sugar into a large mixing bowl and beat well with a wooden spoon or electric mixer for about 2 minutes until fluffy. Scrape down the side of the bowl, then beat in the eggs, a little at a time – don't worry if the mixture starts to curdle a little.

3 When all the eggs have been added, sift the flour, baking powder, cinnamon and salt into the bowl. Gently stir in with the wooden spoon or a plastic spatula until the flour has almost, but not quite, disappeared.

4 Mash the bananas on a plate with a fork – they should still be a bit lumpy rather than a smooth purée. Add to the bowl with the crème fraîche and stir in. Transfer the mixture to the tin and spread evenly.

5 Bake in the heated oven for about 1 hour until golden and a wooden cocktail stick inserted into the centre comes out clean. Leave to firm up and cool in the tin for about 15 minutes before lifting out (use the ends of the lining paper to help) on to a wire rack to finish cooling. Once cold, wrap the bread in foil or greaseproof paper and eat within 3 days.

STREUSEL-TOPPED BANANA BREAD

Put 100g each of plain flour, caster sugar and unsalted butter (chilled and diced) into a mixing bowl. Rub in until the mixture looks like breadcrumbs. Mix in 100g walnut pieces (chopped a bit finer). Scatter the mixture evenly on top of the uncooked banana mixture in the tin and press on to the surface firmly but gently. Bake as above, allowing an extra 5–10 minutes in the oven, then cool. Dust with sifted icing sugar before serving, cut in thick slices.

HOT CROSS BUN LOAF

A Good Friday tradition, small buns marked with a cross have been eaten since Saxon times. The light-textured sweet fruit dough, made with plenty of spice, can also be baked as one giant bun. You can use a bag of regular dried fruit mix (currants, raisins, sultanas and peel) or a luxury type (which can include cherries, apricots, cranberries and pineapple pieces). Or make up your own mixture from the wide choice of dried fruit available now.

MAKES ONE LARGE LOAF

250ml milk
60g unsalted butter, diced
500g strong white bread flour
7g sea salt, crushed
2 teaspoons ground mixed spice
1/2 teaspoon freshly grated nutmeg
1 x 7g sachet fast-action dried yeast
50g light brown muscovado sugar
150g mixed dried fruit
1 medium free-range egg, at room temperature, beaten to mix

For the cross

4 tablespoons strong white bread flour
3 tablespoons cold water

For the glaze

4 tablespoons very hot milk
2 tablespoons caster sugar

1 x 20.5cm sandwich tin, very well greased with butter; a small disposable piping bag OR a plastic bag

1 Gently warm the milk with the butter until melted. Remove from the heat and cool until the mixture just feels comfy when you dip a finger in.

2 Tip the flour into a large mixing bowl (or the bowl of a free-standing electric mixer fitted with the dough hook). Add the salt, mixed spice, nutmeg, yeast, sugar and dried fruit and mix thoroughly so there are no lumps of sugar or clumps of fruit. Make a well in the mixture and pour in the beaten egg and the buttery milk. Mix everything together with your hand (or the mixer on the slowest speed) to make a very soft and slightly sticky dough.

3 Turn out the dough on to a lightly floured worktop and knead for 5 minutes (3 minutes in the mixer on slowest speed). Cover the dough with the upturned bowl and leave to rest for 5 minutes, then knead it again for 5 minutes (3 minutes in the mixer) until the dough feels very elastic and firmer, though still soft. It's important this dough doesn't become tough and dry, so only work in more flour if the dough still feels sticky.

4 Return the dough to the bowl and cover with a snap-on lid or clingfilm. Leave to rise on the worktop until doubled in size – 1–1¹/₂ hours, depending on the temperature in your kitchen.

5 Lightly flour your knuckles and punch down the risen dough to deflate it. Turn it out on to a lightly floured worktop and knead it gently for a minute. Shape the dough into a neat ball about 16cm across and set it into the buttered tin. Slip the tin into a large plastic bag, slightly inflate it so the plastic won't stick to the dough as it rises and secure the ends. Leave to rise as before for about 1 hour until the dough almost fills the tin.

6 Towards the end of the rising time, heat your oven to 200°C/400°F/gas 6, and make the paste for the cross. Mix together the flour and water to make a thick, smooth paste that can be piped. Spoon the paste into the piping bag and cut off the tip.

7 Pipe a cross on top of the dough, taking care you don't glue the mixture to the side of the tin. Bake in the heated oven for about 30 minutes until the bun is a good, rich brown colour and sounds hollow when you tap the underside (see the Baker's Guide page 11 for more information). Transfer to a wire rack.

8 To glaze the bun, stir the hot milk with the sugar until dissolved, then quickly brush over the bun while it is still hot from the oven. Leave to cool before slicing. This is best eaten the same or the next day, or toasted, or even used for a special bread and butter pudding.

INDIVIDUAL HOT CROSS BUNS

If you would rather bake a dozen small buns, make up the dough and leave it to rise as above. When you get to Step 5 weigh the ball of dough and divide it into 12 equal portions. Shape each into a neat ball. Arrange the balls well apart on a baking sheet lined with baking paper, then slip the sheet into a slightly inflated, large plastic bag. Leave to rise at room temperature for about 45 minutes until doubled in size (or overnight in the fridge if you want to eat freshly baked buns for breakfast on Good Friday – let them return to room temperature for about 20 minutes while you heat up the oven). Pipe a cross on each bun, then bake (at the same temperature as above) for about 15 minutes. Brush the buns with the hot glaze as soon as they come out of the oven, then cool on a wire rack. Makes 12.

PAUL'S CHOCOLATE & CHERRY LOAF

MAKES ONE LOAF

500g strong white flour, plus extra
  for dusting
2 teaspoons salt
2 tablespoons olive oil
10g fast-action dried yeast
320ml cold water
390g jar black cherries, well drained
100g dark chocolate chips
100g white chocolate chips

1 baking sheet, dusted with flour

1 Put the flour into a bowl with the salt, olive oil and yeast. Slowly add the water, mixing with your hand to make a pliable dough.

2 Tip the dough out on to a lightly floured worktop and knead for 4-7 minutes until smooth and elastic. Add the cherries to the dough and work them in (you may need to add a little more flour if the dough becomes too sloppy), then work in the chocolate chips until they are evenly distributed.

3 Put the dough back into the bowl, cover and leave to rise for 1 hour until doubled in size.

4 Shape the dough into a 2-strand plait and place on the baking sheet. Dust with flour. Put the baking sheet into a large plastic bag, seal and leave to prove for 1 hour.

5 Heat your oven to 230°C/425°F/gas 8. Remove the baking sheet from the plastic bag and bake the bread in the heated oven for 20 minutes. Reduce the oven temperature to 200°C/400°F/gas 6 and bake for a further 20–25 minutes. Transfer to a wire rack to cool.

PAUL'S CIABATTA

MAKES FOUR LOAVES

500g strong white bread flour
10g salt
10g fast-action dried yeast
440ml cold water
flour and fine semolina, for dusting

1 x 3-litre square plastic container
    with a lid; a large baking sheet; stand
    mixer with dough hook

1 Put the flour, salt and yeast in a free-standing electric mixer fitted with the dough hook (don't put the salt directly on top of the yeast). Add three-quarters of the water, then begin mixing on a slow speed.

2 As the dough starts to come together, slowly add the remaining water, drip by drip. Then mix for a further 5–8 minutes on a medium speed until the dough is smooth and stretchy.

3 Lightly oil the plastic container (it's important to use a square tub as it helps shape the dough). Tip the dough into the oiled container and seal with the lid. Leave for $1\frac{1}{4}$–$1\frac{1}{2}$ hours until at least doubled or even trebled in size.

4 Dust the baking sheet with flour and semolina. Also dust your worktop heavily with flour and semolina.

5 Carefully tip out the dough (it will be very wet), trying to retain a rough square shape. Rather than knocking it back, handle it gently so you can keep as much air in the dough as possible. Coat the top of the dough with more flour and/or semolina.

6 Cut the dough lengthways, dividing it into 4 equal pieces. Stretch each piece of dough lengthways a little and place on the prepared baking sheet. Leave the ciabatta to rest for 30–45 minutes.

7 Heat your oven to 220°C/425°F/gas 7. Bake the ciabatta loaves for about 25 minutes until they are golden brown and sound hollow when tapped on the base. Cool on a wire rack.

PAUL'S POVITICA

For the dough

300g plain flour
40g caster sugar
7g salt
10g fast-action dried yeast
30g unsalted butter, melted
1 large egg, beaten to mix
150ml lukewarm whole milk
$\frac{1}{2}$ vanilla pod, split open lengthways

For the filling

60g unsalted butter
4 tablespoons whole milk
280g walnut pieces
100g caster sugar
2 tablespoons cocoa powder
$\frac{1}{2}$ vanilla pod, split open lengthways
1 egg yolk, beaten to mix

To assemble

15g unsalted butter, melted
1 egg white, beaten to mix
100g icing sugar

1 x 1kg loaf tin, greased with butter;
  a clean bedsheet; stand mixer with
  dough hook

1 Start with the dough. Tip the flour and sugar into the bowl of a free-standing electric mixer fitted with the dough hook. Add the salt to one side of the bowl and the yeast to the other side. Add the butter, egg and milk. Scrape the vanilla seeds out of the pod and add them, then begin mixing on slow speed. When the dough starts to come together, turn up to medium speed and mix for a further 5–8 minutes to make a soft, smooth and stretchy dough.

2 Tip the dough into a large oiled mixing bowl and cover with clingfilm. Leave to rise for about 1 hour until at least doubled in size.

3 Meanwhile, make the filling. Put the butter and milk in a small pan and heat until the butter has melted; remove from the heat. Put the walnuts, sugar and cocoa powder into the bowl of a food processor and add the seeds scraped from the vanilla pod. Blitz to a sandy powder. Add the egg yolk and the milk and butter mixture and pulse to combine. Set aside at room temperature.

4 Spread a clean bedsheet over your worktop and dust with flour. Turn the risen dough out on to the sheet and, without knocking it back, roll out into a large rectangle about 50 x 30cm. Brush the surface with the 15g melted butter.

5 Dust your hands with flour, then ease them, palms down, underneath the dough. Using the tops of your hands, stretch the dough out from the centre until it is very thin and opaque (you should be able to see the sheet through the dough). The rectangle should now measure about 1 metre x 60cm.

6 If the filling has been standing for a long time and seems too thick to spread easily, add a little warm milk to loosen it. Spread the filling gently over the dough – take care as the thin dough could tear – until evenly covered.

7 Starting at one long edge of the dough, lift the sheet and gently roll the dough up tightly, like a Swiss roll. Carefully lift the rolled dough and place one end in a bottom corner of the prepared loaf tin. Ease the roll around the base of the tin to form a U shape, then continue laying the roll over the first U shape to form a second U shape on top.

8 Put the loaf tin inside a clean plastic bag, seal and leave to prove for 1 hour. Towards the end of this time, heat your oven to 180°C/350°F/gas 4.

9 Remove the tin from the bag and brush the dough with beaten egg white. Bake in the heated oven for 15 minutes, then reduce the oven temperature to 150°C/300°F/gas 2 and bake for a further 45 minutes – if the top is beginning to burn, cover with foil.

10 Remove from the oven and leave to cool in the tin for 30 minutes before turning out on to a wire rack to cool completely.

11 When the loaf is cold, mix the icing sugar with a few drops of cold water to make a runny icing and drizzle it over the top.

PAUL'S ROQUEFORT & WALNUT-FILLED LOAF

MAKES ONE LOAF

450g strong white bread flour
50g rye flour
10g salt
8g fast-action dried yeast
350ml cool water
200g walnuts, chopped
200g Roquefort cheese, cut
 into 2cm cubes
1 egg, beaten, tp mix

1 x 20cm springclip cake tin, lightly
 greased with oil

1 Mix the flours in a large bowl (or in a free-standing electric mixer fitted with the dough hook). Add the salt to one side of the bowl and the yeast to the other. Add 250ml of the water and mix it into the flour with the fingers of one hand. Add as much of the rest of the water as you need to form a soft dough – rye flour takes a lot of water so you will probably need most or all of it.

2 Knead by hand or with the dough hook for 5–10 minutes to make a smooth dough.

3 Add the chopped walnuts to the dough and continue kneading until they are incorporated.

4 Place the dough in a lightly oiled bowl, cover with clingfilm and leave to rise for 1–2 hours until at least doubled or trebled in size.

5 Turn the dough on to a lightly floured worktop and knock back by pushing down on the dough with the heels of your hands, then with your knuckles and fingertips, and folding the dough in on itself several times. Divide into 4 equal pieces.

6 Flatten each piece of dough into a 15 x 8cm rectangle. Place a quarter of the Roquefort alongside a long edge of one of the rectangles and roll up like a Swiss roll. Continue rolling under your hands until the dough is a 25cm-long sausage. Repeat with the remaining 3 pieces of dough and remaining Roquefort.

7 Carefully coil each sausage of dough into a spiral. Place them in the prepared cake tin, like a four-leaf clover. Leave to prove for a further hour.

8 Heat your oven to 220°C/425°F/gas 7. Brush the loaf with egg wash and bake for 45–50 minutes. Cool in the tin for 10 minutes, then remove the loaf and transfer to a wire rack to cool completely.

PAUL'S CHOCOLATE & RASPBERRY DOUGHNUTS

MAKES EIGHTEEN

250g strong white bread flour
4g salt
25g caster sugar, plus extra for rolling
5g fast-action dried yeast
70ml lukewarm full-fat milk
2 large eggs
125g unsalted butter, softened
9 large raspberries
100g dark chocolate (36% cocoa solids), broken into 9 squares
sunflower oil, for deep-frying

To decorate
50g dark chocolate, chopped
50g white chocolate, chopped

1 large baking sheet; a deep-fat fryer and cooking thermometer; 2 small disposable piping bags; stand mixer with dough hook

1 Put the flour into the bowl of a free-standing electric mixer fitted with the dough hook. Add the salt and sugar to one side of the bowl and the yeast to the other. Add the milk and eggs and mix on slow speed for 2 minutes. Turn up to medium speed and continue mixing for 6–8 minutes until you have a soft, glossy, elastic dough.

2 Add the soft butter and mix for a further 4–5 minutes, scraping down the bowl periodically to ensure that the butter is thoroughly incorporated. The dough will be very soft.

3 Tip the dough into a plastic bowl and cover with a snap-on lid or clingfilm. Leave in the fridge for at least 7 hours, or overnight, until it is firmed up enough to shape.

4 Tip the dough out on to a lightly floured worktop and knock it back by kneading it a few times. Divide the dough into 18 portions (about 30g each). Shape each into a ball, then flatten out slightly. Place a raspberry or a piece of chocolate in the centre of each piece. Gently fold the dough up and over the raspberry or chocolate to enclose and shape into a ball again.

5 Place the shaped doughnuts on the baking sheet, spaced apart (keep the chocolate-filled doughnuts separate from the raspberry-filled doughnuts). Put the sheet into a large plastic bag and seal, then leave to prove for 20 minutes.

6 Heat oil in the deep-fat fryer to 170°C. Lower the chocolate doughnuts carefully into the hot oil and deep-fry each side for about 3 minutes until golden brown. Remove from the fryer with a slotted spoon, drain on kitchen paper and leave to cool.

7 While you heat the oil to 170°C again, spread some caster sugar on a sheet of baking paper. Lower the raspberry doughnuts carefully into the hot oil and deep-fry each side for about 3 minutes until golden brown. Remove from the oil with a slotted spoon and immediately roll in the caster sugar to coat all over – the hot fat helps the sugar stick. Leave to cool.

8 Melt the dark chocolate in a heatproof bowl set over a pan of steaming hot water. Spoon into a disposable piping bag. Melt the white chocolate in the same way, then spoon into the other piping bag. Snip off the ends. Pipe a zigzag pattern of dark chocolate over each chocolate doughnut, then repeat with the white chocolate. Leave to set.

CAKES

SUMMER BERRY & NUT CAKE

Just the cake for a tea party in summer, when British berries taste best and are good value too. The simple sponge has a jammy covering of berries and then a nut topping. The layers bake together to make an exceptional cake – crunchy yet juicy, and buttery!

For the topping
75g marzipan, diced
25g unsalted butter, chilled and diced
2 tablespoons plain flour
75g light brown muscovado sugar
$\frac{1}{2}$ teaspoon ground cinnamon
50g walnut pieces

For the berry mix
150g each dessert blackberries, raspberries, blueberries and strawberries

For the sponge mixture
125g unsalted butter, softened
145g caster sugar
2 medium free-range eggs, at room temperature
$\frac{1}{2}$ teaspoon vanilla extract
250g plain flour
$1\frac{1}{2}$ teaspoons baking powder
$\frac{1}{4}$ teaspoon bicarbonate of soda
$\frac{1}{2}$ teaspoon ground cinnamon
125ml buttermilk
50g walnut pieces, chopped smaller
icing sugar, for dusting

1 x 23cm springclip tin, greased with butter and base-lined*

1 Heat your oven to 180°C/350°F/gas 4. To make the topping, put all the ingredients into the bowl of a food processor and run the machine briefly, just until the mixture looks like gravel – stop the machine before the mix starts to come together to form a paste. Set on one side for now.

2 Put the blackberries, raspberries and blueberries into a mixing bowl (if you rinse them first, make sure they are well drained and then dried on kitchen paper to prevent them from becoming soggy). Hull the strawberries and halve any larger ones. Add to the bowl and toss gently just to combine the berries. Put on one side while you make the sponge mixture.

3 Put the soft butter and caster sugar into a mixing bowl (or the bowl of a free-standing electric mixer fitted with the whisk attachment). Beat with a wooden spoon or a hand-held electric mixer (or in the free-standing mixer) until fluffy and light. Scrape down the sides of the bowl. Using a fork beat the eggs with the vanilla extract in a small bowl, just until frothy. Gradually add the egg mixture to the creamed butter mixture, a tablespoon at a time, beating well after each addition. Sift the flour, baking powder, bicarbonate of soda and cinnamon into the bowl. Add the buttermilk and walnuts. Gently but thoroughly fold everything together using a large metal spoon or a plastic spatula. The mixture will be fairly stiff.

4 Spoon into the prepared tin and spread evenly. Scatter the berries on top, distributing them evenly (so each slice of cake has a selection of fruit); avoid mounding them up in the middle as this will slow the rate at which the centre of the cake bakes. Sprinkle the topping mixture over the berries in an even layer.

5 Bake in the heated oven for about $1\frac{1}{4}$ hours until the topping is a good golden brown with the berry juices bubbling up through it. Test to be sure the sponge is cooked by inserting a wooden cocktail stick into the middle – it should come out clean (because of the jammy fruit mixture it's best to test in several spots).

6 Set the cake, in its tin, on a wire rack. Run a round-bladed knife around the inside of the tin to loosen the cake, then leave to cool for 15 minutes before gently unclipping the tin side. Dust the cake with icing sugar and serve slightly warm or at room temperature. Best eaten the same day.

VERY QUICK CUPCAKES

Chocolate cupcakes made in a food processor from storecupboard ingredients are a wonderfully easy treat for a wet afternoon. The icing is also simple – just melt and mix. You can leave the cupcakes plain or add whatever decorations you like or have at hand, such as chocolate buttons or sweets, grated chocolate or sugar sprinkles.

MAKES TWELVE

For the cake mixture

140g self-raising flour
40g cocoa powder
200g caster sugar
125ml sunflower oil
1 medium free-range egg, at room
    temperature, beaten to mix
175ml milk OR water, at room
    temperature
1 teaspoon vanilla extract

For the icing

75g icing sugar
25g cocoa powder
50g unsalted butter
50g caster sugar
2 tablespoons strong coffee OR water

To decorate (optional)

chocolate sprinkles OR small sweets
    (smarties/dolly mixtures/mini
    marshmallows)

1 x 12-hole cupcake tray, lined with
    muffin or cupcake cases

1 Heat your oven to 190°C/375°F/gas 5. Put the flour, cocoa and caster sugar into the bowl of a food processor and 'pulse' a few times, just until everything is thoroughly combined.

2 Pour the oil into a measuring jug, add the egg, milk and vanilla, and mix with a fork. With the machine running, pour the liquid into the processor through the feed tube. As soon as it is all in the bowl, stop the machine and scrape down the sides. Run the machine again just for 10 seconds or so until the mixture looks extremely smooth and even.

3 Remove the blade, then pour the cake mixture into the paper cases, filling them equally – they will be almost half full. Bake in the heated oven for 18–20 minutes until the cupcakes feel springy when you press them lightly in the centre – rotate the tray after 15 minutes so they bake evenly. Carefully transfer the cupcakes to a wire rack and leave to cool completely.

4 To make the icing, sift the icing sugar and cocoa into a heatproof mixing bowl. Put the butter, caster sugar and coffee into a small pan, set over low heat and stir gently until the mixture is melted and smooth. Bring to the boil, then pour into the bowl of icing sugar and cocoa and stir with a wooden spoon until very smooth. Leave to cool at room temperature for about 10 minutes until thick enough to spread before topping the cold cupcakes. Leave plain or decorate before the icing sets. Store the cupcakes in an airtight container and eat within 2 days.

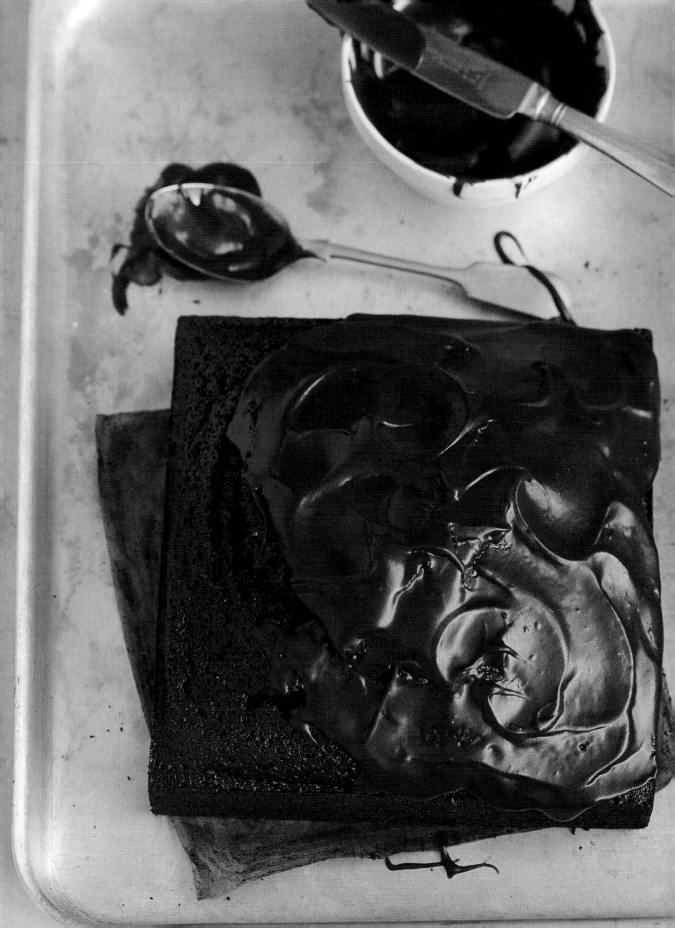

STICKY GINGERBREAD

An outstanding combination of fresh and ground ginger, black treacle and dark porter gives this cake its unique rich taste, colour and texture. It's all the better if kept for two or three days before cutting. There's a butterscotch topping if you want to add a sticky-sweet note.

For the gingerbread
300g black treacle
200ml chocolate stout OR good, dark stout
1/2 teaspoon bicarbonate of soda
3 medium free-range eggs, at room temperature
200g dark brown muscovado sugar
80g piece fresh root ginger, peeled and grated
175ml sunflower oil
350g plain flour
1 tablespoon ground ginger
1 teaspoon ground cinnamon
1 teaspoon ground mixed spice
couple of grinds of black pepper
good pinch of salt

For the butterscotch topping (optional)
200g dark brown muscovado sugar
100g unsalted butter
125ml double cream
1/2 teaspoon vanilla extract

1 x 20.5cm square, deep cake tin, greased with butter and base-lined*

1 Put the black treacle and stout into a medium-sized pan and set over low heat. Stir gently until the treacle has melted and the mixture is very hot but not quite boiling. Remove from the heat and whisk in the bicarbonate of soda – the mixture will froth up and become thick. Leave the mixture to cool to room temperature, which will take about 20 minutes.

2 Meanwhile, heat your oven to 180°C/350°F/gas 4. Put the eggs and dark brown sugar into a large mixing bowl (or the bowl of a free-standing electric mixer fitted with the whisk attachment). Whisk with a hand-held electric mixer (or in the free-standing mixer) for about 4 minutes until very smooth, thick and foamy. This mixture won't form a 'ribbon' (see the Baker's Guide page 9 for information about the 'ribbon stage').

3 Measure the grated ginger – you need 2 slightly rounded tablespoons (discard any excess) – and whisk into the egg mixture. Whisk in the oil, pouring it in a thin, steady stream.

4 Turn down the mixer to the lowest possible speed, then whisk in the cooled treacle mixture. Sift the flour, all the spices and the salt into the bowl and stir in with a plastic spatula or wooden spoon. When thoroughly combined. pour the mixture into the prepared tin and spread evenly.

5 Bake in the heated oven for 1-1 1/4 hours until the gingerbread is firm and a wooden cocktail stick inserted into the centre comes out clean. Set the tin on a wire rack and leave the gingerbread until cold before turning out. Wrap in fresh greaseproof paper or foil and keep in an airtight container for at least 2 days before cutting or covering with the optional butterscotch topping. The plain gingerbread can be kept for a week.

6 To make the butterscotch topping, put the sugar, butter and cream into a medium-sized pan and heat gently until the butter has melted. Bring to the boil, then simmer for about 4 minutes until thick and toffee-coloured. Remove from the heat and stir in the vanilla. Pour into a heatproof bowl and leave to cool. Cover and chill for 2–3 hours until just spreadable before spreading thickly on top of the cold cake. Leave to firm up before slicing. The cake can be kept, in a cool spot, for up to 2 days.

CLAIRE

Where is your current hometown?
Ashton on Mersey, Cheshire.

How would you define yourself as a baker?
I'm definitely an adventurous baker. I like to try new things all the time –
although they don't always work!

How long have you been baking for?
I have baked all my life. There were always scones and cherry and
coconut cake and chocolate bar crispie cakes in our house. Baking really
helps me to relax and focus.

How did you get into baking?
My mum and my nana taught me and my sister to bake. There has always
been an emphasis on home-cooked food and home-baked treats – they
are infinitely better than shop-bought. And you get more! My mum is
quite a haphazard baker, as she will just throw stuff into the mix, whereas
my husband, Carl, who is a scientist, has taught me to be more precise.
I feel that a bit of both is always good! Sometimes I have disasters, and
sometimes it is beautiful!

What are your favourite 3 items of kitchen equipment?
Mixer (with silicone spatula attachment).
Lots of big lovely cooking bowls.
Decent knives.

CLAIRE'S
MINIATURE CHOCOLATE & CHERRY CAKES

▼▼

Ultra-rich chocolate and cherry sponges are covered in a bitter chocolate ganache and beautifully decorated.

MAKES SIXTEEN

For the sponge mixture

1 x 440g jar/can cherries in syrup, preferably Amarena (Italian) cherries
200g dark chocolate (50–70% cocoa solids), broken or chopped up
200g unsalted butter, softened
200g caster sugar
50g dark brown muscovado sugar
4 large free-range eggs, at room temperature, beaten to mix
200g self-raising flour
1 teaspoon baking powder
70g cocoa powder
145ml buttermilk, at room temperature

For the cherry syrup

40g caster sugar
125ml cherry brandy

For the ganache

200g dark chocolate (50–70% cocoa solids), finely chopped
110ml double cream

To decorate

2 x 65g cartons sugar sprinkles
coloured ready-to-roll sugar paste
edible gold lustre dust/paste

1 x 20cm square tray of 16 mini cake tins (each 6.5cm wide and deep), each tin brushed with melted butter, base-lined* and dusted with flour; a large disposable piping bag; a food syringe; cutters for sugar paste decorations; a small paintbrush

1 Heat your oven to 180°C/350°F/gas 4. Prepare the mini cake tins following the manufacturer's instructions or as below left.

2 Thoroughly drain the cherries, reserving the syrup for later. Quarter 24 of the cherries (you won't need the rest).

3 Put the chocolate into a heatproof bowl, set over a pan of steaming hot water and melt gently, stirring occasionally. Remove the bowl from the pan and leave to cool until needed.

4 Put the butter and both sugars into a mixing bowl and beat with a wooden spoon or electric mixer until creamy and light. Gradually beat in the eggs. Sift in the flour, baking powder and cocoa and fold in with a large metal spoon or plastic spatula. Add the melted chocolate and fold in, followed by the buttermilk and 125ml of the reserved cherry syrup. Once combined, gently fold in the quartered cherries.

5 Spoon into the large piping bag and pipe the mixture into the tins until about three-quarters full. (If you have left-over mixture, pipe it into muffin cases and bake with the cakes.) Bake in the heated oven for 25–30 minutes until a wooden cocktail stick inserted into the centre comes out clean.

6 Meanwhile, make the cherry syrup. Put the sugar, brandy and 50ml of the reserved syrup into a small pan. Heat until the sugar has dissolved, then bring to the boil. Leave to cool.

8 Remove the cakes from the oven and leave for a minute, then carefully unmould on to a wire rack. While still warm, inject the syrup into them using the syringe (inject in several spots and use just 2 teaspoons per cake). Leave until cold.

9 To make the ganache, put the chocolate into a heatproof bowl. Heat the cream until steaming hot, then pour over the chocolate. Leave for a minute before stirring gently until smooth. Cool until the mixture is firm enough to spread.

10 To finish, spread the ganache evenly over the top and side of each cake, then roll in sugar sprinkles to coat. Leave on the wire rack in a cool spot until set before adding sugar paste shapes that have been dusted with edible gold dust.

GLUTEN-FREE ORANGE CAKE

Ground almonds plus polenta replace the flour in this light-textured, moist cake that's dense with flavour. As soon as the cake comes out of the oven it is soaked in orange syrup, to which you could add a dash of orange brandy or liqueur. The cake is delicious served with caramelised oranges.

MAKES ONE MEDIUM CAKE

For the sponge
250g unsalted butter, softened
finely grated zest and juice of
  1 large navel orange
225g golden caster sugar
4 medium free-range eggs, at room
  temperature, beaten to mix
250g ground almonds
60g polenta
2 teaspoons baking powder
  (gluten-free)

For the orange soaking syrup
3 tablespoons golden caster sugar
1 tablespoon toasted flaked almonds,
  to finish

1 x 20.5cm springclip tin, greased
  with butter and base-lined*

1 Heat your oven to 180°C/350°F/gas 4. Put the soft butter and orange zest into a mixing bowl (or a free-standing electric mixer fitted with the whisk attachment). Beat well with a wooden spoon or hand-held electric mixer (or in the free-standing mixer) until creamy. Gradually beat in the sugar, a couple of tablespoons at a time, then continue beating for 2–3 minutes until the mixture is light and fluffy. Scrape down the sides of the bowl before gradually adding the eggs, a tablespoon at a time, beating well after each addition.

2 Sift the ground almonds, polenta and baking powder into the bowl and add 1 tablespoon of the orange juice (save the remaining juice for the orange soaking syrup). Gently fold in with a large metal spoon or plastic spatula. Spoon the mixture into the prepared tin and spread evenly. Bake in the heated oven for about 50 minutes until the sponge is golden and springs back when gently pressed in the middle.

3 While the sponge is baking make the orange soaking syrup. Put 5 tablespoons of the saved orange juice and the caster sugar into a small pan. Heat gently until the sugar has completely dissolved, then simmer for a couple of minutes to make a light syrup. Keep warm.

4 As soon as the cake is ready set it, in the tin, on a wire rack. Prick the cake all over with a wooden cocktail stick, then spoon the warm syrup over the hot sponge. Scatter the almonds over the cake, then leave until cold.

5 Run a round-bladed knife around the inside of the tin and carefully unmould the cake. Serve the same or the next day, with thick plain yoghurt or crème fraîche, if you like.

DUNDEE WHISKY CAKE

Not as rich or heavy as a traditional dark fruit cake, this cake dates from the seventeenth century when it was a favourite at the court of Mary Queen of Scots. There are no cherries in the cake because the Queen (reportedly) disliked them. The cake's flavour depends on leaving the dried vine fruits to macerate in whisky overnight, and allowing the baked cake to mature for several days before cutting.

MAKES ONE LARGE CAKE

500g mixed vine fruits
  (raisins/sultanas/currants)
50g chopped mixed peel
5 tablespoons whisky
275g plain flour
salt
1 teaspoon baking powder
65g ground almonds
225g unsalted butter, softened
finely grated zest of 1 large
  unwaxed lemon
225g light brown muscovado sugar
4 medium free-range eggs, at room
  temperature, beaten to mix
18 blanched (skinned) almond halves

For the glaze
2 tablespoons milk
4 teaspoons caster sugar

1 x 20cm round, deep cake tin, greased
  with butter and lined with baking
  paper*; a baking sheet

1 Put the fruit and peel into a bowl, add the whisky and stir well. Cover the bowl and leave to soak overnight, at room temperature.

2 Next day, heat your oven to 180°C/350°F/gas 4. Sift the flour, a couple of good pinches of salt, the baking powder and ground almonds into a bowl; put on one side for now. Put the soft butter and lemon zest into a large mixing bowl (or the bowl of a free-standing electric mixer fitted with the whisk attachment). Beat until creamy using a wooden spoon or a hand-held electric mixer (or in the free-standing mixer). Scrape down the sides of the bowl, then gradually beat in the sugar, a couple of tablespoons at a time. Continue beating for about 3 minutes until the mixture is very light in colour and texture.

3 Scrape down the sides of the bowl again. Gradually add the eggs, a tablespoon at a time, beating well after each addition. Add a tablespoon of the flour mixture with each of the last 2 portions of egg to prevent the mixture from curdling.

4 Add half of the remaining flour mixture to the bowl and fold in with a large metal spoon or plastic spatula. Fold in half of the fruit and whisky mixture, followed by the rest of the flour mixture and, finally, the rest of the fruit mixture. When thoroughly combined, spoon the mixture into the prepared tin and spread evenly.

5 Tap the tin on the worktop to dislodge any air pockets. Make a slight hollow in the centre of the cake's surface so it will rise evenly. Dip your fingers into cold water, then press them lightly over the surface of the cake – this will prevent the crust from becoming too hard. Press the halved almonds on to the cake in neat concentric circles.

6 Tie a folded newspaper around the outside of the tin, then set the tin on top of another folded newspaper on the baking sheet (doing this will prevent the outside of the cake from over-baking). Bake in the heated oven for 40 minutes, then reduce the temperature to 170°C/325°F/gas 3 and bake for a further 1 $^3/_4$ hours until a wooden cocktail stick inserted into the middle of the cake comes out clean. During baking, check the cake now and then and, if the top looks as if it is getting a bit dark, cover lightly with a sheet of baking paper or foil.

7 Towards the end of the baking time, heat the milk until it boils, then add the sugar and stir until dissolved. As soon as the cake is ready, quickly brush the top with the glaze mixture and return to the oven to bake for another minute – this will give the almond decoration a lovely glossy shine.

8 Set the tin on a wire rack and leave overnight, or until the cake is completely cold, before turning out and removing the lining paper. Wrap the cake in foil and keep for a week before cutting. Store in an airtight container.

VICTORIA SANDWICH CAKE

It is hard to better this classic vanilla sponge cake, made by the creaming method where butter is beaten until creamy, sugar is beaten in followed by eggs and vanilla, and finally flour is gently folded through. The sponge layers are usually sandwiched simply with a layer of jam, but this combination of fresh raspberries and thick, creamy filling is well worth the extra effort.

MAKES ONE LARGE CAKE

For the sponge cake
180g unsalted butter, at room
   temperature
180g caster sugar
3 medium free-range eggs, at room
   temperature
$^3/_4$ teaspoon vanilla extract
180g self-raising flour
1 tablespoon warm water from the tap

For the filling
150g full-fat cream cheese
75g mascarpone
$2^1/_2$ tablespoons icing sugar
1 teaspoon vanilla extract
200g raspberries
icing sugar, for dusting

2 x 20.5cm round, deep sandwich tins,
   greased with butter and base-lined*

1 Heat your oven to 180°C/350°F/gas 4. Put the soft butter in a mixing bowl (or a free-standing electric mixer fitted with the whisk attachment). Beat with a wooden spoon or a hand-held electric mixer (or in the free-standing mixer) until the butter is very creamy, with a consistency like mayonnaise. Scrape down the sides of the bowl with a plastic spatula, then gradually beat in the sugar a couple of tablespoons at a time. Scrape down the sides of the bowl again.

2 Put the eggs and vanilla into a small jug or bowl and beat with a fork, just to mix. Gradually add to the butter mixture a tablespoon at a time, beating well after each addition (don't forget to scrape down the sides of the bowl from time to time). To prevent the mixture from 'splitting' or 'curdling' (looking a bit blobby rather than smooth and creamy), it is a good idea to add a tablespoon of the measured flour with each of the last 2 additions of egg.

3 Sift the rest of the flour on to the mixture. Start gently folding in with a large metal spoon or plastic spatula; after 2 or 3 movements add the warm water. Continue folding until the flour is thoroughly amalgamated.

4 Divide the mixture equally between the 2 prepared tins (for the best results do this by weight rather than by eye). Spread evenly. Bake in the heated oven for 20–25 minutes until the sponges are a light golden brown and starting to shrink away from the side of the tin and will spring back when lightly pressed in the middle – check the sponges after 15 minutes and rotate them if necessary so they bake evenly.

5 Run a round-bladed knife around the inside of each tin to loosen the sponge, then leave for a minute or so to firm up before turning out on to a wire rack (see the Baker's Guide page 10 for more information). Leave to cool completely.

6 When you're ready to assemble the cake, put the cream cheese into a mixing bowl and beat well with a wooden spoon or electric mixer. Add the mascarpone, icing sugar and vanilla extract and beat for a couple of minutes until the mixture is light and creamy.

7 Set one sponge, crust side down, on a serving plate. Spread the creamy filling evenly over the sponge. Press the raspberries into the filling, then top with the second sponge, crust side up, and gently press in place. Dust with icing sugar. Serve immediately or store in an airtight container in the fridge; for the best flavour remove from the fridge about 20 minutes before cutting. The cake is best eaten within 48 hours.

SUMMER STRAWBERRY GATEAU

When strawberries are at their absolute peak, this is the perfect summer dessert. Sandwich the sponges with 4 rounded tablespoons of the best strawberry jam or conserve that you can find. Spread the cream cheese mixture over the top of the assembled cake, then decorate with 200g hulled strawberries (leave small berries whole; halve or quarter larger berries). Dust with icing sugar before serving.

BUTTERCREAM ICING

This icing can be used to fill a 20-23cm round sandwich cake (double the ingredients to top as well as fill). Or it can be spooned, spread or piped (with a piping bag fitted with a star tube) on top of 12 fairy cakes. If you want to have lavishly topped cupcakes just double the quantities.

VANILLA BUTTERCREAM

Put 65g soft unsalted butter into a mixing bowl and beat with a wooden spoon or an electric mixer until creamy and pale, with the consistency of mayonnaise. Sift 200g of icing sugar into the bowl. Add 2 tablespoons of milk and ½ teaspoon of vanilla extract, then beat (use the lowest speed on an electric mixer) until very smooth and thick. Use straight away or cover and keep in the fridge. If the icing has been chilled, leave it to soften at room temperature until spreadable before using.

CHOCOLATE BUTTERCREAM

Add 1½ tablespoons cocoa powder and sift with the icing sugar into the creamed butter.

COFFEE BUTTERCREAM

Omit the vanilla extract and replace the milk with 2 tablespoons cold strong coffee (or to your taste).

LEMON BUTTERCREAM

Omit the milk and vanilla, and add 2 rounded tablespoons Lemon Curd (see page 154).

FAIRY CAKES

Miniature sponge cakes – just two or three bites – are a treat whatever your age.
The basic mixture is the classic all-in-one vanilla sponge, but you can add a range
of flavours (or colour the mixture with food-colouring gels and pastes).
Top with buttercream plus as many sprinkles and decorations as you can find!

MAKES TWELVE

115g unsalted butter, softened
115g caster sugar
2 medium free-range eggs, at room
   temperature
1 tablespoon milk
115g self-raising flour
$\frac{1}{4}$ teaspoon baking powder
$\frac{1}{2}$ teaspoon vanilla extract
Vanilla or Lemon Buttercream
   (see opposite page)

12 paper fairy cake cases, set in a
   bun tray OR mince pie tray

1 Heat your oven to 180°C/350°F/gas 4. Put the soft butter, sugar, eggs and milk into a mixing bowl (or the bowl of a free-standing electric mixer fitted with the whisk attachment). Sift the flour and baking powder into the bowl and add the vanilla extract. Beat with a wooden spoon or a hand-held electric mixer (or in the free-standing mixer) for 2–3 minutes until the mixture is light and very smooth. Stop beating and scrape down the sides of the bowl a couple of times so the mixture is thoroughly combined.

2 Spoon the mixture into the paper cases. Make sure they are equally filled – you can do this by eye or by weight (easy with digital scales).

3 Bake in the heated oven for about 15 minutes until the sponges are light gold and springy to the touch. Check after 12 minutes and rotate the tray, if needed, so they bake evenly.

4 Carefully transfer the cakes (in their cases) to a wire rack and leave to cool. Leave plain or ice with Buttercream.

COFFEE & WALNUT FAIRY CAKES

Make up the cake mixture but replace the vanilla extract with 1$\frac{1}{2}$ teaspoons instant coffee (granules or powder) dissolved in 1$\frac{1}{2}$ teaspoons boiling water and cooled. When the mixture is thoroughly combined stir in 50g walnut pieces that have been chopped a bit finer. Leave the fairy cakes plain or finish with a swirl of Coffee Buttercream (see opposite page).

DEVIL'S FOOD FAIRY CAKES

Make up the cake mixture in the same way, using 115g soft unsalted butter; 115g light brown muscovado sugar; 2 medium free-range eggs, at room temperature; 20g cocoa powder, mixed with 3 tablespoons boiling water and cooled; 100g self-raising flour; $\frac{1}{4}$ teaspoon baking powder; and $\frac{1}{2}$ teaspoon vanilla extract. Finish the fairy cakes with a swirl of Vanilla or Chocolate Buttercream (see opposite page).

GATEAU DE L'OPERA

The spiritual home of this most elegant of French cakes is the Dalloyau Pâtisserie in Paris. It's the attention to detail as well as the exquisite taste that makes Opéra Cake so special. There is a lot of work involved, but the six elements can be prepared in advance and then assembled when you have everything at hand. The finished cake can be kept in the fridge for a day or so (the flavour will improve).

MAKES ONE LARGE CAKE

For the nut sponge

6 medium free-range egg whites, at room temperature
good pinch of cream of tartar
30g caster sugar
6 medium free-range eggs, at room temperature
225g icing sugar
225g ground roasted hazelnuts (or ground almonds)
75g plain flour
45g unsalted butter, melted and cooled

For the coffee syrup

60g caster sugar
1½ tablespoons instant coffee (granules or powder)
1 tablespoon brandy

For the coffee buttercream

85g caster sugar
2 medium free-range egg yolks, at room temperature
150g unsalted butter, at room temperature, diced
4 teaspoons instant coffee (granules or powder), dissolved in 1 tablespoon boiling water and cooled

1 Heat your oven to 220°C/425°F/gas 7. Cut each sheet of parchment-lined foil to a square with 26cm sides, then fold in the sides to make a square, shallow cake case with 25cm sides (use the cake board to help form the shape). Set each cake case on a baking sheet (if you have only 1 or 2 sheets, you can bake the sponge mixture in batches).

2 To make the sponge mixture, put the egg whites and cream of tartar into a large, spotlessly clean bowl (or the bowl of a free-standing electric mixer fitted with the whisk attachment). Whisk with a hand-held electric mixer on high speed (or in the free-standing mixer) until the whites reach 'soft peak' stage (see the Baker's Guide page 9 for more information). Sprinkle the caster sugar over the whites and whisk again, just for a few seconds, to make a stiff and glossy meringue. Put the bowl on one side for now.

3 Put the whole eggs into a second mixing bowl and sift in the icing sugar. Add the ground nuts. Whisk on high speed (there's no need to wash the beaters) for about 4 minutes until very thick and massively increased in volume. Sift the flour on top and fold in with a large metal spoon or plastic spatula. Once the flour has been thoroughly incorporated, fold in the meringue in 3 batches. Finally, trickle the cooled melted butter over the top and gently fold in until just combined.

4 Divide the sponge mixture equally among the 3 cake cases and spread it carefully to fill the corners and be exactly flat and even (each sponge layer needs to be the same depth all over so the cake will be level when assembled). Bake in the heated oven for 8–10 minutes until the sponges are lightly browned and spring back when gently pressed in the centre (it's a good idea to rotate the sponges after 5 minutes so they bake evenly).

5 While the sponges are baking, cover 2 wire racks (or the worktop) with some baking paper. Flip the baking sheets over on to the racks to turn out the sponges in their cake cases. Carefully peel off and remove the cake cases. Leave

For the ganache

200g dark chocolate (about 70% cocoa solids), finely chopped
175ml whipping cream
25g unsalted butter, at room temperature, diced

For the under-glaze

50g dark chocolate (about 70% cocoa solids), finely chopped

For the top glaze

100g unsalted butter
150g dark chocolate (about 70% cocoa solids), finely chopped

To decorate (optional)

50g dark chocolate (about 70% cocoa solids), finely chopped
edible gold leaf

3 sheets parchment-lined foil; 1–3 baking sheets (see recipe); a sugar thermometer; a 25cm square cake board; a small disposable piping bag

the sponges to cool, loosely covered with a dry tea towel or a sheet of baking paper. (Once cold the sponges can be wrapped, individually, in baking paper and clingfilm, then left at room temperature overnight.)

6 To make the coffee syrup, put the sugar, coffee and 125ml water into a small pan. Set over low heat and stir until the sugar and coffee have dissolved. Bring to the boil, then simmer for a minute. Remove from the heat and stir in the brandy. Leave to cool to room temperature. (Once cold the syrup can be kept at room temperature for a couple of hours or stored in a jam jar in the fridge overnight – bring back to room temperature before using.)

7 For the coffee buttercream, put the caster sugar and 4 tablespoons cold water into a small, heavy-based pan and set over low heat. Stir gently until the sugar has dissolved, then bring to the boil. Boil rapidly for 4–5 minutes until the syrup reaches 115°C on a sugar thermometer.

8 While the syrup is boiling, put the egg yolks into a heatproof mixing bowl and whisk for a minute until frothy (if you are using a hand-held electric mixer, set the bowl on a damp cloth to prevent it from wobbling). As soon as the syrup is the right temperature, pour it on to the egg yolks in a steady stream while whisking at full speed – try not to let the syrup trickle down the sides of the bowl. Continue whisking for about 5 minutes until the mixture is very thick, pale and mousse-like. If the mixture is still warm at this point, whisk for another minute until cold.

9 Whisk in the soft butter a few pieces at a time, then whisk in the coffee to make a very smooth and thick buttercream. Cover the bowl and chill just until spreadable – check every 5 minutes. (The buttercream can be kept in the fridge overnight; bring it back to spreadable room temperature before using.)

10 To make the ganache put the chopped chocolate into a heatproof bowl. Heat the cream until steaming hot and pour over the chocolate. Leave for a minute, then stir gently until melted and smooth. Gradually stir in the butter to make a glossy, smooth ganache. Cover the bowl and chill until spreadable – check every 5 minutes. (The ganache can be made a day ahead and stored in the fridge; bring it back to spreadable room temperature before using.)

11 When you are ready to assemble the cake, gently melt the chocolate for the under-glaze in a small heatproof bowl set over a pan of steaming hot water. Set one sponge square, crust-side up, on a sheet of baking paper. Brush a thin and even layer of melted chocolate over the sponge. Leave until set and hard (you can chill for 5 minutes to save time), then flip the sponge over on the baking paper so the chocolate side is underneath. Brush the upper surface with coffee syrup – do this carefully and thoroughly so the whole surface is evenly moistened. Leave for 10 minutes, so the syrup can be properly absorbed, then spoon three-quarters of the buttercream on to the sponge and spread evenly. It's vital the cake has a flat surface and doesn't slope down at the sides, so spread the buttercream carefully.

12 Set a second sponge square, crust-side down, on the first sponge, making sure all the sides are aligned. Brush this second sponge layer with coffee syrup as before and leave for 10 minutes, then spoon all the ganache on to the sponge and spread evenly. Set the third sponge, crust down, on top and gently press it in place – make sure the surface is level. Brush with coffee syrup and leave to soak in, then spread over the last of the buttercream in a thin, even layer. Chill for about 15 minutes until firm.

13 Meanwhile, make the top glaze. Melt the butter in a small pan, then skim off the foam. Pour the clear butter into a small bowl, leaving behind the milky residue at the bottom of the pan. Discard the milky residue. Reheat the clarified butter until bubbling. Put all but 25g of the chopped chocolate into a heatproof bowl and pour in the very hot butter. Stir gently until the chocolate has melted, then stir in the reserved 25g chocolate until the mixture is smooth and glossy.

14 Remove the cake from the fridge and set it on the worktop, still on the sheet of baking paper. Quickly pour the glaze over the top of the cake to cover completely (if necessary, help the glaze to spread out with a warmed off-set palette knife: you need to work fast). Let the glaze drip down the sides – there's no need to neaten them up as they will be trimmed off. Return the cake to the fridge and chill until the glaze is set and firm.

15 To finish the cake, dip a large sharp knife in very hot water, then carefully trim the sides to make a neat, perfectly square cake. Transfer to the cake board. Melt the chocolate for the decoration and spoon into a small disposable piping bag. Snip off the very tip, then pipe 'Opéra' diagonally across the top of the cake. Decorate the top and along each top edge with elegant dashes and dots (or musical signs). Finish with gold leaf (handle this with care, using the tip of a small knife or tweezers to set the flakes in place). Chill until firm.

16 The completed cake can be stored in an airtight container in the fridge for up to 48 hours. Remove from the fridge about 20 minutes before serving so the cake is chilled but not hard. To serve cut with a large knife dipped in hot water – keep a roll of kitchen paper handy for cleaning the knife between slices.

EMERGENCY CHRISTMAS CAKE

There are times when you need a cake with all the fragrance and flavour of a traditional, nicely matured Christmas cake, yet one that can be made at the last minute – just in the time it takes to heat up the oven. Instead of a basketful of ingredients – packs of fruit, nuts, peel and lots of spices – all you need to add to the all-in-one cake mixture here is a jar of mincemeat, an apple and a dash of spirit.

MAKES ONE LARGE CAKE OR TWELVE TINY LOAF CAKES

300g mincemeat
1 tablespoon brandy, sherry OR rum
1 medium eating apple
175g unsalted butter, softened
125g dark brown muscovado sugar
3 medium free-range eggs, at room
    temperature, beaten to mix
250g self-raising flour
good pinch of salt
coarse sugar sprinkles OR crushed
    sugar cubes, to finish (optional)

1 x 20cm round, deep cake tin, greased
    and lined with baking paper*,
    OR 12 card mini-loaf cake cases, set
    on a baking sheet

1 Heat your oven to 170°C/325°F/gas 3. Spoon the mincemeat into a bowl and stir in the alcohol. Peel, quarter and core the apple. Chop finely and stir into the mincemeat. Put on one side for now.

2 Put the soft butter, sugar, eggs, flour and salt into a large mixing bowl (or the bowl of a free-standing electric mixer fitted with the whisk attachment). Beat with a wooden spoon or with a hand-held electric mixer (or in the free-standing mixer) – start at slow speed until the ingredients are mixed. Beat thoroughly for about 2 minutes until the mixture is very smooth, light and creamy in texture. Add the mincemeat mixture and gently stir in with a wooden spoon or plastic spatula.

3 Transfer the mixture to the prepared cake tin and spread evenly. Gently bang the tin on the worktop to dislodge any air pockets, then make a slight hollow in the centre of the cake's surface so it will rise evenly. If you are baking the mixture in loaf cake cases, spoon the mixture into the cases so they are equally filled (they will be about half full). Tap each case on the worktop to settle the mixture, then smooth it so it fills the corners and the surface is flat. If you are adding the sugar finish, sprinkle the top of the cake or cakes evenly with plenty of coarse sugar crystals.

4 Bake the cake in the heated oven for about $1\frac{1}{4}$ hours until a wooden cocktail stick inserted in the centre comes out clean. Bake the mini loaf cakes on the baking sheet in the heated oven for 20 minutes, then rotate the sheet so the cakes bake evenly, and bake for a further 10–15 minutes until a wooden cocktail stick inserted into the centre comes out clean.

5 Set the cake tin, or the little cakes in their cases, on a wire rack and leave to cool completely before turning out. Once cold the cake or cakes can be stored in an airtight container at room temperature.

FOR NUT LOVERS

When the cake is cold brush a thick layer of warmed apricot jam or apricot glaze (about 2 tablespoons) over the top, then press on large whole nuts – brazils, almonds, hazelnuts, pistachios, walnut halves – to cover completely. Lightly brush the nuts with a little jam or glaze, to make sure they stay in place. Finish with a colourful ribbon tied around the side of the cake.

FOR A GLAMOROUS FRUIT FINISH

Cover the top with mixed glacé or crystallised fruits, of varying colours and sizes, sticking them on to the cake with apricot jam or glaze as above. (You can finish the little cakes with nuts or glacé fruits in the same way.)

FOR A FONDANT-ICED CAKE

You will need 1 tablespoon warmed apricot jam or apricot glaze, 400g marzipan and 250g ready-to-roll white fondant icing/sugar paste (plus a little icing sugar or cornflour for dusting the worktop). Start by brushing the top of the cake with the jam, to make it sticky enough for the marzipan to stay in place. Gently knead the marzipan into a ball, then roll it out on the dusted worktop to a circle 20cm across. Set the empty cake tin on top and cut around it with a sharp knife to give it a neat, precise edge. Gently press the marzipan disc on to the top of the cake, smoothing it with the flat of your hand. If time allows, lightly cover and leave for a couple of hours (or overnight) so the marzipan can firm up a bit. When you are ready to carry on, gently knead the white icing (make sure your hands, the worktop and rolling pin are all perfectly clean, and there are no crumbs). Roll out the icing on the lightly dusted worktop to about 2.5mm thick (thinner than the marzipan). Cut around the tin, as before, to get a neat 20cm disc. Lightly moisten the marzipan with a teaspoon of brandy or sherry – just enough to make it sticky – then set the icing disc on top. Gently press it

down so there are no air bubbles before using the flat of your hand to lightly smooth and 'polish' the icing (it will gain a slight silky sheen as you gently rub it, but take care not to dent it). Leave for a couple of hours, if possible, so the icing can firm up, then decorate with fondant shapes (see below) or with edible Christmas cake decorations.

FOR LITTLE FONDANT-ICED LOAF CAKES

Brush the tops with apricot jam. Roll out the marzipan to a thin 16.5 x 40cm rectangle. Cut into 12 rectangles, each 5.5 x 10cm, using a ruler and a large sharp knife or pizza wheel-cutter. Press a piece of marzipan on the top of each loaf cake. Roll out the white fondant icing/sugar paste in the same way, cut into rectangles and gently press on top of the moistened marzipan, gently tucking the edges into the loaf cases.

TO DECORATE WITH FONDANT SHAPES

Roll out 250g white fondant icing/sugar paste 2mm thick and stamp out decorations with shaped cutters or plunger-cutters. The shapes can be coloured or painted with edible colouring gels or pens. Fix the decorations to the cake (top and sides) by dampening the underside or using a dab of glacé icing (see page 170) or royal icing (see opposite page). Once the decorations are in place they can be sprayed with silver or gold cake shimmer spray (check to be sure the spray is the correct edible type – some cannot be used for food) or brushed with edible lustre.

Larger supermarkets, cookware shops and on-line cake decorating suppliers have a vast range of decorations for every possible occasion, and many have specialist advisors to help with decorating problems. As well as decorating tools, colours and materials, there are some quirky bits of kit that work well: mats and rollers for embossing rolled-out icing, plunger-cutters for intricate shapes the easy way and press-in silicone moulds for quick bows, leaves or flowers.

FOR A ROYAL-ICED CAKE/LITTLE CAKES

Often known as the 'traditional' Christmas icing as it sets hard, royal icing is a quick and easy alternative to fondant icing to top the marzipan layer, and can be spread smooth or pulled and swirled into snowy peaks. It can also be used for piping. You will need 250g Royal Icing Sugar. Put 2$\frac{1}{2}$ tablespoons cold water into a mixing bowl and gradually sift in the icing sugar, a tablespoon at a time, beating with a wooden spoon (or a hand-held electric mixer on low speed) until the icing is thick and smooth. To check if the icing is the correct consistency lift out the spoon: the tips of the icing peaks should just flop over. If the icing is a bit too floppy or even runny beat in more sugar a teaspoon at a time; if it is too thick to spread or pipe stir in more water a few drops at time. It is easy to colour royal icing: just add a tiny amount of food colouring paste or gel on the end of a cocktail stick. Use immediately, while the icing is spreadable. Add any sprinkles or decorative figures while the icing is soft, then leave uncovered at room temperature until it has set firm.

CHERRY & ALMOND BATTENBERG CAKE

This pink and white cake was first made in 1884 to honour the marriage of Queen Victoria's granddaughter Princess Victoria to Prince Louis of Battenberg. Our version has added glacé cherries to the pink-coloured sponge and almonds to the white (actually a light golden yellow) sponge.

MAKES ONE MEDIUM CAKE

For the sponge
50g glacé cherries
100g self-raising flour
50g ground almonds
125g unsalted butter, softened
125g caster sugar
2 medium free-range eggs
few drops of almond essence
few drops of cherry pink or red
    food colouring
25g flaked or chopped almonds

To finish
350g white marzipan
cornflour OR icing sugar, for dusting
8 tablespoons cherry or apricot jam

To decorate
icing sugar, for dusting
3 glacé cherries
flaked almonds

1 Battenberg tin, 20 x 15cm, greased
  with butter and lined with baking
  paper*, OR a 20cm square shallow
  tin, greased with butter, plus a large
  sheet of parchment-lined foil or
  baking paper (see recipe for details
  of how to prepare the tin)

1 Heat your oven to 180°C/350°F/gas 4. Halve the cherries and rinse under the hot tap to remove the sticky syrup. Drain well, then pat dry on kitchen paper. Leave to dry on a clean sheet of kitchen paper.

2 If you don't have a special Battenburg tin, prepare the square tin: cut a 20 x 28cm rectangle of parchment-lined foil or baking paper. (If using parchment-lined foil, use it paper side up.) Fold the paper in half widthways, then open out and push up the centre fold to make a 4cm pleat, creasing it firmly. Line the base of the greased tin with the paper so the pleat runs down the centre, dividing the tin into 2 separate containers each 20 x 10cm.

3 Chop the cherries fairly finely, then sprinkle with a teaspoon of the weighed flour and toss to separate the pieces. Put on one side.

4 Sift the rest of the flour and the ground almonds into a bowl or on to a sheet of greaseproof paper; set aside for now. Put the butter into a mixing bowl (or the bowl of a free-standing electric mixer fitted with the whisk attachment). Beat with a wooden spoon or a hand-held electric mixer (or in the free-standing mixer) until very creamy. Add the caster sugar and beat thoroughly until the mixture is very light and fluffy, scraping down the sides of the bowl from time to time.

5 Beat the eggs with the almond essence in a small bowl using a fork, just to mix, then gradually add to the butter mixture a tablespoon at a time, beating well after each addition. Add the sifted flour mixture to the bowl and fold in with a large metal spoon or plastic spatula. Divide the mixture in half (by weight if possible), putting one half into a clean bowl.

6 Add the food colouring, a few drops at a time, to one portion to tint it pink, mixing well so there are no streaks, then mix in the chopped cherries. Spoon into 2 sections of the prepared Battenberg tin or one side of the prepared square tin (check to be sure that the pleated divider is still straight and dead centre). Add the flaked or chopped almonds to the second portion of cake mixture and mix well, then spoon into the remaining 2 sections of the Battenberg tin or the other side of the divided square tin. Spread each portion of cake mixture so the surface is level and the corners are evenly filled.

7 Bake in the heated oven for 20–25 minutes until the sponges are well risen and springy when gently pressed. Set the tin on a wire rack and run a round-bladed knife around the inside to loosen the sponges. Leave to cool until the sponges are just warm, then carefully turn out on to the rack and peel off the lining paper. Cool completely.

8 When ready to assemble, set the cold sponges on a chopping board. If you baked 2 sponges in a square tin, use a serrated bread knife to cut each in half lengthways, to make 4 cake strips (2 pink and 2 yellow). Trim all the strips so the short sides are exactly square (they may have risen unevenly).

9 Roll out the marzipan on a worktop lightly dusted with cornflour or icing sugar to a 20 x 30cm rectangle. Heat the jam just enough so it will spread easily (if it seems a bit thick add a tablespoon of water). Brush one long side of one pink cake strip very lightly with jam, then set it jam-side down on one short side of the marzipan rectangle, lined up next to the edge. Brush the

3 other long sides of this cake strip lightly with jam. Next, brush one long side of a yellow cake strip with jam and set it jam-side down on the marzipan next to the pink strip and touching it. Brush the top of this strip with jam.

10 Set the second yellow cake strip on top of the pink strip that is in place on the marzipan. Lightly brush one long side of the second pink cake strip with jam and set it next to this second yellow cake strip (and on top of the yellow strip already on the marzipan). Looking at the end of the layered strips, you will have created a chequerboard pattern.

11 Brush the top and long sides of the assembled cake with jam, then roll the cake or wrap the marzipan neatly around and over the cake, leaving the ends visible. Press the marzipan join to seal it (it should be along one bottom edge). If necessary, turn the cake so the join is at the base. Gently smooth the marzipan with your hands to give it a neat finish (no air pockets), then trim the ends to neaten them. Crimp the top edges of the marzipan by pinching it between your thumb and first finger at a slight angle and at regular intervals.

12 Lightly dust the cake with icing sugar, then set it on a serving plate. Decorate with whole glacé cherries and flaked almonds, pressing them gently into the soft marzipan. Store in an airtight container for up to 5 days.

DIANA

Where do you live?
Whitchurch, Shropshire.

What do you get up to when you are not baking?
I love upholstery, I dabble in art on Tuesday mornings at the art club and when the old bones allow it, my garden takes up a lot of my time. I really love auction sale rooms but have to be restrained because I spend too much money... I also enjoy travelling in the U.K.

How would you define yourself as a baker?
Having baked for 60 long years, I would describe myself as classically adventurous, with flair.

Why do you enjoy baking?
Being able to produce something to share with family and friends, and I can't deny that I do enjoy the compliments.

How did you get into baking?
Nobody taught me to bake but my mother and grandmother were superb bakers so I must have absorbed their skills. My Domestic Science teacher, Miss Morris, obviously had something to do with it too. I did learn a lot through the W.I. and its baking courses.

Who do you tend to bake for?
I suppose it's the Old Boy I've looked after these past 48 years, but also our 2 nephews and their families (5 children between them) are always grateful for any offerings. Or our younger daughter who is always busy working and needing emergency rations.

What are your favourite 3 items of kitchen equipment?
The same washer-upper I've had for 48 years. And just in case he gets uppity, a very sharp knife and a rolling pin that was my mother's.

DIANA'S
MUM'S SUNDAY TEA LEMON CURD SWISS ROLL

This simple whisked sponge is very light in texture. It is filled while warm with a traditional lemon curd, which infuses it with incredible flavour.

MAKES ONE LARGE SWISS ROLL

For the lemon curd

145g slightly salted butter, diced
145g white caster sugar
finely grated zest and juice of 2 large
  (or 2$\frac{1}{2}$ medium) unwaxed lemons
2 medium free-range eggs, at room
  temperature, beaten to mix

For the sponge

3 medium free-range eggs plus 1 yolk,
  at room temperature
160g white caster sugar, plus extra
  for sprinkling
160g self-raising flour

1 large baking sheet, 26 x 40cm,
  greased with butter and lined with
  baking paper

1 Start by making the lemon curd so it has time to cool. Put the butter and sugar into a large heatproof bowl and add the lemon zest and juice. Set the bowl over a pan of gently simmering water (don't let the base of the bowl touch the water). Heat, stirring frequently with a wooden spoon, until the sugar has completely dissolved.

2 Strain the beaten eggs into the mixture, then stir constantly until the mixture becomes very thick and opaque. As soon as you can draw a finger through the mixture on the wooden spoon and make a clear path, remove the bowl from the pan (keep the pan of hot water for later). Pour the lemon curd into a smaller heatproof bowl. Leave to cool, then cover with clingfilm and chill.

3 To make the sponge, heat your oven to 190°C/375°F/gas 5. Wash and dry the large heatproof bowl, then put the 3 whole eggs and the yolk into it. Whisk together, just to mix, using an electric mixer or a rotary whisk, then whisk in the sugar. Set the bowl over the pan of gently simmering water and whisk for about 3 minutes until the mixture is thick and feels lukewarm when you dip in your little finger. Remove the bowl from the pan and set it on a heatproof surface. Continue whisking until the mixture has returned to room temperature and is thick enough to leave a ribbon-like trail when the whisk is lifted (see the Baker's Guide page 9 for more information).

4 Sift the flour on to a sheet of greaseproof paper, then sift it again on to the whisked mixture. Gently but thoroughly fold in with a large metal spoon or plastic spatula. Tip the mixture on to the prepare baking sheet and spread evenly, leaving a 1cm clear border all around, between the sponge and the edges of the baking sheet.

5 Bake in the heated oven for 8–9 minutes until the sponge is a good golden brown and the middle springs back when gently pressed. While the sponge is baking, lay a large sheet of baking paper (slightly larger than your baking sheet) on the worktop and sprinkle it with caster sugar.

6 When the sponge is baked, tip it on to the sugared paper and lift off the baking sheet, then carefully peel off the lining paper. Spread the lemon curd evenly over the sponge, then, working quickly, trim off the edges of the sponge with a sharp knife (a serrated bread knife works best). Make a deep cut about 1.5cm in from one short edge, then fold in this edge quite tightly – it will be in the centre of the roll. Using the sugared paper to help you, roll up the sponge from this end. Leave the paper wrapped around the sponge roll to keep the shape. Transfer the roll to a wire rack and leave to cool.

7 When the sponge is cold, remove the paper. Dust the Swiss roll lightly with caster sugar and set it on a serving plate.

SWEDISH CARDAMOM ALMOND CAKE

A gloriously aromatic, buttery, rich sponge cake studded with almonds (you'll need about 80g nuts in total). The flavours develop as the cake matures so plan to bake this a day or so before cutting. If possible use bright green cardamom pods from a fresh pack – the pods quickly stale once exposed to the air, so buy in small amounts. This is a great cake to go with a pot of really good coffee.

For the coating
10g unsalted butter, melted
2½ tablespoons chopped almonds

For the cake mixture
250g plain flour
good pinch of salt
1½ teaspoons baking powder
4 tablespoons milk
125ml full-fat crème fraîche
175g unsalted butter, softened
seeds from 10 cardamom pods, finely ground
200g caster sugar
3 medium free-range eggs, at room temperature
¼ teaspoon almond extract (not flavouring)
3 tablespoons chopped almonds

To decorate
2 tablespoons chopped almonds
icing sugar, for dusting

1 x 900g loaf tin, about 26 x 12.5 x 7.5cm, greased with butter and lined with a long strip of baking paper*

1 Heat your oven to 180°C/350°F/gas 4. Brush the inside of the lined tin with a thick coating of melted butter, then sprinkle with the chopped almonds so they stick to the sides and base. Set the tin aside.

2 Sift the flour, salt and baking powder into a bowl and put on one side. Stir the milk into the crème fraîche in a small bowl; set this aside as well. Put the soft butter and ground cardamom seeds into a large mixing bowl (or a free-standing electric mixer fitted with the whisk attachment) and beat with a wooden spoon or hand-held electric mixer (or in the free-standing mixer) until creamy, with the consistency of mayonnaise. Scrape down the sides of the bowl, then gradually beat in the sugar, a couple of tablespoons at a time. When all the sugar has been added, scrape down the bowl again, then beat thoroughly for a further minute or so until the mixture is very light and fluffy.

3 Beat the eggs with the almond extract in a small bowl using a fork, just to combine, then gradually add to the butter mixture a tablespoon at a time, beating well after each addition. Scrape down the bowl from time to time so the mixture is thoroughly combined. It's a good idea to add a tablespoon of the sifted flour with the last 2 portions of egg so the mixture doesn't curdle.

4 Add about a third of the rest of the flour to the bowl and gently fold in with a large metal spoon or plastic spatula. Add half the crème fraîche mixture and fold in, followed by half of the rest of the flour. When this has completely disappeared, fold in the last portion of crème fraîche and then the last of the flour together with the 3 tablespoons chopped nuts. When you can no longer see any streaks of flour or crème fraîche, carefully spoon the mixture into the prepared tin and spread evenly.

5 Scatter the 2 tablespoons chopped nuts evenly over the top. Bake in the heated oven for about 1 hour until the cake is a good golden brown and a wooden cocktail stick inserted into the centre comes out clean – check the cake after 50 minutes and cover lightly with a sheet of greaseproof paper or foil if you think it is getting too brown.

6 Set the tin on a wire rack. Run a round-bladed knife around the inside edge of the tin to loosen the cake, then leave to firm up for 10 minutes. Lift the cake out of the tin, using the long ends of the lining paper, and leave to cool completely on the wire rack.

7 Once the cake is cold peel off the lining paper. Wrap the cake in greaseproof paper or foil and leave overnight before cutting. Dust with icing sugar just before serving. Store in an airtight container for about 5 days.

PLUM MUFFINS

Muffins fall somewhere between cupcakes and scones: plainer and not as sweet or rich as the small cakes, but softer, more moist, lighter and less bread-like than the latter. You can also use nectarines in this recipe, when they are available, as they work very well with the lemon-scented muffin mix.

MAKES TWELVE

3 large, ripe but firm plums
85g unsalted butter, softened
75g light brown muscovado sugar
finely grated zest of 1 medium
  unwaxed lemon
1 medium free-range egg, at room
  temperature, beaten to mix
75g plain flour
75g plain wholemeal flour
1½ teaspoons baking powder
5 tablespoons milk
3 tablespoons demerara sugar,
  for sprinkling

1 x 12-hole muffin/cupcake tray,
  lined with paper cases

1 Heat your oven to 180°C/350°F/gas 4. Cut the plums in half and twist apart. Remove the stones. Cut each half into 6 wedges. Set aside for now.

2 Put the soft butter, muscovado sugar and lemon zest into a mixing bowl (or the bowl of a free-standing electric mixer fitted with the whisk attachment). Beat thoroughly with a wooden spoon or hand-held electric mixer (or in the free-standing mixer) until the mixture looks light and fluffy. Scrape down the sides of the bowl, then add the beaten egg in 3 batches, beating well after each addition.

3 Sift the 2 flours and the baking powder into the bowl; add the bits of bran left in the sieve too. Pour in the milk, then fold everything together with a large metal spoon or plastic spatula.

4 Spoon the mixture into the paper cases, filling them equally (the cases will be about half full). Set 3 plum wedges, skin side up, on top so they are almost vertical (the sponge will bubble up). Sprinkle with the demerara sugar. Bake in the heated oven for about 25 minutes until a wooden cocktail stick inserted into the centre of a muffin comes out clean.

5 Transfer to a wire rack and leave to cool. Best eaten the same or the next day.

MARTHA

Where do you live?
Ascot, Berkshire

What do you get up to when you are not baking?
I am a sixth form student so I spend most of my time studying, going out with friends and generally enjoying life!

How would you define yourself as a baker?
I would define my baking style as a little bit spontaneous and very messy, but it is based on scientific understanding of how food works. I have been baking since I was about 7 years old, when brightly coloured rock cakes were my speciality (luckily I've improved a lot since then!)

Why do you enjoy baking?
I like baking because it is my escape from the cruel world of exams and studying, and it makes people happy because no one says no to cake!

How did you get into baking?
I got into baking largely because my parents allowed 7 year old me to experiment in the kitchen (and make a mess!). But I found my love for baking when I attended my school's cooking club and realised that I am actually quite good at it; it gave me confidence to try new things.

What is the trickiest bake you've ever mastered?
Macarons – the nemesis of the home baker.

What are your favourite 3 items of kitchen equipment?
Dough-scraper.
Sugar thermometer.
Palette knife.

MARTHA'S
DARK CHOCOLATE & ALMOND LIQUEUR SAVARIN

▼▼▼▼▼▼▼▼▼▼▼▼▼▼▼▼▼▼▼▼▼▼▼▼▼▼▼▼▼▼▼▼▼▼▼▼▼

A very rich but light triple-chocolate cake with a soft sponge-like texture. It's made with yeast, and soaked after baking in a sweet almond liqueur syrup. The decoration is a crunchy flaked almond brittle and drizzled melted chocolate.

MAKES ONE LARGE CAKE

For the savarin dough

50g dark chocolate (about 70% cocoa solids), broken up
300g strong white bread flour
1½ teaspoons fast-action dried yeast (from a 7g sachet)
½ teaspoon salt
4 tablespoons caster sugar
5 tablespoons cocoa powder
2 large free-range eggs, at room temperature
200ml lukewarm full-fat milk
55g unsalted butter, softened
100g dark chocolate chips

For the amaretti brittle

50g caster sugar
25g salted butter
a few drops each almond extract and almond liqueur extract
50g toasted flaked almonds

For the soaking syrup

150g caster sugar
4 tablespoons almond liqueur (or to taste)

1 To make the dough for the savarin, gently melt the broken-up chocolate in a small heatproof bowl set over a pan of steaming-hot water (don't let the base of the bowl touch the water). Remove the bowl from the pan and leave the chocolate to cool until needed.

2 Put the flour, yeast, salt, sugar and cocoa powder into a large bowl (or the bowl of a free-standing electric mixer fitted with the dough hook). Mix thoroughly with your hand (or the dough hook). Make a well in the middle. Stir the eggs into the milk with a fork, then pour the mixture into the well. Work the flour into the liquid with your hand (or the dough hook on low speed). When all the dry ingredients have been incorporated, add the soft butter and mix in followed by the melted chocolate – the mixture will feel like a heavy, sticky cake mixture rather than a bread dough.

3 Scrape down the sides of the bowl and beat the mixture with your hand (or the dough hook) for 4–5 minutes until it feels very smooth and elastic. Cover the bowl with clingfilm (or a shower cap) and leave to rise at normal room temperature for about 1 hour until doubled in size.

4 While the dough is rising make the brittle. Put the sugar, butter and 2 tablespoons water into a small pan and stir over a low heat until the sugar has dissolved. Bring to the boil (take care as it will froth up) and stir until the mixture turns a light caramel colour. Remove the pan from the heat and stir in the extracts and the almonds. Pour the mixture onto the oiled baking sheet and spread out into an even layer. Leave to cool and set, then break up into shards. Set aside for the decoration.

To decorate

50g good-quality white chocolate, broken up

50g dark chocolate (about 70% cocoa solids), broken up

1 baking sheet, lightly greased with oil; a 2-litre bundt tin (22cm across the top), greased with butter; 2 small disposable piping bags

5 Scatter the chocolate chips over the risen dough and work them in for a couple of minutes using your hand (or the dough hook on low speed). Scoop the dough into the prepared bundt tin and spread evenly. Cover with clingfilm and leave to rise at room temperature for 50–60 minutes until doubled in size. Towards the end of the proving time heat your oven to 180°C/350°F/gas 4.

6 Uncover the risen dough and place in the heated oven. Bake for about 35 minutes until the savarin is lightly coloured and firm, and a wooden cocktail stick inserted halfway between the side of the tin and the centre comes out clean (test in several spots in case you hit chocolate chips). Note that the baking time will depend on the type/weight of your tin so start testing after 25 minutes.

7 While the savarin is baking make the syrup. Put the sugar and 275ml water in a medium pan and stir over low heat until the sugar has dissolved. Bring to the boil and simmer for a minute to make a light syrup. Add the almond liqueur, then bring back to the boil. Remove from the heat and keep warm.

8 As soon as the savarin is baked, carefully turn it out on to a clean baking sheet. Pour enough warm syrup into the hot bundt tin (no need to wash it first) to make a layer about 1cm deep. Carefully replace the hot savarin in the tin, on to the syrup. Prick the top of the savarin all over with a cocktail stick, then pour the rest of the warm syrup slowly over the surface so it is almost swimming. Leave to soak and cool. When cold, and most of the syrup has been absorbed, carefully turn out the savarin on to a serving platter or cake stand with a lip.

9 Melt the white and dark chocolates in separate bowls, as before, then spoon into separate piping bags. Snip off the ends, then pipe chocolate over the top and sides of the moist sponge to decorate. Scatter the almond brittle over the savarin, then leave to set. Serve at room temperature.

COFFEE & WALNUT PRALINE CAKE

A coffee and walnut cake never goes out of fashion. This ultimate version is made of three layers of well-flavoured coffee sponge sandwiched with a rich, light-textured coffee buttercream and finished with plenty of walnut praline – nuts cooked with sugar to a crunchy bittersweet caramel.

For the sponge
175g unsalted butter, softened
175g caster sugar
3 medium free-range eggs, at room temperature, beaten to mix
175g self-raising flour
$\frac{1}{2}$ teaspoon baking powder
1 tablespoon instant coffee (powder or granules), dissolved in 1 tablespoon boiling water and cooled

For the praline
100g walnut halves
100g caster sugar (white, not golden)

For the filling and icing
150g unsalted butter, softened
325g icing sugar
3 tablespoons instant coffee (powder or granules), dissolved in 2 tablespoons boiling water and cooled
75ml whipping or single cream

2 or 3 (see recipe) x 20.5cm round, deep sandwich tins, greased and base-lined;* a baking sheet, greased with oil

1 Heat your oven to 180°C/350°F/gas 4. Put the soft butter into a mixing bowl (or the bowl of a free-standing electric mixer fitted with the whisk attachment). Beat until creamy with a wooden spoon or hand-held electric mixer (or in the free-standing mixer). Scrape down the sides of the bowl, then gradually beat in the sugar. Scrape down the sides again, then continue beating for a minute or so until the mixture is very pale in colour and lighter in texture. Scrape down the sides of the bowl once more, then gradually add the eggs, a tablespoon at a time, beating the mixture well after each addition. To prevent the mixture from separating, add a tablespoon of the weighed flour with each of the last 2 portions of egg.

2 Scrape down the sides of the bowl once more. Sift the remaining flour and the baking powder on to the creamed mixture and, using a large metal spoon or a plastic spatula, start to fold the flour in. After a couple of folding movements add the cooled coffee, then continue folding gently together until the mixture is evenly combined, with no streaks of flour or coffee.

3 Divide the mixture equally among 3 prepared tins and spread evenly. If you have only 2 tins, divide the mixture equally into 3 portions and put a portion into each tin, then cover the bowl containing the third portion to bake later (you will need to wash, dry, grease and base-line a tin for this third sponge layer).

4 Bake in the heated oven for 13–15 minutes until the sponges are springy when gently pressed in the middle and starting to shrink away from the side of the tin. Run a round-bladed knife around the inside of each tin to loosen the sponge, then leave to cool and firm up for a couple of minutes before carefully turning out on to a wire rack. Leave until cold.

5 While the sponges are cooling make the walnut praline. Put the nuts and sugar into a medium-sized heavy-based pan and set over fairly low heat. Stir occasionally with a metal spoon until the sugar starts to melt, then stop stirring. When all the sugar has melted turn up the heat to medium and cook until the sugar syrup starts to colour, shaking the pan now and then so the walnuts cook evenly. Continue cooking, stirring gently, until the mixture turns chestnut brown. Immediately spoon on to the oiled baking sheet and quickly spread the caramel as evenly and thinly as possible. Leave to cool. Once set hard, break up into chunks, then chop up in a food processor until the praline looks like rubble – it should still have some texture and not be finely ground. Put on one side for now.

6 For the coffee buttercream filling and icing, heat the butter in a small pan until it starts bubbling, then let it cook gently for a minute until it turns a light golden brown colour. Meanwhile, sift the icing sugar into a large heatproof mixing bowl (or the bowl of a free-standing electric mixer fitted with the whisk attachment). Pour the hot butter on to the icing sugar quickly followed by the cooled coffee and cream. Beat well with a wooden spoon or a hand-held electric mixer (or in the free-standing mixer), using low speed to start with, to make a thick, smooth, creamy icing. If it is too soft to spread, leave it in a cool place to firm up a bit, or cover and chill briefly.

7 When you are ready to assemble the cake, set one sponge, crust-side down, on a cake board or serving plate. Spread over about a quarter of the coffee buttercream, then set a second sponge on this, crust-side up, and cover it with buttercream. Top with the third sponge, crust-side up. Use the rest of the buttercream to cover the top and sides of the assembled cake.

8 Pick out the largest lumps of praline 'rubble' and set aside for the top of the cake. Press the rest of the praline on to the side of the cake so it is evenly covered. Scatter any leftover praline on top, then add the saved larger pieces.

9 Leave the cake in a cool place – not the fridge – for at least an hour (or overnight, stored in a large plastic container) to firm up a bit before cutting. The flavours will deepen the longer the cake is kept, but the praline may start to soften after 24 hours.

CLASSIC CHOCOLATE FUDGE SANDWICH CAKE

A very dark and rich chocolate sponge, made with melted chocolate plus cocoa powder, this can be filled and covered with either a chocolate fudge icing or a vanilla buttercream – the latter makes a dramatic black and white cake. Finish off your creation with a large chocolate flower rosette, made from rolled-out modelling chocolate ribbons.

For the sponge mixture
200g dark chocolate (about 70% cocoa solids), roughly chopped
200g unsalted butter, diced
4 medium free-range eggs, at room temperature
1 teaspoon vanilla extract
325g caster sugar
175g self-raising flour
$\frac{1}{2}$ teaspoon baking powder
45g cocoa powder
salt

For the chocolate fudge filling and icing
300g icing sugar
150g dark chocolate (about 70% cocoa solids), chopped
150g unsalted butter, at room temperature, diced
$\frac{1}{2}$ teaspoon vanilla extract

OR

For the vanilla buttercream filling and icing
550g icing sugar
250g unsalted butter, softened
1 teaspoon vanilla extract
4 tablespoons milk

1 Heat your oven to 180°C/350°F/gas 4. Put the chopped chocolate and butter into a heatproof bowl and set over a pan of steaming-hot but not boiling water (don't let the base of the bowl touch the water). Leave to melt very gently, stirring now and then. Remove the bowl from the pan and leave to cool until needed.

2 Put the eggs and vanilla into a mixing bowl (or the bowl of a free-standing electric mixer fitted with the whisk attachment). Whisk until frothy using a hand-held electric mixer (or in the free-standing mixer). Add the sugar and whisk until the mixture is very thick and mousse-like and will make a distinct ribbon-like trail when the whisk is lifted out (see Baker's Guide page 9 for more information about whisking to the 'ribbon stage').

3 Turn down the speed of the whisk to its lowest setting and pour in the melted chocolate, whisking all the while. Once all the chocolate has been incorporated scrape down the sides of the bowl. Sift the flour, baking powder, cocoa and a couple of good pinches of salt into the bowl and fold in with a large metal spoon or plastic spatula. The mixture will be quite heavy – take your time so there are no streaks.

4 Divide the mixture equally between the 2 prepared tins and spread evenly. Bake in the heated oven for 30–35 minutes until the sponges are just firm to the touch and have started to shrink away from the side of the tin; a cocktail stick inserted into the centre of the sponge should come out clean. Run a round-bladed knife around the inside of each tin to loosen the sponge, then carefully turn it out on to a wire rack. Leave until completely cold.

5 Meanwhile, make the filling and icing. For the chocolate fudge mixture, sift the icing sugar into a mixing bowl. Put the chopped chocolate into a large heatproof mixing bowl set over a pan of steaming-hot water and melt gently. Remove the bowl from the pan and leave to cool for a couple of minutes until barely warm before adding the butter and a couple

To decorate

1 x 150g pack dark chocolate cocoform
  or modelling chocolate OR make
  your own (see opposite page)
edible gold lustre or gold food
  shimmer spray

2 x 20.5cm round, deep sandwich tins,
  greased with butter and base-lined*

of tablespoons of the icing sugar. Beat well with a wooden spoon or an electric mixer on low speed. Gradually beat in the remaining icing sugar, a few tablespoons at a time, to make a thick, spreadable icing. Beat in the vanilla.

6 To make the vanilla buttercream, sift the icing sugar into a large bowl. Add the soft butter, vanilla and milk and beat everything together very thoroughly using a wooden spoon or electric mixer (on lowest speed) until light and creamy.

7 When ready to assemble the cake, cut each sponge into 2 equal layers (see the Baker's Guide page 10 for how to do this). Use half of the filling/icing mixture to sandwich the 4 layers together. Coat the top and sides of the assembled cake with a very thin layer of icing (use slightly less than half the remaining mixture) – this acts as a 'crumb catcher' layer so the final cake looks pristine and not flecked with chocolate crumbs. Chill for about 10 minutes until firm.

8 Cover the whole cake with the rest of the icing. Use a large palette knife or cake scraper to smooth and neaten the icing. Leave in a cool spot – not the fridge – to firm up. The cake can now be stored in an airtight container for up to 2 days.

9 To make the decoration, take about a quarter of the chocolate cocoform and gently knead it in your hand just until it feels supple, like playdough. Place it between 2 large sheets of clingfilm and roll out very thinly to a large oblong at least 20cm long and no more than 1.5mm thick. Peel off the top sheet of clingfilm, then cut the chocolate into shiny ribbons about 3.5cm wide and 20cm long. Gently pleat or concertina the strips, pinching the pleats together along one long edge, a bit like making a paper fan. Continue making ruffles like this until you have used all the cocoform.

10 Carefully arrange the ruffled strips on the worktop into a pompom or rosette shape, starting with a ring of ruffles about 15cm across and then gradually building up the layers and working in towards the centre. The beauty of modelling chocolate is that you can easily re-knead and re-roll any mistakes and trimmings, so there's no waste. Once you have a pompom shape you like, carefully dismantle it and re-build it on the top of the cake. For a final touch brush the edges of the ruffles lightly with gold lustre or spray with shimmer.

11 Store the decorated cake in an airtight container in a cool spot (not the fridge) and eat within 3 days.

TO MAKE YOUR OWN CHOCOLATE FOR MODELLING

Melt 150g chopped dark chocolate (about 70% cocoa solids) in a heatproof bowl set over a pan of steaming-hot water. Remove the bowl from the pan and gently stir in 3 tablespoons liquid glucose. Leave at room temperature to thicken. Once the mixture is firm and almost set, shape it into a ball. Knead and work the mixture in your hands until it softens and feels pliable, like playdough. As soon as it feels smooth, shape it into a sausage, then put it between 2 long sheets of clingfilm and roll out as thinly as possible. Cut into strips and make into a rosette as opposite.

MARY'S CHERRY CAKE

SERVES TEN TO TWELVE

200g glacé cherries
225g self-raising flour
175g butter, softened
175g caster sugar
finely grated zest of 1 lemon
50g ground almonds
3 large eggs

To decorate
175g icing sugar, sifted
juice of 1 lemon
15g flaked almonds, toasted
5 glacé cherries, quartered

1 x 23cm savarin mould or bundt tin,
    greased with butter

1 Heat your oven to 180°C/350°F/gas 4. Cut the cherries into quarters, put in a sieve and rinse under running water. Drain well, then dry thoroughly on kitchen paper. Toss in 2 tablespoons of the flour.

2 Combine all the remaining ingredients – including the rest of the flour – in a large bowl and beat well for 2 minutes to mix thoroughly. Lightly fold in the floured cherries.

3 Turn the mixture into the prepared mould. Bake in the heated oven for 35–40 minutes until well risen and golden brown, and a skewer inserted into the centre comes out clean. Leave to cool in the mould for 10 minutes, then turn out on to a wire rack and cool completely.

4 For the icing, mix the icing sugar with the lemon juice to make a thick paste. Drizzle from the back of a spoon over the cooled cake. Finish by scattering the toasted almonds and cherries over the top.

MARY'S DOBOS TORTE

MAKES ONE LARGE CAKE

For the caramel buttercream
800g granulated sugar
100ml water
400ml double cream
450g unsalted butter, softened

For the sponge layers
8 large free-range eggs
350g caster sugar
300g sifted self-raising flour

For the almond praline and caramel-coated hazelnuts
75g flaked almonds
16 blanched (skinned) hazelnuts
300g granulated sugar
6 tablespoons water

For the caramel topping
100g granulated sugar
2 tablespoons water

baking paper; 2 or more baking sheets; a piping bag fitted with a medium star tube

1 First make the caramel buttercream. Put the sugar and water in a large saucepan. Bring to the boil over medium heat, stirring until the sugar has dissolved. Once there is no grittiness left, turn up the heat and boil to a golden caramel. Take off the heat, add the cream and give it a quick stir, then pour into a bowl. Leave to cool, then chill until set.

2 Put the soft butter in the bowl of a free-standing electric mixer and whisk until light and fluffy. Add to the cooled caramel mixture a spoonful at a time, whisking between each addition and scraping down the bowl regularly. Keep in the fridge until ready to use.

3 Heat your oven to 200°C/400°F/gas 6. Draw 6 x 20cm circles and 6 x 15cm circles on sheets of baking paper cut to fit your baking sheets (you'll probably need to bake in batches).

4 To make the sponge layers, break the eggs into a large bowl, add the sugar and whisk until the mixture is light and foamy and the whisk just leaves a trail when lifted out of the mixture. Lightly fold in the flour, a little at a time. Divide the mixture among the 12 marked circles on the baking paper, spreading the mixture out evenly.

5 Bake the sponge layers in the heated oven for 8–10 minutes until pale golden and springy to the touch. Remove the baking sheet from the oven and set on a heatproof surface. With a sharp knife, trim the sponge layer to neaten it, then peel off the parchment and leave to cool on a wire rack.

6 Now make the almond praline and caramel-coated hazelnuts. Spread the flaked almonds over a silicone mat or sheet of baking paper on the worktop. Stick a wooden cocktail stick into each of the 16 hazelnuts. Have ready an orange or piece of foam on the worktop.

7 Dissolve the sugar in the water in a small pan over low heat, then increase the heat and boil the syrup until it turns a deep golden colour. Allow the caramel to cool slightly, then pour three-quarters of it over the flaked almonds to make the praline. Dip the hazelnuts in the remaining caramel, twisting the sticks so they are completely coated. Carefully invert and push the sticks into the orange or foam. Leave to cool and set.

8 Take one of the 15cm sponge layers and place it on a sheet of baking paper, ready to be topped with caramel. To make this, dissolve the sugar in the water in a small pan over low heat, then increase the heat and boil the syrup until it turns a deep golden colour. Allow the syrup to cool slightly, then pour it over the sponge layer to cover evenly. When the caramel is just beginning to set, mark it and then cut into 8 wedges using an oiled knife. These will be used for the top layer of the assembled cake.

9 Sandwich the 20cm sponge layers with some of the caramel buttercream. Spread buttercream over the top and side of this cake stack.

10 Sandwich the remaining 5 x 15cm sponge layers with buttercream. Spread buttercream around the side and top of the stack, then place it on top of the 20cm cake stack to form a second tier. Spoon the remaining buttercream into the piping bag.

11 Break the almond praline into small pieces and press into the side of both tiers of the cake.

12 Remove the caramel-coated hazelnuts from the cocktail sticks. Pipe 16 rosettes of buttercream around the top edge of the 20cm cake. Top each rosette with a caramel-coated hazelnut. Pipe 8 buttercream rosettes on top of the 15cm cake. Place a caramel-topped wedge of cake at an angle leaning against each rosette to form the top layer. This is best eaten on the day, but it can be kept in the fridge for up to 3 days – however the caramel will melt when kept in the fridge.

MARY'S PRINSESSTÅRTA

SERVES TWELVE TO SIXTEEN

For the vanilla custard
600ml milk
1 vanilla pod, split open lengthways
6 free-range egg yolks
100g caster sugar
50g cornflour
50g unsalted butter
600ml double cream

For the jam
200g raspberries
175g jam sugar
2 tablespoons water

For the sponge
4 large free-range eggs
150g caster sugar
75g cornflour
75g plain flour
1 teaspoon baking powder
50g unsalted butter, melted

For the fondant rose
25g pink ready-to-roll fondant icing

For the marzipan
400g ground almonds
150g caster sugar
250g icing sugar, sifted
2 medium free-range eggs, beaten
   to mix
1 teaspoon almond extract
green paste food colouring

To decorate
150ml double cream
50g dark chocolate, melted

1 x 23cm springclip tin, greased and
base-lined*; a piping bag; a small
plain and a small star nozzle; a small
disposable piping bag

1 To make the vanilla custard, pour the milk into a heavy-based saucepan. Scrape the seeds from the vanilla pod and add to the pan with the pod. Heat gently until just simmering. Remove from the heat.

2 Whisk the yolks with the sugar and cornflour in a bowl until light and creamy. Remove and discard the vanilla pod from the warm milk, and pour over the egg mixture, stirring. Return the mixture to the pan and cook over low heat, whisking constantly, for 4–5 minutes until the custard starts to thicken and the whisk leaves a trail. Remove from the heat and beat in the butter. Transfer to a bowl. Cover the surface with clingfilm to prevent a skin from forming. Leave to cool, then chill.

3 For the jam, tip the raspberries into a medium-sized pan and add the sugar and the water. Cook over low heat, stirring occasionally, until the sugar has dissolved. Bring to the boil and boil vigorously for about 4 minutes until the temperature reaches 104°C on a sugar thermometer, or setting point. Transfer to a heatproof bowl and leave to cool and set.

4 Next make the sponge. Heat the oven to 180°C/350°F/gas 4. Put the eggs and sugar into a large bowl and whisk together using an electric mixer until the mixture is very pale and thick, and leaves a ribbon-like trail on the surface when the whisk is lifted out. This will take about 5 minutes. Sift the cornflour, flour and baking powder over the mixture and carefully fold in using a large metal spoon or plastic spatula. Fold in the melted butter, taking care not to over-mix.

5 Pour the mixture into the prepared tin and bake in the heated oven for 25–30 minutes until the sponge is golden and has just started to shrink away from the side of the tin. Remove from the oven and set on a heatproof surface. When cool enough to handle, turn out the sponge on to a wire rack and leave to cool completely.

6 To make the fondant rose, dust 2 small pieces of greaseproof paper with icing sugar. Divide the icing into 10 little pieces and roll each into a small ball about the size of a cherry stone. One at a time, place the balls of icing between the sheets of greaseproof (sugar side in) and flatten with your fingers to a thin circle about 2cm in diameter. These will be the petals. Roll one petal up like a sausage to form a bud and wrap the remaining petals around this to form a rose. Curl the petal edges, to make them look more realistic. Dry for at least 1 hour.

7 To assemble the cake, use a serrated knife to cut the sponge horizontally into 3 equal layers. Place the first sponge layer on a serving plate. Spread a very thin layer of vanilla custard over the sponge. Spoon a quarter of the remaining vanilla custard into a piping bag fitted with the plain nozzle and pipe a border around the edge of the sponge – this is to contain the jam. Spoon the jam over the sponge, and spread evenly within the piped border.

8 Whip the 600ml double cream to firm peaks. Fold half of the cream into the remaining vanilla custard. Spread a third of this creamy vanilla custard over the jam. Place the second sponge layer on top and spread the remaining creamy vanilla custard over it.

9 Set the third sponge on top. Spoon the remaining whipped cream over the sponge and spread to cover the top and sides, smoothing the cream into a small dome shape on the top. Chill in the fridge for 1 hour.

10 Meanwhile make the marzipan. Mix the ground almonds and 2 sugars in a free-standing electric mixer fitted with the dough hook. Add the eggs and almond extract and knead in the bowl to make a stiff dough. Turn out on to a worktop dusted with icing sugar. Using a cocktail stick, add a tiny amount of green food colouring and knead into the marzipan to tint it an even pastel green colour.

11 Roll out the marzipan on the sugar-dusted worktop to a circle about 40cm in diameter, or large enough to cover the cake completely. Lift the marzipan up over the cake and, using your hands, shape the marzipan around the side of the cake to get a smooth finish. Trim off any excess marzipan.

12 Whip the 150ml cream for decoration to medium peaks. Spoon into the washed piping bag fitted with the star tube. Pipe around the base of the cake.

13 Melt the chocolate in a heatproof bowl set over a pan of steaming hot water. Remove the bowl from the pan and stir the chocolate until smooth, then leave to cool. Spoon the chocolate into the disposable piping bag and snip off the end, then pipe rings over the top of the cake. Finish with the fondant rose.

PAUL'S BLACKCURRANT & LIQUORICE SWISS ROLL

For the decorative sponge paste

70g unsalted butter, softened
70g icing sugar, sifted
2 medium free-range egg whites
80g plain flour, sifted
1 teaspoon liquorice essence
1/2–1 teaspoon black food colouring paste

For the sponge

3 large free-range eggs, at room temperature
75g caster sugar, plus extra for sprinkling
75g self-raising flour

For the filling

75g unsalted butter, softened
225g icing sugar
1 tablespoon milk
1/2 teaspoon liquorice essence
200g blackcurrant jam

1 20cm x 30cm Swiss roll tin, greased and lined with baking paper; a piping bag fitted with a piping 1 1/2 plain nozzle

1 Heat your oven to 200°C/400°F/gas 6.

2 For the decorative sponge paste, cream the butter and icing sugar together until light and fluffy. Gradually add the egg whites, beating constantly. Fold in the flour, then add the liquorice essence and food colouring paste and beat until the mixture is black. Spoon into the piping bag and pipe 6 diagonal lines across the base of the prepared tin.

3 To make the sponge, put the eggs and caster sugar into a large bowl and whisk with an electric mixer until the mixture is light and frothy and it will make a ribbon trail on itself when the whisk is lifted. Sift the flour over the mixture and carefully fold in using a large metal spoon or rubber spatula.

4 Pour the sponge mixture into the tin and give the tin a little shake so the mixture finds its own level; gently push the mixture into the corners if necessary. Bake for 10–12 minutes until the sponge is golden and starting to shrink away from the sides of the tin.

5 Lay 2 sheets of baking paper (cut a little larger than the size of the tin) on the worktop and sprinkle one with caster sugar. As soon as the sponge is ready, turn it out on to the sheet of sugared paper and carefully peel off the lining paper. Lay the other sheet of paper over the striped top and flip the sponge over, so that the black lines are underneath. Leave the sponge to cool on a wire rack.

6 Make the buttercream filling by beating together the butter, icing sugar, milk and liquorice essence in a bowl until smooth.

7 Once the sponge has cooled, trim the edges with a sharp knife. Score a line across the sponge 2cm in from one of the short edges.

8 Spread the buttercream over the sponge in an even layer, then cover with an even layer of jam. Roll up the sponge firmly from the scored end.

MARY'S MINI COFFEE & WALNUT CAKES

MAKES SIXTEEN

For the sponge

150g butter, softened
150g light brown muscovado sugar
3 large eggs
150g self-raising flour
1 level teaspoon baking powder
1 tablespoon chicory and coffee
   essence
75g walnuts, chopped

For the filling and decoration

150g butter, softened
450g icing sugar, sifted
2 tablespoons milk
1 tablespoon chicory and coffee
   essence
200g walnuts, finely chopped
16 chocolate-covered coffee beans

16 x 5cm mini cake tins; a piping bag
   fitted with a small star (2D) tube

1 Heat your oven to 190°C/375°F/gas 5. Line each cake tin with a piece of baking paper. Grease the base tray and line with baking paper.

2 Measure the butter, sugar, eggs, flour, baking powder and chicory and coffee essence into a bowl and beat until thoroughly blended and smooth. Fold in the walnuts.

3 Spoon or pipe the mixture into the mini cake tins, dividing it evenly. Bake in the heated oven for 12–15 minutes until the cakes are well risen and the top springs back when lightly pressed with a finger.

4 Leave to cool in the tins for a few minutes. When cool enough to handle, turn the cakes out of the tins and remove the paper. Trim each cake neatly across the top and slice them in half. Leave to cool completely on a wire rack.

5 To make the buttercream for the filling and topping, beat together the butter, icing sugar, milk and chicory and coffee essence in a bowl until smooth.

6 When the cakes are cold, sandwich the halves together with buttercream, using about a quarter of it.

7 Spread a thin coat of buttercream around the side of each cake, then roll in chopped walnuts to coat the side.

8 Spoon the remaining buttercream into the piping bag and pipe over the top of each cake. Set a chocolate-covered coffee bean in the centre of the top.

MALTED CHOCOLATE TARTS • SOMERSET APPLE TART • LUIS' TROPICAL MANCHESTER TART • SNOWBALL MERINGUES • APPLE TREACLE TART • MORELLO CHERRY BAKEWELL • CHOCOLATE FUDGE TART • CHOUX CARAMEL PUFFS • KATE'S RHUBARB & CUSTARD TART WITH ALMOND & RASPBERRY PASTRY • GOLDEN MILLEFEUILLES • RASPBERRY & LEMON CREAM HORNS • SUMMER FOUR-BERRY PIE • APRICOT CUSTARD TART • PAUL'S KOUIGN AMANN • MARY'S LEMON & RASPBERRY ÉCLAIRS • MARY'S CHOCOLATE ORANGE TART • MARY'S DOUBLE CHOCOLATE MOUSSE ENTREMETS

SWEET PASTRY & PATISSERIE

MALTED CHOCOLATE TARTS

The cases for these glamorous tarts are made from a rich shortbread-like dough and they're baked in a bun tray rather than individually. The ganache filling is made quickly in the food processor with milk and dark chocolates and malted drink powder. For the best flavour, look for milk chocolate with a fairly high percentage of cocoa solids and an 'original' malted milk-drink powder – the kind you add to milk.

MAKES TWELVE INDIVIDUAL TARTS

For the chocolate pastry
150g plain flour
good pinch of salt
20g cocoa powder
60g icing sugar
120g unsalted butter, chilled and diced
1 medium free-range egg yolk

For the filling
200g good-quality milk chocolate, broken up
100g dark chocolate (about 70% cocoa solids), broken up
25g malted milk drink powder
250ml whipping cream

To decorate
175ml whipping cream, well chilled
2 teaspoons malted milk drink powder
12 malted milk chocolate balls OR grated dark chocolate

1 x 7.5cm plain round cutter; a 12-hole bun tray; a baking sheet; a piping bag and star tube (optional)

1 This chocolate pastry is best made in a food processor and handled as little as possible. Put the flour, salt, cocoa and icing sugar into the processor bowl and 'pulse' several times to combine. Add the cold butter and run the machine just until the mixture looks like fine crumbs. Add the egg yolk and run the machine again until the mixture comes together to make a ball of heavy, slightly sticky dough. Carefully remove the dough, flatten it into a disc and wrap it in clingfilm. Chill for 30 minutes until firm.

2 It's easiest to roll out the dough between 2 large sheets of clingfilm because touching it with a rolling pin or hands dusted with flour can leave white marks. Roll out the dough (between the clingfilm sheets) to a large rectangle 4mm thick and the size of your bun tray. Slide the whole thing (clingfilm-dough sandwich) on to the baking sheet and chill for about 10 minutes until firm.

3 Remove the top sheet of clingfilm and cut out discs of chocolate pastry using the plain round cutter. One at a time, peel them off the bottom sheet of clingfilm and gently press into each hole in the bun tray – the pastry will be quite thick. Prick the base of each pastry case with a fork, then put the bun tray in the fridge to chill for 15 minutes while you heat your oven to 180°C/350°F/gas 4.

4 Cut a large sheet of greaseproof paper into 12 x 7cm squares. Crumple up the squares, to make them more flexible, then gently press one into each pastry case to line it. Fill the cases with baking beans and bake blind in the heated oven for about 12 minutes until the pastry is just set and firm.

MALTED CHOCOLATE TARTS CONTINUED...

5 Very carefully remove the paper and beans – the pastry will be very fragile – then return the bun tray to the oven and bake for a further 5–7 minutes until the pastry is thoroughly cooked and crisp (watch like a hawk as this pastry is very rich and you don't want it to get too dark and scorch). Remove the tray from the oven, set it on a wire rack and leave to cool.

6 Once the pastry is cold and has firmed up, gently ease each case out of the tray, then replace it – the tart cases are easier to fill, and less likely to become damaged, if they are in the bun tray.

7 To make the filling put both chocolates and the malted milk drink powder into the bowl of the clean food processor and blitz until the chocolate is finely chopped. Heat the cream until it just comes to the boil. With the machine running, pour into the processor bowl through the feed tube. As soon as you have a very smooth, thick liquid, turn off the machine and scrape down the sides of the bowl. Spoon the chocolate mixture into the tart cases, right to the top so that they are completely filled. Chill for about 20 minutes until the filling is firm.

8 To decorate the tarts, pour the chilled cream into a mixing bowl, add the malted milk drink powder and whip until thick enough to form stiff peaks. Spoon into the piping bag fitted with a star tube (if using), then pipe – or spoon – the cream on top of the chocolate filling. Decorate with chocolate balls or grated chocolate, then chill for 10 minutes. If not serving straight away, the tarts can be kept in a large plastic box in the fridge for up to 24 hours; remove from the fridge about 20 minutes before serving.

SOMERSET APPLE TART

This is a recipe for using up windfalls at harvest time, as long as the variety of apples you grow are well-flavoured, with a sweet/tart taste, and will keep their shape when baked.

> MAKES ONE MEDIUM TART

For the rich sweet shortcrust pastry

175g plain flour
pinch of salt
30g icing sugar
100g unsalted butter, chilled and diced
1 medium free-range egg yolk
about 1 tablespoon icy-cold water, to mix

For the filling

800–900g Braeburn or Jazz apples (about 5 or 6 large apples)
125ml single cream
1 medium free-range egg
35g caster sugar OR vanilla caster sugar
2 teaspoons Somerset apple brandy or brandy OR ½ teaspoon vanilla extract
3 tablespoons sieved apricot jam OR apricot glaze, warmed

1 x 23cm fluted, deep, loose-based flan tin; a baking sheet

1 To make the pastry, sift the flour, salt and sugar into a mixing bowl. Add the pieces of butter and toss in the flour so they are lightly coated, then gently rub the butter into the flour until the mixture looks like fine crumbs. Add the egg yolk and water and stir into the crumbs with a round-bladed knife to make a firm dough. If there are dry crumbs, work in more cold water a teaspoon at a time. Shape the dough into a flat disc, wrap in clingfilm and chill for 20 minutes.

2 Roll out the pastry on a lightly floured worktop to a large circle about 32cm across and use to line the flan tin (see the Baker's Guide page 9). Leave the excess pastry hanging over the rim. Prick the base with a fork, then chill for 15 minutes. Meanwhile, heat your oven to 190°C/375°F/gas 5.

3 Carefully neaten the pastry rim, trimming off the excess pastry. Line the case with greaseproof paper, fill with baking beans and bake blind in the heated oven for 12–15 minutes until the pastry is set and firm. Remove the paper and beans, then return to the oven and bake for a further 5 minutes until the pastry is crisp and lightly coloured (see the Baker's Guide page 10 for more information).

4 Set the flan tin on a heatproof surface. Put the baking sheet into the oven to heat up, and reduce the oven temperature to 180°C/350°F/gas 4.

5 While the pastry case cools, peel and quarter the apples. Cut out the cores, then cut the apples into very thin slices. Arrange the apple slices, slightly overlapping, in the cooled pastry case, starting from the edge and working round in neat concentric circles. Make sure the pastry case is completely filled to the top, with no gaps, and the top layer looks pretty.

6 Measure the cream in a jug. Add the egg, sugar and brandy (or vanilla) and mix well until smooth. Slowly pour this mixture evenly over the apples, letting it seep through the layers.

7 Set the flan tin on the heated baking sheet in the oven and bake for about 35 minutes until the custard is just set when you jiggle the tart and the apples are a golden colour. Set the tin on a wire rack and quickly brush the top of the tart with apricot jam or glaze to give a glossy sheen. Carefully unmould the tart and leave to cool. Eat warm or at room temperature.

LUIS

Where do you live?
Poynton in Cheshire.

What do you get up to when you are not baking?
I enjoy keeping honey bees – they give me an enormous amount of pleasure
and are fascinating creatures. Spending time with family and friends outside
of work is always a must and I love cooking for them, especially BBQs – no
matter what the time of year!

How would you define yourself as a baker?
Integrating my design skills into my baking is always a must. Baking
definitely lets me express my creative side. I like my baking to be big,
bold, experimental and enjoy coming up with new flavour combinations,
and have done so for the last 5 years.

How did you get into baking?
I'm a totally self-taught baker. Having been brought up in a Spanish house-
hold and around restaurants, food and cooking played a massive role in my
younger years. Having discovered I was a good home cook, baking was the
next step. I was fascinated by how many things could be made from so few
base ingredients.

What are your favourite 3 items of kitchen equipment?
My mixer.
My fine grater.
My bench scraper!

LUIS'
THE TROPICAL MANCHESTER TART

This is a citrus-flavoured egg custard tart with a real difference! Exotic fruit purées and spicy rum enhance the orange and lime zests in the smooth, creamy custard.

> MAKES ONE LARGE TART

For the rich sweet pastry

320g plain flour
45g icing sugar
180g unsalted butter, chilled and diced
3 medium free-range egg yolks
2 tablespoons icy-cold water
2 medium free-range egg yolks, beaten to mix, for brushing

For the custard filling

10 medium free-range eggs, at room temperature
3 oranges
finely grated zest of 3 limes
225g caster sugar
1 ripe mango
6 ripe passion fruits
1½ tablespoons spiced rum OR dark rum
200ml double cream

To decorate

4 tablespoons desiccated coconut
1 ripe mango, peeled and sliced
100g physalis fruit (cape gooseberries), leaves/husks removed

1 x 26cm loose-based, deep flan tin, greased with butter and base-lined; a baking sheet; a cooking thermometer; a digital probe thermometer (optional)

1 To make the pastry, put the flour and icing sugar into the bowl of a food processor and 'pulse' a few times to mix. Add the butter and 'pulse' just until the mixture looks like fine crumbs. Tip the mixture into a large mixing bowl and make a well in the centre. Add the egg yolks and icy water to the well and mix everything together with your hands.

2 As soon as the mixture comes together, tip it out of the bowl on to the worktop and knead briefly, just until it comes together to make a smooth and supple dough. Flatten to a thick disc. If it is very warm you may need to wrap the dough in clingfilm and chill it for 15 minutes; otherwise just carry on to roll it out.

3 Roll out the dough on a lightly floured worktop and use to line the flan tin (see the Baker's Guide page 9 for how to do this). Prick the base with a fork, then put the pastry case into the fridge to firm up for 15 minutes while you heat your oven to 200°C/400°F/gas 6.

4 Set the flan tin on the baking sheet. Line the pastry case with baking paper and fill with baking beans. Bake blind for about 15 minutes until the pastry is set and firm. Carefully remove the paper and beans, then paint the base of the pastry case with beaten egg yolks. Bake for a further 5–8 minutes until the pastry is thoroughly dry and golden (see the Baker's Guide page 10 for more information).

5 Remove the flan tin from the oven – do not unmould the pastry case – and set on one side while you make the filling. Reduce the oven temperature to 140°C/275°F/gas 1.

6 Break the eggs into a large heatproof mixing bowl. Finely grate the zest from the oranges and add to the bowl with the lime zest. Add the caster sugar and stir gently until the sugar has dissolved.

7 Peel the mango, cut the flesh into chunks and purée in a food processor. Sieve the purée into a small bowl, then weigh out 70g purée and add it to the egg mixture (you won't need the rest of the purée).

THE TROPICAL MANCHESTER TART CONTINUED...

8 Cut the passion fruits in half and scoop out the flesh and seeds into a sieve set over a measuring jug. Press to extract the juice, then measure it and make it up to 130ml with juice squeezed from one of the zested oranges. Add this juice to the egg mixture along with the rum and cream. Mix well.

9 Set the bowl over a pan of gently simmering water (don't let the base of the bowl touch the water) and put the cooking thermometer into the mixture. Stir constantly until it reaches 55°C. Pour the mixture into a large jug.

10 Return the flan tin, on the baking sheet, to the oven and warm the pastry case for a couple of minutes. Then pull out the oven shelf a little and carefully pour the warm custard into the pastry case, filling it up to the rim. (If your pastry has shrunk you may not need all the custard.) Slide the shelf back in, close the oven door and bake for 50-55 minutes until the custard filling has set with just a slight wobble in the centre (70°C if you have a digital probe thermometer). Remove from the oven and leave to cool in the tin set on a wire rack.

11 When completely cold, unmould the tart and set it on a cake stand or serving platter. Decorate with the desiccated coconut and slices of mango. Set the physalis fruit around the tart.

SNOWBALL MERINGUES

Fluffy, snowy-white balls of meringue covered in whipped cream and then in white chocolate – a bit of fun to make and eat! You can experiment with different chocolate, or use finely chopped nuts or desiccated coconut (try tinting the coconut with a few drops of food colouring; leave to dry before using).

MAKES ABOUT FIVE

For the meringue
3 medium free-range egg whites, at
    room temperature
good pinch of cream of tartar
90g caster sugar (white, not golden)
90g icing sugar (white, not golden)

To decorate
250ml whipping cream, well chilled
$1\frac{1}{2}$ tablespoons icing sugar
$\frac{1}{2}$ teaspoon vanilla extract
85g good-quality white chocolate,
    grated, OR 50g unsweetened
    desiccated coconut OR finely
    chopped almonds

2 baking sheets, lined with baking
    paper; pretty paper or foil
    cupcake cases

1 Heat your oven to 110°C/225°F/gas $\frac{1}{4}$. Put the egg whites into a large, clean and grease-free mixing bowl (or the bowl of a free-standing electric mixer fitted with the whisk attachment). Add the cream of tartar – this helps to build and strengthen the structure of the meringue – then start to whisk with a hand-held electric mixer (or using slow speed in the free-standing mixer).

2 Once the whites look frothy – this barely takes a minute – increase the speed and whisk until the mixture is fairly thick and frothy (but not yet at 'soft peak' stage). Whisk in a third of the caster sugar, a tablespoon at a time, and continue whisking just until the mixture will form soft, slightly floppy peaks when the whisk is lifted from the bowl. Whisk in half the remaining caster sugar in the same way, then whisk until the mixture will form stiff peaks. Quickly whisk in the rest of the caster sugar and carry on whisking for exactly 1 minute to make a very stiff and glossy meringue. Set a sieve over the bowl and sift the icing sugar on to the meringue, then carefully but thoroughly fold in with a large metal spoon or plastic spatula.

3 Shape the meringue into balls about 5.5cm across: to make each one, scoop up some meringue with a soup spoon and use a second spoon to gently push the ball of meringue on to the lined baking sheet. If necessary, carefully tidy up and smooth the ball shape with a palette knife, but don't fiddle too much as the meringue will eventually be covered with cream. Set the meringues slightly apart on the lined baking sheet to allow for expansion.

4 Bake in the heated oven for about 3 hours until crisp and dry, but still very pale. Turn off the oven and leave the meringues in the cooling oven to finish drying. Once cold, they can be stored in an airtight container for up to 5 days before decorating.

5 When you are ready to finish the snowballs, pour the cream into a chilled bowl, add the icing sugar and vanilla, and whip until the cream is very thick.

SNOWBALL MERINGUES CONTINUED...

6 Put the grated chocolate, or coconut or nuts, on to a large plate and have a clean baking sheet or board ready for the decorated snowballs. Holding one meringue by its base, balancing it on your fingers, use a palette knife or small spatula to cover the rest of the ball with whipped cream in an even layer.

7 Hold the ball, still by the base, over the plate of grated chocolate and sprinkle the chocolate over the cream to coat completely; the excess chocolate will fall back on to the plate (if you tried to press the chocolate on to the cream, or to roll the ball in the chocolate, it would be very messy indeed). Set the balls well apart on the clean baking sheet, then chill for about 30 minutes until firm. Transfer to paper cases and eat immediately, or keep in an airtight container in the fridge. These are best the same day.

APPLE TREACLE TART

A twist on an old favourite – rich and crumbly shortcrust pastry plus the unique taste of golden syrup mixed with grated apple and lemon to cut the sweetness. The pastry, made with half white flour and half wholemeal with just a touch of baking powder, has a lovely nutty flavour and light texture, perfect with the sticky filling.

MAKES ONE LARGE TART

For the pastry
100g plain white flour
100g plain wholemeal flour
good pinch of salt
$\frac{1}{4}$ teaspoon baking powder
150g unsalted butter, chilled and diced
2$\frac{1}{2}$–3 tablespoons icy-cold water,
   to mix

For the filling
150g golden syrup (from a tin, not a
   squeezy bottle)
1 medium Bramley apple (about 225g)
65g fresh white or wholemeal
   breadcrumbs
finely grated zest and juice of 1 large
   unwaxed lemon

1 x 25cm round, deep pie plate

1 First make the rich shortcrust pastry, either in a food processor or by hand. If using a processor, put both flours, the salt and baking powder into the processor bowl and blitz just to combine. Add the chunks of butter and process until the mixture looks like fine crumbs. With the machine running, slowly add 2$\frac{1}{2}$ tablespoons icy water through the feed tube; stop the machine as soon as the dough starts to come together. Add more water a teaspoon at a time if the mixture seems too dry and crumbly to form a dough. Gather up the dough and flatten into a thick disc, then wrap in clingfilm and chill for 20 minutes.

2 To make the dough by hand, mix the flours, salt and baking powder in a mixing bowl, add the pieces of butter and rub into the flour using the tips of your fingers until the mixture looks like fine crumbs. Using a round-bladed knife, stir in enough icy water to bind the mixture together to make a firm dough.

3 Roll out the dough on a lightly floured worktop to a round about 3cm larger than your pie plate, then use to line it (see the Baker's Guide page 9 for how to do this). Leave any excess pastry hanging over the edge of the plate for now. Put the pastry case into the fridge to chill while making the filling.

4 Heat your oven to 180°C/350°F/gas 4. Gently warm the syrup in a medium-sized saucepan over low heat, just until runny. Remove the pan from the heat and set on a heatproof surface. Peel and quarter the apple, then cut out the core. Coarsely grate the apple into the warm syrup. Add the breadcrumbs and the lemon zest and juice and mix well.

5 Spoon the filling mixture into the pastry case and distribute it evenly (use a fork so you don't compress the filling). Trim off any overhanging pastry with a sharp knife. If you like, gently knead the trimmings together, roll out and cut into leaf or other small shapes (use a small sharp knife or shaped cutter). Gently set the pastry decorations on the filling. Finish the pastry rim by pressing down with back of a fork.

6 Bake in the heated oven for 30 minutes until the pastry is golden. Serve warm or at room temperature with custard.

SWEET PASTRY & PATISSERIE

197

MORELLO CHERRY BAKEWELL

There are so many recipes for this classic tart. This is one of the best, with an old-fashioned soft and rich frangipane filling baked in a buttery, flaky puff pastry case.

½ quantity Puff Pastry (see page 242)
  OR 1 x 375g pack all-butter puff
  pastry, thawed if frozen

For the filling

2 medium free-range eggs, at room
  temperature
150g caster sugar
150g ground almonds
1 tablespoon double cream
2 teaspoons almond liqueur
4 tablespoons Morello cherry
  preserve or jam
1 tablespoon flaked almonds
2 tablespoons sieved apricot jam OR
  apricot glaze, warmed, for brushing

1 x 20.5cm round, deep, loose-based
  flan tin (straight-sided if possible)
  OR deep, loose-based sandwich tin;
  a baking sheet

1 Make sure home-made puff pastry is well rested and chilled; if using ready-made pastry, follow the pack instructions. Roll out the pastry on a lightly floured worktop to a round about 30cm across, then use to line the flan tin (see the Baker's Guide page 9). Leave the excess pastry hanging over the rim. Prick the base, then chill for 30 minutes.

2 Towards the end of this time, heat your oven to 190°C/375°F/gas 5, and put the baking sheet into the oven to heat up.

3 Neaten the rim of the pastry case, trimming off the excess pastry with a sharp knife – take care not to drag the pastry as you cut it. Line the case with a sheet of crumpled greaseproof paper and fill with baking beans. Set the tin on the hot baking sheet in the oven and bake blind for 12–15 minutes until the pastry is set. Remove the paper and beans, then return the tin to the oven. Reduce the temperature to 180°C/350°F/gas 4 and bake for 12 minutes or so until the pastry is cooked through, golden and crisp (see the Baker's Guide page 10).

4 Remove the tin from the oven and set on a heatproof surface; leave the baking sheet in the oven. Leave the pastry case to cool, still in its tin, while you make the filling.

5 Put the eggs and sugar in a mixing bowl (or the bowl of a free-standing electric mixer fitted with the whisk attachment). Whisk with a hand-held electric mixer (or in the free-standing mixer) for 4–5 minutes until the mixture is very thick, pale and mousse-like (it won't quite reach 'ribbon stage' – see the Baker's Guide page 9). Gently fold in the ground almonds, cream and liqueur with a large metal spoon or plastic spatula.

6 Spread the cherry preserve over the base of the pastry case, then pour the almond mixture evenly on top. Scatter the flaked almonds over the surface. Set the tin on the hot baking sheet in the oven again and bake for 40 minutes until the filling is golden brown and just firm when pressed in the centre.

7 Remove the tin from the oven and set it on a wire rack. Quickly brush the surface with the warm jam to give a thin, shiny glaze. Cool for 15 minutes – the tart will sink slightly – then carefully unmould by setting the tin on a can of food and letting the ring fall down. Leave to cool to room temperature before cutting and serving.

CHOCOLATE FUDGE TART

A feast of chocolate and walnuts – crisp shortcrust pastry plus a soft chocolate filling.
The cocoa gives the fudge an intense flavour to balance the muscovado sugar.

MAKES ONE MEDIUM TART

For the walnut pastry

175g plain flour
pinch of salt
50g walnut pieces
1 teaspoon caster sugar
110g unsalted butter, chilled and diced
2¹/₂ tablespoons icy-cold water

For the filling

150g walnut pieces
3 medium free-range eggs, at room
   temperature
150g light brown muscovado sugar
150g dark brown muscovado sugar
1 teaspoon vanilla extract
175g unsalted butter, melted and
   cooled
60g cocoa powder
50g plain flour
good pinch of salt

1 x 22cm loose-based flan tin;
   a baking sheet

1 Make the pastry in a food processor: put the flour, salt, walnuts and sugar into the processor bowl and run the machine until the nuts are finely chopped and the mixture looks sandy. Add the pieces of cold butter and process again until the mixture looks like fine crumbs. With the machine running, slowly add the icy water through the feed tube and process until the mixture comes together to make a ball of dough. If there are dry crumbs and the mixture won't form a dough, add more water a teaspoon at a time. Carefully remove the ball of dough and flatten it to a thick disc, then wrap it in clingfilm and chill for 20 minutes.

2 Roll out the pastry on a lightly floured worktop to a round about 30cm across. Use to line the flan tin (see the Baker's Guide page 9 for how to do this). Chill for 15 minutes while your oven is heating to 190°C/375°F/gas 5.

3 Line the pastry case with a crumpled sheet of greaseproof paper and fill with baking beans. Bake blind for 15 minutes until the pastry is firm. Carefully lift out the paper and beans, then bake for a further 7-10 minutes until the pastry is fully cooked, crisp and lightly golden (see the Baker's Guide page 10).

4 Remove the flan tin from the oven and set it on a heatproof surface. Turn down the oven to 180°C/350°F/gas 4 and put the baking sheet in to heat up.

5 To make the filling, tip the walnut pieces into a small baking dish and toast in the oven for 5-7 minutes until they turn a light gold colour. Remove and leave to cool.

6 Put the eggs into a mixing bowl (or the bowl of a free-standing electric mixer fitted with the whisk attachment). Whisk with an electric mixer until frothy. Add both the sugars and the vanilla and whisk for 4-5 minutes until the mixture is very thick and mousse-like, and the whisk will leave a distinct ribbon-like trail when it is lifted out of the mixture. Whisking constantly, pour in the butter in a thin, steady stream. Sift the cocoa, flour and salt on to the mixture and fold in with a large metal spoon or plastic spatula – take your time doing this to make sure there are no streaks. Lastly, fold in the cooled nuts.

7 Spoon the mixture into the pastry case (still in the tin) and spread it evenly. Set the tin on the heated baking sheet in the oven and bake for about 30 minutes until the filling is slightly puffed and just firm when gently pressed in the centre. Start checking after 25 minutes because you don't want the filling to be overcooked – it will continue cooking for a few minutes after it comes out of the oven and you want it to have a fudgy rather than set and firm texture. If it seems to be becoming too dark, cover it with a sheet of greaseproof paper.

8 Leave the tart to cool for 10 minutes before carefully unmoulding. Eat warm or at room temperature with whipped cream or vanilla ice cream.

CHOUX CARAMEL PUFFS

Choux pastry is that strange creature that's cooked twice – the basic flour, butter and water dough is made in a saucepan, then eggs are beaten in, and the resulting glossy, supple mixture is piped or spooned into shapes and baked until crisp and dry. Weird but wonderful to watch! Here, the mixture is piped into chubby fingers and filled with a rich caramel and whipped cream. There are other ideas for you too.

MAKES FOURTEEN

For the choux pastry
100g plain flour
75g unsalted butter, diced
$1/4$ teaspoon sea salt flakes, crushed
175ml water
3 medium free-range eggs, beaten
  to mix
25g chopped almonds

For the caramel filling
200g caster sugar
4 tablespoons water
100g unsalted butter, diced
100ml whipping cream
good pinch of sea salt flakes

For the whipped cream
250ml whipping cream, well chilled
2 tablespoons icing sugar, sifted
icing sugar, for dusting

1–3 large piping bags; a 1.5cm plain
  piping tube; 2 baking sheets, lined
  with baking paper; a large star
  piping tube

1 Heat your oven to 200°C/400°F/gas 6. To make the choux pastry, sift the flour on to a sheet of greaseproof paper; put on one side for now. Put the butter, salt and water into a medium-sized pan and heat gently until the butter has melted – don't let the water boil and start to evaporate. Quickly bring the mixture to the boil, then tip in the flour all in one go. Take the pan off the heat and beat furiously with a wooden spoon. The mixture will look an unpromising, lumpy mess but keep beating and it will turn into a smooth, heavy dough.

2 Put the pan back on low heat. Beating at a more gentle speed, slightly cook the dough for a couple of minutes until it will come away from the sides of the pan to make a smooth and glossy ball. Tip the dough into a large mixing bowl (or the bowl of a free-standing electric mixer fitted with the whisk attachment) and cool for a couple of minutes. Then, using an electric mixer (you can also use a wooden spoon but it won't give the same result), gradually add the eggs, whisking well after each addition. Add only enough of the beaten eggs to make a very shiny, paste-like dough that just falls from the spoon when you lightly shake it; you may not need the last spoonful or so of egg (save the last teaspoon of beaten egg for glazing the puffs). The dough needs to be stiff enough to pipe or spoon into shapes. If it is too wet and thin it will spread out rather than puff up in the oven.

3 Fit a large piping bag with the large plain tube. Spoon the choux paste into the bag and twist the top to prevent the mixture from escaping and to push the choux paste down the tube. Pipe into fingers 3cm wide and 8cm long on the lined baking sheets (you can also spoon the mixture into oval shapes the same size). Space the fingers well apart to allow for rising and expansion.

4 Brush the top of each finger very lightly with beaten egg and sprinkle with chopped almonds. Bake in the heated oven for 15 minutes without opening the door. Turn down the oven to 180°C/350°F/gas 4, and quickly open and close the oven door to let out the steam. Bake for a further 20 minutes until the choux fingers are puffed, firm and golden.

5 Remove the sheets from the oven. Using the tip of a small sharp knife or skewer, quickly make a small hole in the end of each finger to release the steam trapped inside. Return the sheets to the oven and bake for a further 10–12 minutes until the choux fingers are really firm, crisp and dry, and a good golden brown (under-baked choux is flabby rather than crunchy, so don't rush it). Transfer the puffs to a wire rack and leave to cool.

6 To make the caramel filling, put the sugar and water into a medium-sized heavy-based pan and heat gently, stirring occasionally with a wooden spoon, until the sugar has completely dissolved. Add the lumps of butter and melt gently, then turn up the heat a little so the mixture boils. Leave to boil for 7–10 minutes until the mixture turns a good caramel colour – don't stir it as it boils, but carefully swirl it in the pan now and again so it doesn't get stuck in the corners.

7 As soon as the mixture is the right colour take the pan off the heat. Cover your hand with a cloth and carefully pour in the cream – the mixture will froth up and splutter. Gently swirl it in the pan, then return to low heat and stir gently with a wooden spoon until the caramel is smooth and silky. Stir in the salt. Pour the mixture into a heatproof bowl and leave to cool until firm enough to spoon or pipe.

8 With a sharp knife (or a small serrated knife), cut off the top third of each choux puff to make a lid. Fit the plain tube back into the cleaned piping bag (or a new disposable bag) and fill with the caramel. Pipe a finger of caramel into the base of each puff, or spoon the caramel in with a teaspoon.

9 Pour the cream into a large mixing bowl (in warm weather it's a good idea to chill the bowl and whisk first). Add the icing sugar and whip until stiff peaks just start to form when the whisk is lifted from the bowl. Fit the star tube into a clean piping bag (or a new disposable bag) and fill with the whipped cream. Pipe a thick swirled rope of cream on top of the caramel filling in each choux puff. Cover with the lids and dust with icing sugar. Eat as soon as possible.

BANOFFEE BUNS

Make the choux pastry and spoon into 8 large mounds, spaced well apart, on the lined baking sheet. Glaze with beaten egg and sprinkle with nuts. Bake as above, making sure the buns are thoroughly cooked. Leave to cool before carefully cutting off the lids. Spoon the caramel into the base of each bun (you can use a 397g can of ready-made caramel to save time). Cover with a few slices of banana (you'll need 3 medium), then spoon the whipped cream on top. Cover with the lids, dust with icing sugar and serve. Makes 8.

ÉCLAIRS

To make elegant, slim éclairs, spoon the choux pastry into a piping bag fitted with a 1.25cm plain tube and pipe 12 fingers exactly 10cm long on the lined baking sheets; space well apart to allow for expansion. Lightly glaze the top of each finger with beaten egg but don't add the chopped nuts. Bake as above, although after making the steam hole you may not need 10–12 minutes' baking time – just be sure the fingers are well cooked through. Cool on a rack, then split open lengthways. Fill with the whipped cream, spooning or piping it in using the plain tube or a large star tube (omit the caramel). Alternatively, fill with light, fluffy vanilla crème pâtissière (see page 212). For a traditional shiny chocolate glaze, chop up 100g dark chocolate (about 70% cocoa solids) and gently melt with 2 tablespoons whipping or double cream in a small heatproof bowl set over a pan of steaming-hot water (see the Baker's Guide page 9 for more information). Stir until smooth. Cool for a couple of minutes until thick, then spread over the top of each éclair. Leave to set in a cool place – not the fridge – before serving. Makes 12.

KATE

Where do you live?
Brighton.

What do you get up to when you are not baking?
I'm a trained upholsterer and I also enjoy sewing, running and weeding
my allotment. But most of all, I enjoy spending time with my 6-year-old,
my friends and my family.

How would you define yourself as a baker?
A chaotic but extremely enthusiastic newcomer.

Why do you enjoy baking?
I like the concept of mixing simple ingredients and ending up with a bake
that's bigger and better than the sum of its parts. I love watching my
bakes transform through the oven door.

Who do you tend to bake for?
My friends, my family and my street.

What is the trickiest bake you've ever mastered?
I once made an exact replica cake of my friend's head.

What are your favourite 3 items of kitchen equipment?
Whisk.
Dough hook.
A teaspoon for tasting.

KATE'S
RHUBARB & CUSTARD TART WITH ALMOND & RASPBERRY PASTRY

With sweet, rich pastry that tastes like almond and rosemary shortbread plus a creamy egg custard filling shot through with a sharp rhubarb purée, this is a great twist on an old favourite.

MAKES ONE MEDIUM TART

For the almond and rosemary pastry
150g plain flour
100g ground almonds
100g caster sugar
1 small sprig of fresh rosemary (about 6 leaves), or to taste
150g unsalted butter, chilled and diced
1 large free-range egg yolk
beaten egg, for brushing

For the rhubarb purée
500g rhubarb, as red as possible, cut into 2cm chunks
60g caster sugar
1 cinnamon stick, snapped in half
4 tablespoons water

For the custard
9 large free-range egg yolks, at room temperature
80g caster sugar
525ml double cream
fresh nutmeg, for grating

1 x 23cm loose-based, deep flan tin; a large squeezy bottle OR disposable piping bag; a baking sheet

1 Lightly grease the flan tin with soft butter, then line the base with a disc of baking paper. Grease the paper and the sides of the tin again, then dust with flour. Set aside.

2 The pastry is best made in a food processor, although it can also be made by hand. To use a food processor, put the flour, ground almonds, sugar and rosemary leaves into the processor bowl and 'pulse' several times until combined. Add the butter and run the machine just until the mixture looks like fine crumbs. Add the yolk and 'pulse' several times to bring the mixture together into a heavy biscuit-like dough. Gather the dough together and shape into a thick disc, then wrap in clingfilm and chill for 30 minutes to firm up. If making by hand, sift the flour, almonds and sugar into a mixing bowl. Finely chop the rosemary and stir in, then rub in the butter. Add the egg yolk and stir everything together with a round-bladed knife to make a dough.

3 While the dough is chilling, make the rhubarb purée. Put the rhubarb into a medium-sized pan with the sugar, cinnamon and 4 tablespoons of water. Heat, stirring, until the sugar dissolves. Bring to the boil, then simmer gently, stirring now and then, for about 10 minutes until the rhubarb is very soft. Cool, then remove the cinnamon stick and purée with a stick blender or in a food processor. Pass the purée through a sieve into a jug. Pour into the squeezy bottle or piping bag (don't snip off the end just yet). Set aside until needed.

4 Roll out the pastry on a lightly floured worktop and use to line the prepared flan tin (see the Baker's Guide page 9 for how to do this). Don't worry if the pastry tears – it is easy to patch with scraps of excess pastry. Chill for 15 minutes. Meanwhile heat your oven to 180°C/350°F/gas 4.

5 Set the flan tin on the baking sheet. Prick the base of the pastry case with a fork, then line the case with baking paper and fill with baking beans. Bake blind for 15–18 minutes until the pastry is set and firm. Carefully remove the paper and beans (this pastry is fragile), then paint the base of the pastry

case with beaten egg. Bake for a further 12–15 minutes until the pastry is crisp and golden (see the Baker's Guide page 10 for more information).

6 Remove from the oven and set the tin (still on the baking sheet) on a heatproof surface. Leave to cool while making the custard. Turn down the oven to 150°C/300°F/gas 2.

7 Put the egg yolks and sugar into a large heatproof bowl and whisk with an electric mixer or hand whisk until paler and thick – you don't need to whisk to the ribbon stage (see the Baker's Guide page 9). Heat the cream until boiling, then pour it on to the egg mixture while whisking (use slow speed with an electric mixer). You want the custard to be smooth but not foamy. Strain through a sieve into a large jug and leave for 5 minutes so the bubbles can subside.

8 If you put the rhubarb purée into a piping bag, snip off the end. Pipe or squeeze a thick spiral of rhubarb purée into the cold pastry case – still in the tin set on the baking sheet – to cover the base (you'll have purée left). Slowly pour half the custard into the pastry case over the purée.

9 Set the baking sheet on the oven shelf (slightly pulled out if necessary), then carefully pour more custard into the pastry case to fill it right up to the rim. Slowly push the shelf back into place and close the oven door. Bake for 10–12 minutes, just until a skin has formed on top of the custard.

10 Carefully remove the tart from the oven and pipe or squeeze a neat spiral of the remaining rhubarb purée on top of the custard. Return the tart to the oven and bake for 40–45 minutes until the filling is set with just a slight wobble in the centre. Grate nutmeg over the top, then leave to cool for several hours – the tart should be completely cold before you unmould it for serving.

GOLDEN MILLEFEUILLES

This most refined of pastries – rectangles of delicate pastry sandwiched with the fluffiest crème pâtissière – is a challenge even for seasoned bakers. You need to be organised, and to keep to the chilling times so the pastry is as firm as possible; this will ensure that it cuts neatly and keeps its shape in the oven. This is best eaten the same day, but the baked rectangles can be stored in an airtight container at room temperature overnight.

½ quantity Puff Pastry (see page 242) OR 1 x 375g pack all-butter puff pastry, thawed if frozen

For the icing
60g icing sugar
1 medium free-range egg white, at room temperature
¼ teaspoon lemon juice

For the light crème pâtissière filling
200ml milk
1 vanilla pod, split lengthways
2 medium free-range egg yolks, at room temperature
40g caster sugar
15g cornflour
15g unsalted butter, at room temperature
100ml double cream, well chilled

2 baking sheets, lined with baking paper

1 Make sure your home-made puff pastry is well rested and chilled; if using ready-made pastry, follow the pack instructions. Clear a shelf in the freezer or fridge.

2 Lightly dust the worktop and rolling pin with flour, then roll out the pastry to a large rectangle about 3mm thick and measuring 33 x 23cm. Wrap the pastry around the rolling pin and lift it on to a lined baking sheet lined with baking paper. Cover the pastry, fairly loosely, with a sheet of clingfilm and freeze for about 20 minutes, or chill in the fridge for about an hour, so the pastry is very hard. (This will make it less likely to shrink during baking.)

3 With a ruler and a pizza wheel-cutter, or a large, very sharp knife, trim the pastry sheet so it is exactly 32 x 22cm. Cover, as before, and return to the freezer or fridge until very hard again – about 15 minutes in the freezer or 30 minutes in the fridge.

4 While the pastry is resting, make the icing and filling. For the icing sift the icing sugar into a mixing bowl. Lightly beat the egg white in another bowl with a fork so it is well broken up. Let the bubbles subside for a minute, then measure 1 tablespoon and add to the bowl of icing sugar (you probably won't need the rest of the egg white). Add the lemon juice and stir until very smooth, with the consistency of glacé icing. The icing should be thick enough to spread without running everywhere but not as firm as royal icing, so add a bit more egg white, a few drops at a time, if necessary. Cover and set on one side until needed.

5 To make the crème pâtissière, pour the milk into a medium-sized pan. Scrape some of the tiny black seeds from the vanilla pod into the milk, then add the pod too. Heat until the milk is steaming hot. Remove the pan from the heat and leave to infuse for 10 minutes.

6 Put the egg yolks, caster sugar and cornflour into a heatproof bowl and mix together with a wire hand whisk for a couple of minutes until very smooth, creamy and lighter in colour. Remove the vanilla pod from the hot milk, then whisk the milk into the egg mixture. When thoroughly combined pour the mixture back into the pan and whisk over medium heat until it boils and thickens. Set the pan on a heatproof surface and whisk the crème for a minute to make sure it is smooth. Leave to cool for a couple of minutes before whisking in the butter. Transfer the crème to a bowl, press a piece of clingfilm on the surface (so a skin doesn't form) and leave until cold, then chill thoroughly.

7 Whip the cream in another bowl until it will stand in soft peaks, then cover the bowl and keep in the fridge until needed.

8 Cut the pastry sheet in half lengthways, using the ruler and pizza cutter or knife as before (each piece will now be 32 x 11cm). Transfer one piece to another lined baking sheet, or a board; cover and return it to the fridge or freezer for now.

9 Using a palette knife (an off-set one is best for this), spread the icing evenly over the remaining piece of pastry. Put this iced pastry rectangle (uncovered) into the freezer or fridge to firm up – it will need at least 15 minutes in the freezer or 30 minutes in the fridge.

10 Meanwhile, remove the un-iced pastry rectangle from the freezer/fridge and cut it across into 8 very neat and even 4 x 11cm rectangles. Arrange them well apart on the lined baking sheet, cover with another sheet of baking paper and chill in the fridge for 15 minutes while heating your oven to 180°C/350°F/gas 4.

11 To bake the un-iced pastry rectangles, set a second baking sheet, or an upturned wire rack, on top of the baking paper covering the pastry – this will ensure that the pastries rise evenly, so they all look neat, with a flat surface. Bake in the heated oven for 15 minutes. Remove the second baking sheet (or the rack) and the top sheet of baking paper and return to the oven. Bake for a further 12–15 minutes until the pastry rectangles are a good golden brown and cooked through. Transfer to a wire rack and leave to cool.

12 Remove the iced sheet of pastry from the fridge or freezer and very carefully cut into 8 rectangles as before, making sure you handle the pastry as little as possible (use a palette knife to move it around so the icing doesn't have fingermarks). Also, avoid dragging the pastry as you cut it (this would distort the edges and make the pastry rise unevenly). Wipe the pizza cutter or knife if it gets sticky with icing, so the lines stay sharp and clean. Arrange the rectangles well apart on the lined baking sheet and return to the fridge or freezer (uncovered) to firm up for 10 minutes or so.

13 Bake (uncovered) in the heated oven for 15–20 minutes until the icing is a light gold colour and the pastry is cooked through. Transfer to a wire rack and leave to cool. (Avoid leaving the pastries in a steamy kitchen or the crisp icing will soften.)

14 To assemble the pastries, stir the chilled crème pâtissière well until smooth, then carefully fold in the whipped cream. Spread the filling over the 8 pastry bases. Set them on a serving plate and cover with the iced pastry rectangles. Serve immediately.

RASPBERRY & LEMON CREAM HORNS

It's about time cream horns made a comeback as they not only look fantastic, but they are a great combination of textures and flavours. There is an art in getting the pastry strips neat and even – it helps if the pastry is as firm as possible before you try to cut it (in very hot weather pop it in the freezer for a few minutes if it gets too soft to handle). Instead of the usual strawberry and cream, try lemon curd with lemon cream and fresh raspberries.

MAKES TWELVE

¹/₂ quantity Puff Pastry (see page 242) OR 1 x 375g pack all-butter puff pastry, thawed if frozen
1 medium free-range egg white, very lightly beaten
caster sugar, for sprinkling
36 small raspberries, to decorate

For the filling

125g Lemon Curd (see page 152 or use ready-made)
200ml whipping cream, well chilled
finely grated zest of ¹/₂ unwaxed lemon
2 tablespoons icing sugar, sifted

cream horn moulds, 12–14cm long, lightly greased with butter (see recipe); a baking sheet, lined with baking paper; a large piping bag fitted with a star tube (optional)

1 If you have 12 cream horn moulds you can make all the pastries at once; if you have a set of 4 or 6 moulds you will have to work in batches. Follow the manufacturer's instructions for your cream horn moulds – if non-stick, they may not need to be greased. Make sure home-made puff pastry is well rested and thoroughly chilled; if using ready-made, follow the pack instructions for thawing or removing from the fridge.

2 Lightly dust the worktop and rolling pin with flour, then roll out the pastry to a large rectangle about 31 x 41cm. Wrap the pastry around the rolling pin and transfer it to the baking sheet. Unroll the pastry, then cover it with a sheet of clingfilm or greaseproof paper. Chill until firm – about 15 minutes.

3 Using a ruler and a large, very sharp knife or a pizza wheel-cutter, trim the edges of the pastry rectangle to make it exactly 30 x 40cm. Cover and chill again for 10 minutes so the pastry is very firm. This will make it easier to cut into neat strips without dragging or stretching the edges.

4 Using the ruler and knife or pizza cutter, cut the pastry into strips 2.5cm wide and 40cm long. Brush the pastry strips with egg white. Take one strip and coil it, egg-white-side out, around a horn mould, starting at the tip and slightly overlapping the pastry strip as you wrap it round. Avoid stretching the pastry, and try to keep the pastry spiral as neat and even as possible. Set the pastry-wrapped mould on the lined baking sheet so the end of the pastry strip is underneath. Repeat with the rest of the pastry strips and moulds (if making in batches, loosely cover the strips and keep in the fridge until needed).

5 Chill the pastry horns for 30 minutes. Towards the end of this time, heat your oven to 220°C/425°F/gas 7.

6 Lightly brush the pastry with egg white and sprinkle with sugar. Bake in the heated oven for about 15 minutes until crisp and a good golden brown. Transfer the horns to a wire rack and leave to cool for 10 minutes before removing the moulds. If the pastry inside the horns looks at all damp, return the horns to the oven, without the moulds but set on the baking sheet, and bake for an extra 5–7 minutes until crisp and dry. (If baking in batches make sure the moulds and baking sheet are completely cold before using again – you can run them under the cold tap.) Once the horns are baked and cold they can be stored in an airtight container overnight.

7 When ready to finish, spoon the lemon curd into the tip of the horns, making sure it reaches right to the end. Put the cream, lemon zest and icing sugar into a large mixing bowl and whip until very thick and stiff peaks will form. Spoon into the piping bag and pipe into the pastry horns to fill generously; or just spoon the cream into the pastry horns. Decorate with the raspberries and serve as soon as possible.

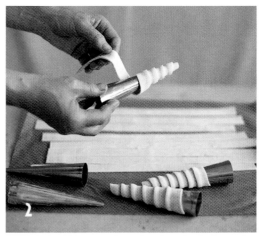

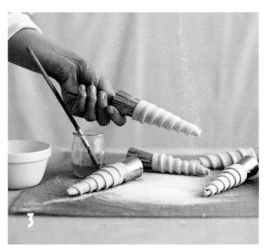

SUMMER FOUR-BERRY PIE

Very easy to make (you do need a food processor) and easy to handle, cream cheese pastry is deliciously crisp, rich and slightly flaky. Have a go if you haven't made it before!

MAKES ONE MEDIUM PIE

For the cream cheese pastry
275g plain flour
pinch of salt
1 tablespoon icing sugar
150g unsalted butter, chilled and diced
150g full-fat cream cheese
1 medium free-range egg yolk
caster sugar, for sprinkling

For the filling
150g raspberries
150g dessert blackberries
300g ripe strawberries, hulled
  and halved
150g blueberries
finely grated zest of $\frac{1}{2}$ medium
  unwaxed lemon
2 teaspoons lemon juice
100g caster sugar
3 tablespoons cornflour

1 x 23–24cm round, deep pie plate;
  a baking sheet

1 Put the flour, salt and icing sugar into the processor bowl and 'pulse' a couple of times to combine. Add the pieces of butter and run the machine just until the mixture looks like fine crumbs. Break up the cream cheese into small lumps and add to the bowl with the egg yolk, then process until the mixture comes together to make a firm, slightly waxy dough (the moisture in the cream cheese means you don't need to add any water). Flatten the dough to a thick disc, wrap in clingfilm and chill for at least 45 minutes (and up to 3 hours).

2 While the pastry is in the fridge, put all the berries, the lemon zest and juice, caster sugar and cornflour into a medium-sized pan. Stir gently to mix. Set the pan over low heat and stir occasionally until the juices start to run, then simmer for about 2 minutes, stirring constantly, until the juices have thickened to make a syrupy sauce. Taste and add more sugar or lemon as you think is needed. Transfer to a heatproof bowl and leave until completely cold before covering and chilling for at least 40 minutes (and up to 3 hours).

3 When ready to assemble and bake the pie, heat your oven to 200°C/400°F/gas 6 and put a baking sheet in to heat up. Divide the pastry in half and roll out one portion on a lightly floured worktop to a round about 3cm wider than your pie plate. Use to line the pie plate (see the Baker's Guide page 9). Leave any excess pastry hanging over the edge.

4 Spoon the filling into the pastry case, slightly mounding it up in the centre and leaving the rim clear. Brush the rim with water to dampen. Roll out the remaining pastry as before and lift over the pie. Gently press the lid on to the rim to seal the edge. Trim off the overhanging pastry with a sharp knife, using short sharp cuts so you don't stretch the pastry too much. Using the back of a small, sharp knife, 'knock up' and 'flute' the edge (see the Baker's Guide page 10 for how to do this). Make a small steam hole in the centre of the lid, then sprinkle evenly with sugar to give the baked pie a crisp, slightly crunchy crust.

5 Set the pie on the heated baking sheet in the oven and bake for 15 minutes. Reduce the oven temperature to 180°C/350°F/gas 4 and bake for a further 25 minutes until the pastry is golden brown and crisp. Leave to cool a little before serving.

APRICOT CUSTARD TART

Here's a custard tart made the French way, with pâte brisée (made from
the same ingredients as shortcrust but using a different method) and a filling of rich
pastry cream (rather like crème pâtissière) that complements good, well-flavoured summer
apricots. The tart has to be thoroughly chilled after baking so it can be cut into
beautiful slices, so plan to make it a day ahead.

For the pâte brisée
200g plain flour
good pinch of salt
110g unsalted butter, chilled
1 medium free-range egg yolk
3 tablespoons icy-cold water
1 1/2 tablespoons caster sugar

For the filling
600ml creamy milk
   (such as Jersey or Guernsey)
1 vanilla pod, split lengthways
2 medium free-range eggs plus 4 yolks,
   at room temperature
150g caster sugar
35g cornflour
6 ripe apricots, halved and stoned
icing sugar, for dusting

1 x 23cm round, deep, loose-based,
   fluted flan tin; a baking sheet

1 To make the pastry, sift the flour and salt on to a clean
worktop and make a large well in the centre. Put the butter
between 2 sheets of clingfilm and pound with a rolling pin
until the butter is very supple but still cold. Cut the butter
into pieces and put them into the well with the egg yolk, water
and sugar. Put the fingertips of one of your hands together to
form a beak shape and use to mash together the ingredients in
the well. When they are thoroughly combined, gradually work
in the flour with your fingers; use a plastic dough scraper (or
metal spatula) to help you draw the flour in. When the mixture
looks like coarse crumbs, gather the whole lot together to
make a ball of dough. If there are dry crumbs and the dough
won't come together, add more water a teaspoon at a time; if
the dough is really sticky work in more flour.

2 Lightly dust the worktop with flour, then start to gently
work the dough: press down on the ball of dough with the
heel of your hand and push it away from you, then gather
up the dough into a ball once more (using the scraper) and
repeat. Continue working the dough for a couple of minutes –
no more – until it is silky-smooth and very pliable, so pliable it
can be pulled off the worktop in one piece. Shape into a ball,
then flatten to a thick disc. Wrap in clingfilm and chill for
about 30 minutes.

3 Roll out the dough on the lightly floured worktop and use
to line the flan tin (see the Baker's Guide page 9 for how to
do this). Leave the excess pastry hanging over the edge of the
tin for now. Prick the base with a fork and chill for 20 minutes.
Meanwhile, heat your oven to 190°C/375°F/gas 5.

4 Carefully neaten the pastry rim and trim off the excess
pastry, then line the pastry case with a crumpled sheet of
greaseproof paper and fill with baking beans. Bake blind for
12 minutes until the pastry is firm. Carefully lift out the paper
and beans, then bake for a further 8–9 minutes until the pastry
is fully cooked, crisp and lightly golden (see the Baker's Guide
page 10 for more information).

5 Remove the tin from the oven and set it on a heatproof surface. Leave to cool while making the filling. Reduce the oven temperature to 180°C/350°F/gas 4 and put a baking sheet into the oven to heat up.

6 For the pastry cream, pour the milk into a medium-sized pan. With the tip of a small sharp knife, scrape the seeds out of the vanilla pod into the milk, then add the pod to the pan too. Heat the milk until steaming hot, but not quite boiling. Remove from the heat and leave to infuse for 5 minutes before removing the pod. (Rinse the pod and dry it thoroughly, then use to flavour a jar of caster sugar.)

7 While the milk is infusing, put the whole eggs and yolks into a heatproof mixing bowl, add the sugar and cornflour, and mix until smooth using a wire hand whisk. Pour the hot milk on to the egg mixture in a thin, steady stream, whisking constantly. When thoroughly combined, return the mixture to the pan and set over medium heat. Whisk constantly until the mixture boils and thickens – take care that the thick, sticky mixture doesn't 'catch' in the corners. Remove from the heat and leave to cool until lukewarm, whisking now and then.

8 Spoon about a third of the pastry cream into the pastry case and spread evenly. Arrange the apricot halves on top rounded side up, making sure they are tightly packed in a single layer and not overlapping (you may not be able to fit in all the fruit, depending on their size). Spoon the rest of the pastry cream over the apricots so they are completely and evenly covered.

9 Set the flan tin on the heated baking sheet in the oven and bake for 30 minutes. Remove the baking sheet with the tin on it and thickly dust the top of the tart with icing sugar. Return to the oven and bake for another 30 minutes until the filling is slightly puffed and (under the icing sugar) has dark brown patches. The filling should wobble slightly when you jiggle the tin. Leave to cool before covering loosely with clingfilm (or put the tin in a plastic container). Chill overnight.

10 The next day, unmould the tart. The icing sugar will have dissolved to give a glossy golden finish to the custard filling. Leave to stand at room temperature for about 20 minutes so that the tart can 'come to' before slicing. Store any leftovers in the fridge.

PAUL'S KOUIGN AMANN

For the initial dough

300g strong plain flour
5g fast-action dried yeast
1 teaspoon salt
200ml warm water
25g unsalted butter, melted

To further enrich

250g unsalted butter, in a block,
   well chilled
100g caster sugar, plus extra for
   sprinkling

1 x 12-hole muffin tin, well greased
   with oil

1 Put the flour into the bowl of a free-standing electric mixer fitted with the dough hook. Add the yeast to one side of the bowl and the salt to the other. Add the water and melted butter and mix on slow speed for 2 minutes. Turn up to medium speed and continue mixing for 6 minutes.

2 Tip the dough on to a lightly floured worktop and shape into a ball. Put it into a lightly oiled bowl, cover with clingfilm and leave to rise for 1 hour.

3 Sandwich the butter between 2 sheets of greaseproof paper and bash with a rolling pin, then roll out to a square about 18 x 18cm. Place in the fridge to keep chilled.

4 Turn out the dough on to the lightly floured worktop and roll out to a square about 20 x 20cm. Place the butter in the centre of the dough so that each side of the butter square faces a corner of the dough square. Fold the corners of the dough over the butter to enclose it.

5 Roll out the dough away from you into a rectangle about 45 x 15cm. Fold the bottom third of dough up over the middle third, then fold the top third down over the middle. You will now have a sandwich of 3 layers of butter and 3 layers of dough. Wrap in clingfilm and chill for 30 minutes. This completes one 'turn'.

6 Repeat twice to complete a total of 3 turns, chilling the dough for 30 minutes after each one.

7 Roll out the dough away from you into a rectangle about 45 x 15cm again. Sprinkle the measured caster sugar evenly over the dough, then fold into thirds as before.

8 Working quickly now, roll out the dough into a larger rectangle 40 x 30cm. Sprinkle with caster sugar, then cut the dough into 3 x 40cm strips. Cut each strip across into 4. You will now have 12 squares, each measuring 10 x 10cm.

9 One by one, gather each dough square up by its 4 corners, pulling the corners towards the centre, and place in a hole in the muffin tin – it will look like a four-leaf clover. Sprinkle with caster sugar. Leave to rise for about 30 minutes until slightly puffed up. Meanwhile, heat your oven to 220°C/425°F/gas 7.

10 Bake the cakes in the heated oven for 30–40 minutes until golden brown – check halfway through this time and cover with foil if they are beginning to brown too much.

11 Remove from the oven and leave to cool for a couple of minutes before turning out on to a wire rack. (The caramelised sugar will be very hot, but don't leave the cakes to cool too long in the tin or the sugar will harden and they will be stuck.)

SHOWSTOPPER
MARY'S LEMON & RASPBERRY ÉCLAIRS

MAKES TWELVE

For the choux pastry
50g unsalted butter, cut into cubes
150ml water
65g plain flour
2 large free-range eggs, beaten

For the filling
600ml double or whipping cream
6 tablespoons lemon curd (see page 152)
2 tablespoons freeze-dried raspberry powder

For the icing
400g icing sugar, sifted
juice of $\frac{1}{2}$ lemon
yellow food colouring paste
pink food colouring paste

To decorate
100g white chocolate drops
100g dark chocolate drops

2 large baking sheets, greased with butter; a large piping bag fitted with a 1cm plain tube; 3 disposable piping bags

1 Heat your oven to 220°C/425°F/gas 7. For the choux pastry, put the butter and water in a saucepan over a low heat. Bring slowly to the boil. Tip in the flour, then remove from the heat and stir vigorously to make a smooth paste.

2 Return the pan to the heat and stir the mixture until it dries out a little and comes away from the side of the pan to form a soft ball. Remove from the heat again and leave the mixture to cool slightly, then gradually add the eggs, beating really well between each addition, until the choux mixture is smooth and glossy.

3 Spoon the mixture into the piping bag. Sprinkle the greased baking sheets with water (a water spray with a fine nozzle is good for this), then pipe the mixture on to the sheets in 7.5cm lengths. Leave space between each éclair for them to spread a bit in the oven.

4 Bake in the heated oven for 10 minutes, then reduce the temperature to 190°C/375°F/gas 5 and bake for a further 20 minutes. Split each éclair in half lengthways and transfer to a wire rack to cool completely.

5 Once the éclairs are cold, make the filling. Whip the cream to soft peaks. Spoon half of the cream into a separate bowl. Fold the lemon curd into one bowl of cream and the freeze-dried raspberry powder into the other bowl.

6 Spoon the lemon cream into the washed piping bag and pipe into the bottom half of 6 of the éclairs. Spoon the raspberry cream into the washed piping bag and pipe into the bottom half of the remaining 6 éclairs.

7 For the icing, put half the icing sugar in a bowl and mix with enough lemon juice to make a very stiff icing. Tint with yellow food colouring and spoon into a disposable piping bag.

8 Tip the remaining icing sugar into another bowl and add enough water to make a very stiff icing. Tint with pink food colouring and spoon into a disposable piping bag.

9 Snip the ends off the piping bags. Pipe the thick pink icing on to the top half of the 6 éclairs filled with raspberry cream. Spread the icing smooth using a palette knife dipped in boiling water. Set the iced tops in place.

10 Repeat with the yellow icing to cover the 6 lemon cream-filled éclairs.

11 To decorate, melt the white chocolate drops in a heatproof bowl set over a pan of steaming-hot water, then drizzle from a spoon over the pink icing in a zigzag pattern. Melt the dark chocolate drops in the same way, then spoon into a small disposable piping bag, snip off the tip and pipe swirls over the lemon icing. Leave to set before serving.

MARY'S CHOCOLATE ORANGE TART

SERVES EIGHT

For the pastry

100g plain flour, plus extra for dusting
50g icing sugar
50g unsalted butter, diced
1 large egg yolk
1 tablespoon cold water

For the chocolate filling

75g unsalted butter
115g dark chocolate (no more than
   60% cocoa solids), finely chopped
115g golden caster sugar
55g plain flour
4 medium eggs

For the orange filling

25g unsalted butter
50g white chocolate, finely chopped
finely grated zest of 1 orange
35g golden caster sugar
25g plain flour
2 medium egg yolks

1 x 23cm round, fluted tart tin, greased
   with butter; a baking sheet

1 To make the pastry, measure the flour and icing sugar into a food processor and pulse to blend, then add the butter and pulse until the mixture resembles fine breadcrumbs. Add the egg yolk and water and run the machine just until the mixture comes together to form a soft dough. Form into a ball, wrap in clingfilm and leave to rest in the fridge for about 30 minutes.

2 Preheat your oven to 200°C/400°F/gas 6. Roll out the pastry on a lightly floured worktop as thinly as you can to a round about 5cm larger than your flan tin. Line the tin with the pastry (see the Baker's Guide page 9 for how to do this). Don't worry if the pastry breaks a little: it is easy to patch up. Chill for 15 minutes.

3 Prick the base of the pastry case with a fork, then line with baking paper and fill with baking beans. Bake blind for 10 minutes until just lightly golden. Remove the paper and beans and bake for a further 5–7 minutes until the pastry case is pale golden and the base is cooked (see the Baker's Guide page 10 for more information). Set the pastry case aside. Leave the oven on.

4 To make the chocolate filling, melt the butter and chocolate in a heatproof bowl set over a pan of steaming-hot water, then stir until smooth. Remove the bowl from the pan and stir in the sugar and flour. Beat in the eggs, one at a time. Set aside.

5 To make the orange filling, melt the butter and chocolate as above. Remove from the heat and stir in the orange zest, sugar and flour. Beat in the egg yolks, one at a time. Pour the mixture into a jug.

6 Place the pastry case in the tin onto the baking sheet. Pour the chocolate filling into the pastry case, then drizzle or pipe the orange filling over the chocolate filling to create swirls. Draw a cocktail stick or skewer through the 2 fillings to create a marbled effect.

7 Bake in the heated oven for 10–12 minutes until the filling is just set around the edges – it should still be slightly wobbly in the centre. Remove from the oven and allow to cool slightly, until warm and not piping hot, before serving.

MARY'S DOUBLE CHOCOLATE MOUSSE ENTREMETS

For the decorative paste
70g unsalted butter, softened
70g icing sugar, sifted
2 large free-range egg whites
40g plain flour, sifted
40g cocoa powder, sifted

For the joconde sponge
2 large free-range egg whites
10g caster sugar
60g ground almonds
60g icing sugar, sifted
2 large free-range whole eggs
20g plain flour, sifted
20g unsalted butter, melted

For the dark chocolate mousse
150g dark chocolate (36% cocoa
  solids), broken into small pieces
knob of butter
2 large free-range eggs, separated
1 tablespoon brandy (optional)
100ml double cream

For the white chocolate mousse
300g white chocolate, broken into
  small pieces
1 large egg white
100ml double cream

1 Cut the sheet of silicone to fit the base of the Swiss roll tin. Lay the silicone sheet on the lined baking sheet.

2 To make the decorative paste, cream the butter and icing sugar together until light and fluffy. Gradually add the egg whites, beating constantly. Fold in the flour and cocoa powder. Spread the paste thinly and evenly over the silicone sheet using a palette knife. Drag a pastry comb or fork diagonally through the paste to form a pinstripe pattern, scraping off the excess paste after each drag. Place the baking sheet in the freezer for 15 minutes.

3 Meanwhile, make the mixture for the joconde sponge. Heat your oven to 220°C/425°F/gas 7. Whisk the egg whites in a bowl until stiff peaks form when the whisk is lifted. Add the caster sugar, a teaspoon at a time, whisking between each addition to make a glossy meringue. Cover with clingfilm and set aside.

4 Tip the ground almonds and icing sugar into the bowl of a free-standing electric mixer. Add the whole eggs and whisk together for 3–5 minutes until doubled in volume. Fold in the flour, then gently fold in the meringue in 3 batches. Pour the melted butter down the side of the bowl and fold in until incorporated.

5 Remove the silicone sheet, with its pinstripe paste, from the freezer and place it (pinstripe-side up) in the base of the lined Swiss roll tin. Pour the joconde sponge mixture into the tin and level the surface with a palette knife. Bake in the heated oven for 5–7 minutes until pale golden brown and springy to the touch.

6 Lay a sheet of baking paper on a wire rack and turn out the sponge on to it. Peel off the lining paper and silicone sheet from the base of the sponge, then leave to cool completely.

To decorate

50g raspberries
50g blueberries
icing sugar, for dusting

1 Swiss roll tin, 33 x 23cm, greased
and lined with baking paper;
a sheet of silicone paper; a baking
sheet lined with baking paper; a
pastry comb (optional); 6 x 6.5cm
chef's rings or mini cake rings,
lined with baking paper; additional
baking paper; a 4cm round cutter;
2 disposable piping bags

7 Cut out a rectangular template measuring 17 x 5cm from
a piece of baking paper. When the sponge has cooled, trim
the edges, then cut out 6 rectangular strips, using the paper
template as a guide. Wrap a strip of sponge round the inside
of each cake ring, pinstripe side facing out. Once wrapped
inside the ring, gently push and press the ends of the strip to
meet, to make a seamless cake lining. You want the joconde to
be very tightly pressed against the side of the cake ring. Place
the cake rings onto a a baking sheet.

8 Using the 4cm round cutter, cut out 6 small circles from the
sponge trimmings. Push these pinstripe-side down into the
base of the cake rings.

9 For the dark chocolate mousse, melt the chocolate in a
heatproof bowl set over a pan of steaming-hot water. Remove
the bowl from the pan, add the butter and stir until smooth.
Add the egg yolks and brandy (if using) then allow to cool
a little. Whisk the egg whites to stiff peaks and fold into the
chocolate mixture. Whip the cream to soft peaks and fold in.

10 Spoon the mousse into a disposable piping bag and snip off
the tip. Pipe into each cake-lined ring until the mousse comes
three-quarters of the way up the sponge. Chill in the freezer
while you make the white chocolate mousse.

11 Melt the white chocolate as above, but take care not to let it
get too hot. As soon as it has softened, remove the bowl from
the pan and stir the chocolate until smooth, then set aside to
cool a little. Whisk the egg white to a stiff peak, then fold into
the white chocolate. Whip the cream to soft peaks and fold in.

12 Spoon the white chocolate mousse into a disposable piping
bag, snip off the tip and pipe on top of the mousse until it
reaches the top of the cake ring. Chill in the fridge until set.

13 Lift the cake rings off the entremets, peel off the paper
and place on serving plates. Top with the raspberries and
blueberries and dust with icing sugar. Serve chilled.

• •

SALMON COULIBIAC • GAME, PORT &
REDCURRANT CHARLOTTE • FETA & SPINACH
FILO TRIANGLES • ROAST VEGETABLE & GOATS'
CHEESE TORTE • GIANT SAUSAGE ROLL •
BOEUF BOURGUIGNON PIE • CHEESE, HAM &
CHIVE TART • LAMB, APRICOT, CORIANDER &
GREEN CHILLI PIE • CHETNA'S CRISPY LENTIL
KACHORI • AUBERGINE PARMIGIANA CRUMBLE
• SMOKED HADDOCK ROULADE • TAPENADE
TWISTS • SAVOURY PASTRY PARCELS • LITTLE CRAB
SOUFFLÉS • PAUL'S MINI SAUSAGE PLAITS

SAVOURY
BAKES

SALMON COULIBIAC

This version of the grand festive Russian fish pie is is assembled from puff pastry, wholemeal crêpes, salmon fillet and wild rice. It's a real project for a home baker, but everything can be prepared in stages and assembled well ahead, ready for baking at the last minute. Ask the fishmonger, or at the supermarket fish counter, for a piece of salmon fillet cut from the thick centre of a skinless side, with the belly flaps trimmed away.

1 x 600g piece of trimmed skinless
  salmon fillet (see above)
1 quantity Puff Pastry (see page 242)
  OR 2 x 375g packs all-butter puff
  pastry, thawed if frozen
beaten egg, to glaze

For the crêpes

115g plain wholemeal flour
  (wheat or spelt)
good pinch of salt
1 medium free-range egg plus 1 yolk,
  at room temperature
300ml milk, at room temperature
15g unsalted butter, melted
1 sprig of fresh dill, finely chopped
knob of butter, for frying

For the rice mixture

80g mixed basmati and wild rice
  (from a pack)
30g unsalted butter
1 small onion, finely chopped
150g button mushrooms, quartered,
  OR mixed fresh wild mushrooms
1 tablespoon chopped fresh parsley
2 teaspoons chopped fresh dill
salt and black pepper

1 x 19–20cm non-stick frying pan;
  a large baking sheet, lined with
  baking paper

1 To make the crêpe batter, combine the flour and salt in a mixing bowl. Make a well in the centre and add the egg, egg yolk and milk. Using a wire whisk, mix the ingredients in the well, then gradually work in the flour to make a smooth, fairly thin batter. Cover the bowl and leave at room temperature for at least 30 minutes (up to 4 hours).

2 Whisk the crêpe batter just to mix it before whisking in the melted butter and dill. Heat the frying pan over medium heat, then lightly grease the base of the pan by wiping with a small knob of butter held in a thickly folded sheet of kitchen paper. Add about 3 tablespoons of batter to the pan and swirl briskly so the batter evenly covers the base of the pan. Cook for 1½–2 minutes until you can slide a palette knife under the crêpe to loosen it. Check to be sure the underside is a good golden colour, then flip the crêpe over using the palette knife. Cook for a further minute or so until the second side is speckled with brown spots. Tip out the crêpe on to a plate.

3 Cook the rest of the batter in the same way (it will make about 12 crêpes), wiping the pan with the butter paper now and again so the batter doesn't stick. As each crêpe is cooked, tip it out on to the plate, stacking the crêpes on top of each other. (If you aren't going to use the crêpes straight away, interleave them with strips of greaseproof paper and cool completely, then wrap the stack well in foil and keep in the fridge overnight.)

4 To prepare the rice mixture, bring a large pan of water to the boil, add a good pinch of salt and the rice and boil gently until tender – 20–25 minutes, or according to the instructions on the pack. Drain thoroughly. While the rice is boiling, melt the butter in a medium-sized pan over low heat, stir in the onion and cook gently for about 3 minutes until softened. Add the mushrooms and cook, stirring frequently, for about 5 minutes until tender. If the mushrooms have produced a lot of liquid turn up the heat and cook, stirring, until dry (don't let them burn). Tip into a heatproof bowl. Stir in the rice and the herbs and add plenty of seasoning. Leave to cool.

5 Check to be sure the salmon fillet will fit on to your baking sheet (don't forget to add on a bit for the pastry), lying diagonally if necessary. If the fillet is too long trim the tail end; don't throw away the excess piece but slip it under the thinner tail end of the fillet.

6 Before you start to assemble the coulibiac, make sure home-made pastry is well rested, or ready-made pastry thawed/removed from the fridge according to the pack instructions. Cut off slightly less than half of the home-made pastry (or use one pack ready-made) and roll it out on a lightly floured worktop to a rectangle 4cm wider and longer than your piece of fish. Roll up the pastry around the rolling pin and lift it on to the lined baking sheet. Lay a crêpe over each short end, so only half of the crêpe is on the pastry. Now arrange 6 more crêpes in pairs down the length of the pastry rectangle, slightly overlapping each other in the centre; the outer half of each crêpe should extend beyond the pastry edge. Use kitchen scissors to trim off any thick edges or large overlaps. The crêpes should completely cover the pastry, to seal in the juices from the fish and so keep the pastry crisp.

7 Set the salmon skinned-side down on the crêpes. Season it lightly with salt and pepper. Spoon the rice mixture on top and gently press it down to give it a neat and even rounded shape. Brush the outer edges of the crêpes with a little beaten egg, then wrap them up and over the sides of the fish. Cover the top with more crêpes as needed, trimming off any excess as before, so the fish and rice are completely enclosed in crêpes. Brush the edges of the pastry, now visible, with beaten egg.

8 Roll out the remaining pastry to a rectangle 10cm longer and wider than the first. Roll the pastry around the rolling pin and lift it over the fish. Gently unroll the pastry so it drapes over the fish, then press it down to remove any pockets of air and to mould it into a neat even shape. Firmly press the pastry edges together to seal, then cut off the excess pastry leaving a 2cm border.

9 Use the back of a small knife to 'knock up' the pastry edge, then flute it (see the Baker's Guide page 10 for how to do this). Re-roll the pastry trimmings and cut out small decorative shapes – leaves, stars, flowers or fish – and attach to the pie with dabs of beaten egg. Make 4 evenly spaced steam holes along the top of the pie with the tip of a small knife. Cover loosely with clingfilm and chill thoroughly – at least 30 minutes, up to 3 hours.

10 Towards the end of the chilling time, heat your oven to 190°C/375°F/gas 5. Uncover the chilled pie and brush the pastry with beaten egg to glaze. Bake for 20 minutes, then reduce the oven temperature to 180°C/350°F/gas 4 and bake for a further 25 minutes until the pastry is a good crisp, dark golden brown. Transfer to a serving platter or board and serve hot. Any leftovers can be kept overnight in the fridge, tightly wrapped, and eaten cold the next day.

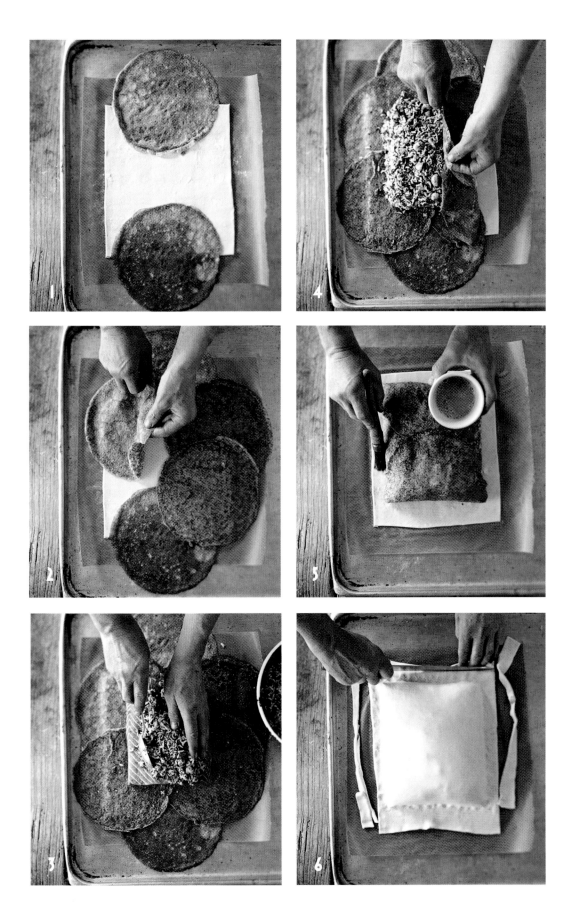

GAME, PORT & REDCURRANT CHARLOTTE

In season you can find mixed game, already diced, in packs at supermarkets, good butchers and farmers' markets. The mix usually includes pheasant, partridge, mallard, rabbit and sometimes venison. If you prefer a lighter flavour replace some of the weight of game with skinless chicken thigh meat. Instead of pastry the filling is baked in a crisp shell of bread – use a good white loaf like the Perfect Soft White Sandwich Bread on page 58.

SERVES SIX

For the game mixture
800g skinless, boneless mixed game meat, diced
1 medium onion, finely sliced
leaves from 1 large sprig of fresh thyme
6 black peppercorns
1 fresh bay leaf
300ml port
20g unsalted butter
150g chestnut mushrooms, quartered, OR mixed wild mushrooms
1 teaspoon plain flour
1 garlic clove, crushed
1 tablespoon redcurrant jelly
small bunch of fresh parsley, chopped
salt and black pepper

For the crust
1 slightly stale loaf of white bread (see above)
60g unsalted butter, melted

1 x 16–18cm round, deep charlotte mould OR cake tin, well greased with butter and base-lined*; a baking sheet

1 Put the game in a large bowl and add the sliced onion, thyme leaves, peppercorns, bay leaf and port. Mix well, then cover and leave to marinate in the fridge overnight.

2 Next day, heat the butter in a heavy-based flameproof casserole (or a pan with a tight-fitting lid) and cook the mushrooms over medium heat for a few minutes until softened and golden. Drain the marinated meat and onions – save the marinade but discard the peppercorns and bay leaf – and add to the mushrooms. Stir well. Sprinkle over the flour and stir, then add the marinade and bring to the boil, stirring. Add the garlic, then turn down the heat so the mixture simmers very gently. Cover with the lid and leave to cook for about 1$\frac{1}{2}$ hours until the meat is very tender, stirring now and then.

3 Using a slotted or draining spoon, transfer the meat and mushrooms to a heatproof bowl; set aside. Add the redcurrant jelly to the liquid in the casserole and boil until reduced and lightly syrupy in consistency. Taste and add salt and pepper as needed – you may want to add an extra splash of port too, just to 'wake up' this gravy.

4 Spoon a little of the gravy over the game and mushroom mixture – just enough to moisten – and save the rest for serving. Leave the game mixture to cool. (At this point the game mixture and gravy can be covered and kept in the fridge overnight.)

5 When ready to assemble and bake the charlotte, heat your oven to 200°C/400°F/gas 6. Thinly cut off all the crusts from the bread, on all sides, then cut the loaf down its length (rather than in the usual way) into long medium-thick slices.

6 Cut a slice (or 2) to fit the base of the prepared mould, making sure it is completely covered, with no gaps. (You may have to squash the bread in.) Once you have cut the pieces to fit the base, remove them and brush one side with melted butter. Re-fit them into the base, buttered-side down.

7 Cut slices 3–4cm wide, and slightly tapered, to fit the side of the mould standing vertically and slightly overlapping. Brush one side of each piece with butter, then press it firmly against the side of the mould. Again, make sure there are no gaps. Cut pieces to fit the top of the mould.

8 Stir the chopped parsley into the game mixture, then pack it into the bread case, making sure it is tightly filled. Bang the mould on the worktop a couple of times to settle the contents. Cover the top with the bread pieces cut to make the lid and press down firmly, then brush with butter. If the bread slices around the sides stick up over above the bread lid, trim them with kitchen scissors so the surface is flat (this will be the base when the charlotte is turned out).

9 Set the mould on the baking sheet and bake in the heated oven for 30–35 minutes until piping hot and the top is golden brown. Hold an upturned warmed serving platter (one with a rim) on top of the mould and invert. Lift off the tin and remove the lining paper. Cut the charlotte open with a sharp knife and serve with the reheated gravy in a warmed jug.

FETA & SPINACH FILO TRIANGLES

There's plenty of filling in these crunchy filo pastries, and they are substantial enough to pop into a lunchbox or take on a picnic. If you can't find tender young spinach, you can use larger leaves, but remove the stalks before weighing.

MAKES TEN

300g fresh young spinach leaves
2 spring onions, finely sliced
1 garlic clove, crushed
1 tablespoon olive oil
2 teaspoons lemon juice
freshly grated nutmeg, to taste
1 tablespoon freshly grated
    Parmesan cheese
40g drained feta cheese, crumbled
6 sheets filo pastry (each about
    48 x 25.5cm), total weight about
    270g, thawed if frozen
50g unsalted butter, melted
1 medium free-range egg, beaten,
    to glaze
1 tablespoon sesame seeds,
    for sprinkling
salt and black pepper

1 x 9.5cm plain round cutter; a baking
    sheet, lined with baking paper

1 Thoroughly wash and drain the spinach. Pack into a large pan, set over medium heat and stir for about 4 minutes until the spinach wilts and softens. Tip into a colander in the sink and leave to drain. (If using microwaveable packs, follow the instructions and then drain.) When the spinach is cool enough to handle, squeeze out as much water as you possibly can. Put the spinach on a chopping board and roughly chop. Tip into a mixing bowl.

2 Add the spring onions, garlic, olive oil, lemon juice, and pepper and nutmeg to taste. Mix well, then mix in the Parmesan and feta. Taste, and add more pepper and nutmeg or a pinch of salt as needed. Cover and set aside.

3 Heat your oven to 200°C/400°F/gas 6. Unwrap the filo sheets, then cover them with clingfilm so they don't dry out while you're working with them. Lay one sheet on the worktop and brush lightly with melted butter. Lay another sheet on top, making sure the edges line up, and brush with butter. Repeat until you have a stack of 6 sheets. Use the round cutter to cut out 10 discs from the pastry stack.

4 Put a rounded tablespoon of spinach filling in the middle of each pastry disc – don't flatten the mound. Lightly brush the pastry edge with beaten egg. With your fingers, fold and pinch 3 'sides' of the pastry disc up around the filling to make a 'three-cornered hat' triangle effect with some filling visible in the centre. The triangles don't have to look neat, so don't worry if some of the pastry starts to flake at the seams.

5 Set the triangles slightly apart on the lined baking sheet. Brush the pastry lightly with the beaten egg, then sprinkle with the sesame seeds. Bake in the heated oven for 20-25 minutes until a good golden brown and crisp. Serve warm or at room temperature.

ROAST VEGETABLE & GOAT'S CHEESE TORTE

Thin wholemeal crêpes (pancakes) are layered with roasted vegetables and creamy goat's cheese to make this colourful and richly flavoured main dish. It's ideal for making use of a glut of summer vegetables; in winter experiment with roots such as carrots, parsnips and sweet potatoes plus onions or leeks, and try other cheeses too.

SERVES FOUR TO SIX

For the crêpe batter
115g plain wholemeal flour
  (wheat or spelt)
1 medium free-range egg and
  1 egg yolk, at room temperature
300ml milk, at room temperature
15g unsalted butter, melted
knob of butter, for frying

For the vegetable layers
1 medium yellow pepper, seeded
2 medium red peppers, seeded
1 medium courgette
1 medium aubergine
3 tablespoons olive oil
few sprigs of fresh thyme
4 garlic cloves, thinly sliced
50g pitted black olives, roughly
  chopped

For the cheese layers
225g log-type goat's cheese
small bunch of fresh basil leaves,
  roughly torn
salt and black pepper

To garnish
black olives
small fresh basil leaves

2 roasting tins OR large baking dishes;
  a 19–20cm non-stick frying pan;
  a 20.5cm springclip tin, lightly
  greased with butter

1 Make the crêpe batter first so it has time to stand before using. Combine the flour and a good pinch of salt in a mixing bowl. Make a well in the centre and add the egg, egg yolk and milk. Using a wire whisk, mix the ingredients in the well, then gradually work in the flour to make a smooth, fairly thin batter. Cover the bowl and leave at room temperature for at least 30 minutes (up to 4 hours).

2 Meanwhile, heat your oven to 225°C/425°F/gas 7. Cut the peppers, courgette and aubergine into 3cm pieces. Divide the vegetables between the roasting tins so the pieces can be spread out in a single layer. Sprinkle the oil over the vegetables and add the leaves from the sprigs of thyme, dividing these evenly between the 2 tins. Mix well, then roast in the heated oven for about 25 minutes until softened and lightly caramelised, stirring occasionally.

3 Remove the tins from the oven and combine the roasted vegetables in one tin. Add the garlic, olives, a little salt and plenty of pepper and stir gently to mix. Set aside to cool while cooking the crêpes. (Once cold, the vegetable mixture can be covered and left at room temperature for up to 4 hours.) Leave the oven on, turning it down to 190°C/375°F/gas 5 – unless you are going to assemble and bake the torte later.

4 Whisk the crêpe batter just to mix it before whisking in the melted butter. Heat the frying pan over medium heat, then lightly grease the base of the pan by wiping with a small knob of butter held in a thickly folded sheet of kitchen paper. Add about 3 tablespoons of batter to the pan and swirl briskly so the batter evenly covers the base of the pan. Cook for 1^1/$_2$–2 minutes until you can slide a palette knife under the crêpe to loosen it. Check to be sure the underside is a good golden colour, then flip the crêpe over using the palette knife. Cook for a further minute or so until the second side is speckled with brown spots. Tip out the crêpe on to a plate.

5 Cook the rest of the batter in the same way (it will make about 12 crêpes), wiping the pan with the butter paper now and again so the batter doesn't stick. As each crêpe is cooked, tip it out on to the plate, stacking the crêpes on top of each other. (If you aren't going to use the crêpes straight away, interleave them with strips of greaseproof paper and cool completely, then wrap the stack in foil and keep in the fridge.)

6 You will need 11 crêpes to make the torte – select the best-looking one of these for the top. Divide the roasted vegetable mixture into 4 equal portions. Roughly crumble the cheese, then divide into 4 equal portions. Layer 2 crêpes in the base of the prepared springclip tin. Spoon one portion of vegetables evenly on top. Press a crêpe on the vegetables and scatter over one portion of cheese. Add a little torn basil, then cover with another crêpe. Spread another portion of vegetables on this, then press a crêpe on top. Continue to layer up until you have 4 layers each of vegetables and cheese separated with crêpes. Lay the last 2 crêpes on top of the final layer of cheese and gently press down with the palm of your hand.

7 Cover the tin with a sheet of buttered foil and bake in the heated oven for 30–35 minutes until piping hot. Unclip the tin and carefully lift off the ring. Garnish the torte with olives and basil leaves, then serve hot cut in wedges, with a salad or a tomato and red pepper sauce (see Aubergine Parmigiana Crumble on page 258).

GIANT SAUSAGE ROLL

It's hard to beat home-made sausage rolls fresh from the oven: they are always crowd-pleasers at parties with all ages. But for a change why not make a large sausage roll? Use your own favourite pastry (puff, rough puff, flaky or shortcrust) or a 375g pack of all-butter puff pastry. Or try the 'quick' rough puff method here. This is filled with a simple mix of minced chicken and spiced mango chutney rather than the usual pork sausagemeat.

SERVES SIX TO EIGHT

For the pastry
125g unsalted butter, chilled
  (see method)
185g plain flour
$\frac{1}{4}$ teaspoon salt
125ml icy-cold water
1 teaspoon lemon juice
beaten egg, to glaze

For the filling
1 small onion, finely chopped
2 garlic cloves, crushed
1 tablespoon olive oil
40g fresh breadcrumbs
finely grated zest of 1 lime
4 tablespoons spicy mango chutney
  (choose mild/medium/hot, to taste)
500g minced chicken (a mix of thigh
  and breast meat)
25g pistachios, roughly chopped
salt and black pepper

1 baking sheet, lined with baking paper

1 To make the pastry, first put the butter into the freezer for 10 minutes so it's very hard. Sift the flour and salt into a mixing bowl. Holding the butter in its wrapper, grate into the flour (use the coarse side of the grater). With a round-bladed knife toss the butter in the flour so the shreds are coated and separate, instead of a clotted mass. Combine the water and lemon juice and stir enough into the flour mixture to make a slightly soft, shaggy-looking dough. Press the dough together – don't knead it – and wrap in clingfilm. Chill for 1 hour.

2 Turn out the dough on to a lightly floured worktop and gently press out, away from you, with a lightly floured rolling pin to a rectangle about 12 x 35cm. Fold the dough in 3: fold the bottom third up to cover the middle third, then fold the top third down to cover the other 2 layers. Press the 2 'open' sides (not the fold) with the rolling pin to seal the 3 layers of pastry, then wrap tightly in clingfilm and chill for at least 1 hour, or for up to 12 hours. (If you are using ready-made puff pastry, thaw it or remove it from the fridge according to the pack instructions.)

3 While the pastry is chilling make the filling. Gently cook the onion and garlic in the olive oil in a small pan for about 5 minutes until softened. Tip into a mixing bowl. Add the breadcrumbs, lime zest and chutney to the bowl and mix well. Leave until cold.

4 Add the minced chicken, pistachios and a little salt and black pepper. Mix thoroughly, then season with a little salt and pepper. Take a teaspoon of the mixture, shape it into a tiny burger and fry it in a non-stick frying pan for about a minute on each side (until piping hot), then taste it. Add more seasoning or a bit more chutney to the rest of the filling as you think necessary.

5 Transfer the filling mixture to a sheet of clingfilm and shape into a 25 x 7.5cm 'sausage', using the clingfilm to help you. Wrap tightly in the clingfilm to keep the shape and chill for at least 1 hour, or overnight, to allow the flavours to develop.

6 When ready to make the sausage roll, lightly flour the worktop and roll out the pastry to a 26 x 30cm rectangle. With a sharp knife trim the edges so they are neat and straight. Lightly score a line across the width of the rectangle to divide it in half. Unwrap the filling 'sausage' and set it on the pastry so it lies crossways, halfway between the scored centre line and the nearest 26cm edge (the sausage will be parallel to this edge).

7 Lightly brush the two 26cm edges with beaten egg, then fold the pastry over the sausage to cover it (the ends of the sausage will not be covered); the 26cm edges should meet neatly at the side of the sausage. Press them together to seal. Use the back of a small knife to 'knock up' the pastry edge, then flute it (see the Baker's Guide page 10 for how to do this).

8 Transfer the roll to the lined baking sheet. Lightly brush the pastry all over with beaten egg, then chill for about 20 minutes while you heat up your oven to 220°C/425°F/gas 7.

9 Brush the pastry again with beaten egg, then use a sharp knife to score the top of the pastry with diagonal lines. Bake in the heated oven for about 35 minutes until the pastry is a good golden brown and the sausage filling is piping hot (to test, insert a metal skewer into the centre of the filling and leave it for 4 seconds; if it feels hot when tapped on the inside of your wrist the filling is cooked). Eat warm from the oven or at room temperature.

SMALL SAUSAGE ROLLS

Roll out the pastry to a 46 x 24cm rectangle. With a floured knife, or pizza wheel-cutter, cut the pastry lengthways down the centre to make 2 narrow rectangular strips. Shape the filling into 2 long sausages about 3cm thick and about 46cm long (or the length of your pastry strips). Set a sausage on each strip of pastry. Lightly brush the 2 long edges of each pastry strip with beaten egg, then fold the pastry over the sausage and press the long edges together to seal. Knock up and flute the edge, then cut across into 5cm lengths. Arrange on the baking sheet. Brush with beaten egg, score with diagonal lines and bake as above for 15–20 minutes. Makes 20 tiny rolls.

BOEUF BOURGUIGNON PIE

A richly flavoured puff pastry pie filled with the French classic stew of beef, mushrooms, lardons and red wine is irresistible. The slow-cooked beef mixture can be prepared a couple of days in advance and then topped with pastry (which can also be made ahead) just before baking.

SERVES FOUR TO SIX

For the filling
10g dried porcini mushrooms
200ml very hot water
100g lardons (diced streaky bacon)
800g lean boneless stewing steak
  (chuck or skirt), cut into 5cm cubes
about 2 tablespoons olive oil (optional)
3 shallots, quartered
1 tablespoon plain flour
500ml red wine
2 garlic cloves, crushed
1 bay leaf
salt and black pepper

For the pastry
½ quantity Puff Pastry (see page 242)
  OR 1 x 375g pack all-butter puff
  pastry, thawed if frozen
beaten egg, to glaze

1 deep pie dish, about 1.5 litre capacity;
  a pie raiser OR egg cup;
  a baking sheet

1 Heat your oven to 150°C/300°F/gas 2. Put the dried mushrooms into a heatproof bowl, pour over the very hot water and leave to soak and rehydrate until needed.

2 Put the lardons into a cold flameproof casserole and set over medium heat. Fry, stirring frequently, until the fat melts and the lardons are golden. Remove from the casserole with a slotted spoon to a small plate, leaving the melted fat behind. Add the beef to the casserole, a few pieces at a time, and fry until browned on all sides – add a little oil if needed. As each batch of beef cubes is browned, transfer to a large plate using the slotted spoon. Add the quartered shallots to the casserole and brown quickly, then add them to the browned beef.

3 Turn the heat down to low and add the flour to the casserole. Stir until lightly coloured, then stir in the wine and the mushrooms with their soaking liquid. Bring to the boil, stirring. Return the beef and shallots to the casserole along with the garlic, bay leaf and a little salt and pepper (go easy on the salt as the lardons are salty). Bring to the boil, then cover the casserole and transfer to the heated oven. Cook for 1½–2 hours until the meat is very tender.

4 Remove the bay leaf from the casserole. Stir in the lardons, then taste and adjust the seasoning as needed. Set the pie raiser (or upturned egg cup) in the centre of the pie dish and spoon the meat filling into the dish. Leave until cold (at this point the filling can kept, tightly covered, in the fridge for a couple of days).

5 Before you cover your pie make sure home-made pastry is well-rested, or ready-made pastry thawed/removed from the fridge according to the pack instructions. Roll out the pastry on a floured worktop to the shape of the pie dish and about 7cm larger all round. Cut off a 1cm wide strip from around the edge of the pastry shape. Dampen the rim of the dish with water and press the strip of pastry on to it, joining the ends

neatly. Dampen the pastry strip. Make a small slit
in the centre of the pastry lid (to fit over the pie
raiser without tearing the pastry). Roll the pastry
around the rolling pin and gently unroll it over
the pie to cover, fitting the pie raiser through the
slit. Press the edges of the pastry lid on to the
strip on the rim to seal firmly. Trim off the excess
pastry with a sharp knife – save the trimmings for
decorations.

6 Use the back of a small knife to 'knock up'
the pastry edge, then flute it (see the Baker's
Guide page 10 for how to do this). Cut the pastry
trimmings into leaf shapes or small discs, using a
small fluted cutter or a knife, and stick on to the
pastry lid with a dab of beaten egg.

7 Chill the pie while heating your oven to
200°C/400°F/gas 6. Set the pie on the baking
sheet. Brush the pastry with beaten egg to
glaze. Bake for 15 minutes, then turn down the
oven to 180°C/350°F/gas 4 and bake for a further
20–25 minutes until the pastry is puffed up, crisp
and a good golden brown. Serve hot with creamy
mashed potatoes.

CHEESE, HAM & CHIVE TART

A simple but favourite combination of lean ham and cheese with a proper 'bite', held together with a creamy custard, generously fills this tart.

MAKES ONE MEDIUM TART

For the cheese shortcrust pastry

175g plain flour
good pinch of salt
$^1/_4$ teaspoon mustard powder
75g extra mature Cheddar cheese,
  chilled and finely grated
85g unsalted butter, chilled and diced
about 3 tablespoons icy-cold water

For the filling

3 medium free-range eggs, at room
  temperature
300ml single cream
small bunch of fresh chives, finely
  snipped
200g thickly sliced lean ham, finely
  diced
100g extra mature Cheddar cheese,
  coarsely grated
salt and black pepper

1 x 20.5cm round, deep, loose-based
  flan tin (straight-sided) OR a deep
  loose-based sandwich tin;
  a baking sheet

1 Sift the flour, salt and mustard powder into a mixing bowl and stir in the grated cheese. Add the diced butter and toss the pieces in the flour so they are lightly coated, then rub in until the mixture looks like breadcrumbs. Using a round-bladed knife stir in enough cold water to make a firm dough. Flatten the dough into a thick disc, wrap in clingfilm and chill for about 25 minutes until cool and firm.

2 Using a lightly floured rolling pin, roll out the pastry on a floured worktop to a round about 28cm across. Use to line the flan tin (see the Baker's Guide page 9 for how to do this); leave the excess pastry hanging over the rim of the tin for now. Prick the base of the case with a fork, then chill for 20 minutes.

3 Heat your oven to 190°C/375°F/gas 5. Trim off the overhanging pastry with a sharp knife, then line the pastry case with a crumpled sheet of greaseproof paper and fill with baking beans. Bake blind for 15 minutes until the pastry is firm. Carefully lift out the paper and beans, then bake for a further 7–10 minutes until the pastry is fully cooked and lightly golden (see the Baker's Guide page 10 for more information).

4 Remove the case from the oven and leave to cool while making the filling. Put a baking sheet into the oven to heat up and reduce the oven temperature to 180°C/350°F/gas 4.

5 Beat the eggs with the cream, chives and some salt and pepper until thoroughly combined. Scatter the ham over the bottom of the pastry case, then add the cheese in an even layer. Pour in half the egg mixture. Set the flan tin on the heated baking sheet in the oven (you may need to pull out the shelf slightly), then pour in enough of the remaining egg mix to fill the pastry case. Gently push the shelf back into place, close the oven door and bake for about 35 minutes until the filling is puffed, golden and firm to the touch in the centre.

6 Remove the tart from the oven and cool for 10 minutes before unmoulding – the filling will sink slightly. Serve warm or at room temperature (if you serve the tart hot from the oven it will be difficult to slice neatly).

LAMB, APRICOT, CORIANDER & GREEN CHILLI PIE

Just perfect for a cold day – a very tender, warmly spiced lamb filling covered with a delicious crisp pastry flavoured with fresh coriander. The suet pastry is light as a feather thanks to the addition of fresh breadcrumbs.

SERVES FOUR TO SIX

For the filling

3cm piece fresh root ginger, peeled
 and sliced
3 garlic cloves, sliced
1 green chilli (mild/medium/hot –
 to taste), quartered and seeded
2 medium onions, roughly chopped
2 tablespoons vegetable oil
2 teaspoons ground coriander
750g lamb neck fillet OR boneless
 stewing lamb, diced
150ml vegetable stock
75g soft-dried apricots, quartered
150g diced butternut squash
lemon juice to taste
salt and black pepper

For the suet crust pastry

200g self-raising flour
50g fresh white breadcrumbs
1 tablespoon chopped fresh coriander
1/4 teaspoon salt
100g beef or vegetable suet
about 200ml icy-cold water, to mix
beaten egg, to glaze

1 pie dish, about 1.25–1.5 litre capacity;
 a pie raiser OR egg cup

1 Heat your oven to 150°C/300°F/gas 2. Put the ginger, garlic, chilli and onions into the bowl of a food processor and process until very finely chopped (or chop with a knife).

2 Heat the oil in a flameproof casserole. Add the ground coriander and the contents of the processor bowl to the casserole and stir over medium heat for 3 minutes. Add the diced lamb and stir over the heat for another 3 minutes until the lamb is thoroughly coated in the spice mixture and lightly coloured. Add the vegetable stock and bring to the boil. Stir well, then cover the casserole and transfer to the oven to cook for 30 minutes.

3 Stir in the apricots and the squash and season lightly with salt and pepper. Cover the casserole again and continue cooking in the oven for 30–45 minutes until the meat is meltingly tender.

4 Stir well. If there is a lot of thin gravy, simmer uncovered on top of the stove until reduced to the consistency of single cream. Taste and add more seasoning and lemon juice to taste. Set the pie raiser (or upturned egg cup) in the pie dish and spoon in the filling. Leave to cool (at this point the pie filling can be covered and kept in the fridge overnight).

5 When you are ready to finish and bake the pie, put the flour, breadcrumbs, coriander, salt and suet into a mixing bowl. Mix well using your hand. With a round-bladed knife, stir in enough icy water to make a slightly firm but shaggy and elastic dough.

6 Turn out on to a lightly floured worktop and knead for a couple of seconds, just to make a smooth ball of dough. Cover with the upturned bowl and leave to rest for about 10 minutes while heating your oven to 180°C/350°F/gas 4.

7 Roll out the pastry on the lightly floured worktop to a shape the same as your pie dish but 3cm larger all round than the dish. Dampen the rim of the dish with water. Cut a strip of pastry about 1.5cm wide from all around the edge of the pastry shape and press it on to the rim of the dish. Brush the strip with water. Wrap the pastry lid around the rolling pin and gently unroll it over the dish, letting the pie funnel poke through (you may need to make a small slit in the pastry lid to avoid tearing it). Using your thumbs, gently press the edge of the lid firmly to the pastry strip on the rim to seal. Cut off excess pastry with a sharp knife.

8 Use the back of a small knife to 'knock up' the pastry edge, then 'flute' or scallop it (see the Baker's Guide page 10 for how to do this). Brush the pastry lid with beaten egg to glaze, and cut a couple of steam holes using the tip of a sharp knife. Bake in the heated oven for 35 minutes until the pastry is a rich golden brown. Serve hot from the oven.

CHETNA

Where do you live?
Broadstairs in Kent.

What do you get up to when you are not baking?
I love to read, and enjoy going for a run or a swim. I love gardening – but only in fair weather!

How would you define yourself as a baker?
I am a very organised home baker and can't work in a messy kitchen. I love to combine my knowledge of Indian flavours with British recipes.

Why do you enjoy baking?
I love to bake as I find it's the perfect outlet for my creativity. I see baking as creating pieces of art that can be enjoyed rather than just be seen. I love to feed my family and friends, and get great pleasure from seeing them enjoy the things I bake.

How did you get into baking?
My first memories of baking are from childhood when I used to bake birthday cakes with my mother. She is the one who taught me everything I know about flavours and has been the inspiration behind my baking. I only really started baking regularly after having kids because I wanted to give them the same experience.

What is the trickiest bake you've ever mastered?
I will always remember making a near-perfect Croquembouche on my very first attempt.

What are your favourite 3 items of kitchen equipment?
My very basic and reliable cheap electric whisk.
A Chakla Belan (an Indian rolling pin).
A wooden board and kitchen knife, which are the oldest things I own in the kitchen.

CHETNA'S
CRISPY LENTIL KACHORI

▼▼▼▼▼▼▼▼▼▼▼▼▼▼▼▼▼▼▼▼▼▼▼▼▼▼▼▼▼▼▼▼▼▼▼▼▼

A delicious and popular deep-fried vegan snack, these have a crisp,
flaky pastry-like dough made with carom seeds (which add a thyme-like flavour) and
a spicy lentil filling. The tamarind chutney is essential for dipping torn-up chunks
of the kachoris – you could become addicted!

MAKES TWELVE

For the dough
400g plain flour
1 tablespoon carom (ajowan) seeds
100ml sunflower oil, plus extra for the
    worktop and for deep-frying
150ml cold water

For the filling
200g urad/urid dal (split black lentils)
500ml water
1 1/2 tablespoons sunflower oil
1 1/2 teaspoons cumin seeds
2cm piece of fresh root ginger, grated
1 large garlic clove, grated
1 1/2 teaspoons ground coriander
1/2 teaspoon chilli powder, or to taste
1 tablespoon mango (amchur) powder
1 1/2 teaspoons garam masala
small bunch of fresh coriander leaves

For the tamarind chutney
55g jaggery OR reduced palm sugar
    and unrefined cane sugar lumps
60g tamarind paste
350ml water
50g pitted dates, roughly chopped
1 teaspoon toasted cumin seeds
1/2 teaspoon chilli powder, or to taste
1 teaspoon ground ginger
toasted fennel seeds, for sprinkling
salt

a deep-fat fryer OR deep pan, plus
    a cooking thermometer

1 To make the dough, put the flour, 1/4 teaspoon salt and the
carom seeds into a large mixing bowl and mix well together.
Trickle the oil over the mixture, then rub it into the flour using
the tips of your fingers until the mixture looks like coarse
crumbs. Using your hand or a round-bladed knife, slowly work
in the cold water to make a firm but not hard dough – you may
not need all the water, it should not feel damp or sticky.

2 Lightly oil the worktop, then turn out the dough onto it.
Knead gently for about a minute until the dough feels smooth
and silky. Return the dough to the bowl and cover the top with
a damp tea towel. Leave to rest (on the worktop) while you
make the filling.

3 Put the lentils into a medium-sized pan with the water and
a good pinch of salt. Bring to the boil, then skim off the foam
that forms on the surface. Turn down the heat and simmer
gently, stirring frequently, for 15–20 minutes until the water has
been absorbed and the lentils are soft (but not mushy).

4 Meanwhile, make the spice mixture for the filling. Heat the
oil in a medium-sized frying pan set over medium heat, then
add the cumin seeds. Once they start to turn golden, stir in
the grated ginger and garlic and cook for a minute, stirring. Stir
in the ground coriander, chilli powder, mango powder, garam
masala and salt to taste to make a thick paste.

5 Add the hot cooked lentils and stir gently over a medium
heat for 2–3 minutes to make a thick, spicy mixture. Taste and
add more spices or salt as needed. Remove the pan from the
heat, stir in the chopped coriander and leave to cool.

6 While the filling is cooling, make the chutney. Put the jaggery,
tamarind, dates and the water into a medium-sized pan and
set over a medium heat. Bring to the boil, then simmer gently,
stirring frequently, for 15–20 minutes until the dates are very
soft and the jaggery has melted. Strain into a smaller pan and
simmer for about 5 minutes until the chutney is the thickness

▼▼▼▼▼▼▼▼▼▼▼▼▼▼▼▼

of double cream. Stir in the cumin seeds, chilli powder, ground ginger and salt to taste. Simmer for a couple of minutes longer, then pour the chutney into a heatproof serving bowl. Scatter a few crushed fennel seeds on top and set on one side until ready to serve.

7 To assemble the parcels, turn out the dough onto a lightly floured worktop. Knead for a few seconds, then weigh the dough and divide into 12 equal portions (about 50g each). Shape one portion into a neat ball and slightly flatten it. Roll out to a neat round about 12cm across. Spoon 2 tablespoons of the lentil filling into the centre of the round. Lightly brush the edges of the dough with water. There are two ways to shape the parcels, just make sure that they are well sealed. Either fold one side of the dough over the filling to create a semi-circle, then fold the open edges back and pinch together to seal and make pleats. Or you can gather the dough edges up over the top and pleat together to make a purse-like parcel or dumpling, then turn it over and gently flatten with your hand or the rolling pin to a neat round about 10cm across. Repeat your chosen method with the rest of the dough and filling.

8 When ready to fry the parcels, heat oil in the deep-fat fryer, or large deep pan, to 180°C. Fry the parcels 2 at a time: drop them into the hot oil and fry, turning occasionally, for 2–3 minutes until lightly coloured, then turn up the heat and fry at 190°C for another 2–3 minutes until a good golden brown. Drain on kitchen paper and serve hot, with the chutney.

AUBERGINE PARMIGIANA CRUMBLE

Here's a colourful twist on an old Italian favourite. It's substantial enough for a main dish for four people with bread and salad, or as a side dish to accompany grilled chicken pieces or chops. Vegetarian mozzarella and Parmesan cheeses are available.

For the aubergines

3 small to medium aubergines
  (about 900g in total)
3 tablespoons olive oil
3 garlic cloves, crushed
small handful of fresh parsley,
  chopped
1 large sprig of fresh thyme, oregano
  or basil, chopped

For the sauce

2 tablespoons olive oil
1 large red onion, finely chopped
1 large red pepper, seeded and
  cut into large chunks
4 garlic cloves, crushed
2 x 400g cans chopped tomatoes
crushed dried chilli, to taste

To finish

100g crustless, slightly stale bread,
  cut into cubes
2 tablespoons olive oil
50g pine nuts
40g Parmesan cheese, freshly grated
2 balls fresh mozzarella, about 250g
  drained weight in total
salt and black pepper

1 large roasting tin, lightly greased with
  oil; a large baking dish OR lasagne
  dish, lightly greased with oil

1 Heat your oven to 200°C/400°F/gas 6. Trim the ends from the aubergines. With a vegetable peeler shave off 4 wide strips of peel down the length of each aubergine – north, south, east and west – so the aubergine looks striped black and white (this will help the flavours permeate the flesh without causing it to disintegrate). Cut each aubergine in half lengthways.

2 Mix the olive oil with the garlic, a little salt and pepper and the herbs. Brush the aubergines all over with the flavoured oil, then pack them cut-side up into the roasting tin. Cover with foil and bake in the heated oven for about 1 hour until just tender when pierced with the tip of a sharp knife – start testing after 45 minutes as smaller ones may be ready sooner. Transfer the tin to a heatproof surface. Leave the oven on.

3 While the aubergines are baking, make the tomato sauce. Heat the oil in a medium-saucepan. Add the chopped onion and stir well, then cover and cook over very low heat for about 10 minutes until soft but not browned. Add the red pepper with the garlic, stir and cook for a further minute before stirring in the chopped tomatoes. Bring to the boil, then cover the pan again, turn down the heat and simmer for 30 minutes, stirring occasionally. If the sauce seems a bit thin and watery, simmer uncovered until thick. Add salt, pepper and chilli flakes to taste. (The sauce can be made ahead and stored in a covered container in the fridge for a couple of days.)

4 Make the topping while the sauce is simmering. Put the cubes of bread into a food processor and reduce to very coarse crumbs. Tip into a mixing bowl and stir in the oil, nuts, Parmesan and a few grinds of black pepper.

5 To assemble, spoon a third of the tomato sauce into the baking dish. Set the aubergines on top in a single layer. Cover with the rest of the sauce. Drain the mozzarella thoroughly on kitchen paper, then tear up into thick strips and arrange on top of the sauce. Scatter the topping evenly over the mozzarella.

6 Bake in the heated oven for 30–40 minutes until golden and bubbling. Serve hot.

SMOKED HADDOCK ROULADE

Made in the same way as a sweet one, this is a light and delicious savoury version.

50g unsalted butter, plus extra melted
   butter for the case
250g skinless undyed smoked
   haddock fillet
300ml creamy milk
6 black peppercorns
1 bay leaf
50g plain flour
3 medium free-range eggs,
   at room temperature
2 teaspoons lemon juice
small handful of fresh parsley sprigs,
   finely chopped

For the filling

250g fresh young spinach leaves,
   rinsed and well drained
25g unsalted butter
1 tablespoon plain flour
2 tablespoons freshly grated Parmesan
   cheese, plus extra for sprinkling
freshly grated nutmeg, to taste
salt and black pepper

1 large sheet of parchment-lined foil;
   a baking sheet

1 Cut a 33 x 37cm rectangle from the foil. Set foil-side down, on the baking sheet and fold in the edges 3.5cm all around. Unfold so they stand vertically, then pinch the corners to make a neat case 26 x 30cm with 3.5cm sides. Brush with melted butter and set aside. Heat your oven to 200°C/400°F/gas 6.

2 Put the haddock into a shallow pan. Pour over the milk, add the peppercorns and bay leaf, and bring to the boil. Turn down to a simmer, then cover and poach gently for 6–8 minutes until the fish flakes easily when prodded with the tip of a knife.

3 Remove the fish with a slotted spoon. Strain the milk into a jug; discard the peppercorns and bay leaf. Flake the fish.

4 Melt the butter in a medium saucepan. Stir in the flour over low heat, then stir in 150ml of the milk (save the rest for the filling). Bring to the boil, stirring constantly, to make a thick, smooth sauce. Simmer, stirring, for a few minutes to 'cook out' the flour. Set on a heatproof surface and stir in the flaked fish.

5 Separate the eggs. Stir the yolks into the fish and put the whites into a spotlessly clean bowl. Season the fish with the lemon juice, a little salt and lots of pepper. Stir in the parsley.

6 Whisk the egg whites with an electric mixer until they stand in stiff peaks when the whisk is lifted from the bowl. Using a large metal spoon or plastic spatula, gently fold the whites into the fish mixture in 3 batches. Spoon the mixture into the case on the baking sheet and spread evenly. Bake in the heated oven for about 12 minutes until golden brown and just firm.

7 Make the filling. Put the spinach into a large pan and stir over medium heat until wilted. Tip into a colander in the sink to drain and cool, then squeeze out the liquid and roughly chop.

8 Melt the butter in a medium-sized pan. Stir in the flour, then stir in 125ml of the reserved poaching milk. Bring to the boil, stirring constantly, to make a smooth thick sauce. Simmer, stirring, for a minute to cook out the flour, then stir in the spinach and Parmesan. Season with salt, pepper and nutmeg.

9 As soon as the base is ready, turn it, in its case, on to a sheet of dampened baking paper on the worktop. Gently undo the corners, then peel it off. Quickly spread the filling over and roll up from one long side, using the paper to help you – don't worry if it doesn't look neat. Transfer it to a serving platter, sprinkle with extra grated Parmesan and serve immediately.

TAPENADE TWISTS

Quick to assemble and bake, these crisp, savoury pastry biscuits are perfect with soup or a soufflé starter, or with drinks. They can be made a day or so in advance and then gently warmed through in a low oven before serving.

MAKES FORTY

½ quantity Puff Pastry (see page 242)
   OR 1 x 375g pack all-butter puff
   pastry, thawed if frozen
5 tablespoons tapenade, or
   black olive paste
1 teaspoon brandy

1–2 baking sheets, lined with baking
   paper

1 Make sure home-made puff pastry is well rested and chilled before you start, or ready-made pastry thawed/removed from the fridge according to the pack instructions. Mix the tapenade or black olive paste with the brandy.

2 Lightly flour your worktop and rolling pin, then roll out the pastry to a rectangle about 40 x 30cm. Spread the tapenade evenly over the pastry, right to the edges.

3 Lightly score a line lengthways down the centre of the pastry, just to mark the centre (rather than cut through it). Roll the pastry inward from each long side to meet in the centre. Cut the double roll across into slices 1cm thick using a large sharp knife – take care not to drag the pastry as this will damage the layer structure. The slices will look like old-fashioned pince-nez specs.

4 Pick up each slice and twist one side so the coil is facing in the opposite direction. Set cut side down (and slightly apart from the other twists) on the lined baking sheet so the twist now look like an S shape. Chill for 15 minutes while you heat the oven to 220°C/425°F/gas 7.

5 Bake in the heated oven for 12–15 minutes until a good golden brown. Transfer to a wire rack and cool slightly. Serve warm. (If making in advance, leave until completely cold before storing in an airtight container in a cool spot – not the fridge – for up to a day; reheat gently in a preheated 180°C/350°F/gas 4 oven for about 5 minutes until warm and crisp.)

LITTLE CRAB SOUFFLÉS

Made with fresh, frozen or canned white crabmeat, this recipe makes a really lovely starter. There's not too much work: a soufflé is really a thick savoury cream sauce mixed with whisked egg whites, which the heat of the oven transforms into a crisp, fluffy, fragrant puff. Add Tapenade Twists (see page 261) and a green salad for a light lunch.

MAKES SIX INDIVIDUAL SOUFFLES

30g unsalted butter, plus extra for greasing
fine dry breadcrumbs OR grated Parmesan, for the dishes
300g white crabmeat (prepared/drained weight)
30g plain flour
300ml single cream
2 tablespoons brandy
1 tablespoon lemon juice
1 teaspoon sweet mild paprika, plus extra for sprinkling
$\frac{1}{4}$ teaspoon hot paprika OR cayenne pepper, or to taste
4 medium free-range eggs plus 2 egg whites, at room temperature
salt and black pepper

6 x 250ml ramekins OR individual soufflé dishes; a baking sheet

1 Heat your oven to 200°C/400°F/gas 6. Grease the inside of the dishes with butter, then coat with breadcrumbs or Parmesan, shaking out any excess.

2 Pick over the crab and discard any pieces of shell or cartilage (frozen crabmeat should be thawed and drained thoroughly). Flake the meat, then set aside for now.

3 Melt the butter in a medium-sized saucepan and whisk in the flour. Cook for a minute over low heat, whisking constantly. Set the pan on a heatproof surface and whisk in the cream. When thoroughly combined and smooth, return the pan to the heat and whisk constantly until the mixture comes to the boil to make a thick, lump-free sauce. Turn the heat down very low and simmer gently, stirring very frequently, for about 5 minutes to 'cook out' the taste of the flour.

4 Remove the pan from the heat and stir in the brandy, lemon juice, the mild and hot paprika (or cayenne), a little salt and plenty of pepper. Stir in the crabmeat, then taste and adjust the seasoning – the mixture should have plenty of flavour as you will be adding a mass of egg whites.

5 Separate the eggs, stirring the 4 yolks into the warm crab mixture and putting the 6 whites into a large, spotlessly clean mixing bowl. Add a good pinch of salt to the whites and whisk them with an electric mixer until they stand in stiff peaks when the whisk is lifted from the bowl. Using a large metal spoon, fold a third of the whites into the crab mixture, just to loosen it. Now spoon the crab mixture into the bowl of egg whites and gently fold them together.

6 Spoon the soufflé mixture into the prepared ramekins so they are filled to slightly below the rim. Run your finger, or the tip of a small knife, just inside the rim of each dish (this will help the soufflés to rise). Set the dishes on the baking sheet and bake in the heated oven for 10–12 minutes until well risen, a good golden brown and just firm in the middle of the crust (the centre should still be moist). Quickly sprinkle the top of each soufflé with mild paprika and serve immediately.

PAUL'S MINI SAUSAGE PLAITS

MAKES TWELVE

For the shortcut puff pastry

600g plain flour
pinch of salt
100g unsalted butter, well chilled
  and cut into cubes
about 300ml cold water
200g unsalted butter, in a block,
  frozen
1 free-range egg, beaten, to glaze
1 tablespoon sesame seeds

For the filling

300g chestnut mushrooms
2 tablespoons fresh thyme leaves
1 tablespoon sunflower oil
25g unsalted butter
2 red onions, thinly sliced
2 teaspoons soft brown sugar
1 tablespoon sherry vinegar
300g good-quality pork sausagemeat
100g black pudding, cut into
  1–2cm pieces
salt and black pepper

1 large baking sheet

1 Mix the flour and salt together in a bowl. Rub in the cubes of chilled butter using your fingertips until the mixture resembles breadcrumbs. Gradually add enough of the cold water (about 4–6 tablespoons) to form a dough.

2 Turn out on to a lightly floured worktop and roll out the dough away from you into a rectangle. Grate all of the frozen butter over the bottom two-thirds of the dough. Fold down the top third, over the butter, then fold up the bottom third – as if folding a business letter. Turn the folded dough through 90 degrees and roll it out into a rectangle again. Fold into 3 as before. Wrap the dough in clingfilm and leave to rest in the fridge for 30 minutes.

3 Repeat the rolling out and folding procedure twice, chilling in between them.

4 To make the filling, put the mushrooms in a food processor and season with salt and pepper. Pulse until the mushrooms are broken down to a rough paste. Add the thyme and give the mix a final pulse. Tip the mushroom mix into a dry frying pan and cook on medium-high heat, stirring often, until all the moisture from the mushrooms has evaporated. Remove from the pan and leave to cool.

5 Meanwhile, heat the oil and butter in the frying pan over medium-low heat, add the onions and sugar, and cook slowly until the onions are very soft and sweet. This will take at least 20 minutes. Stir in the sherry vinegar. Set aside.

6 Heat your oven to 200°C/400°F/gas 6. Roll out the block of pastry on a lightly floured worktop into a large rectangle. Cut into 12 squares, each 15 x 15cm. (On a warm day, chill the pastry squares in the fridge to make them easier to plait.)

7 Divide the mushroom mixture into 12 portions and spread one down the central third of each square of pastry, leaving a 2cm gap at the top and bottom.

8 Mix the sausagemeat with the black pudding and mould into 12 small sausage shapes that will fit on top of the mushroom paste. Set one on top of the paste on each pastry square, then spread the caramelised onions on top of this.

9 Make 2 small diagonal cuts in each corner of a pastry square, to remove a small triangle. Then fold the top and bottom 'wings' to seal in the sausagemeat. Cut 1cm strips all the way down the pastry on each side of the filling. Bring one strip over the filling from one side, then one from the other side and so on, crossing the strips over to form a plaited effect. Tuck the ends of the pastry under the plait, trimming off any excess. Repeat with the remaining 11 pastry squares.

10 Place the sausage plaits on the baking sheet, brush with beaten egg and sprinkle with sesame seeds. Bake in the heated oven for 20 minutes until the pastry is golden brown. Leave to settle for 5 minutes or so before serving hot, or cold.

• • • • • • • • • • • • • • • • • •

HOT WHITE CHOCOLATE SPONGE
PUDDINGS • APPLE, CIDER & RAISIN
CRUMBLE • BITTER CHOCOLATE & STEM GINGER
PUDS • NANCY'S SUMMER PUDDING ALASKA •
ESPRESSO CRÈME CARAMEL • STICKY APPLE
SPONGE PUDDING • BLUEBERRY & LEMON
BREAD PUDDING • CELEBRATION RUM TORTE •
LITTLE ORANGE SOUFFLÉ PUDS • GINGER &
PEAR PUDDING • RICHARD'S BLACK FOREST
CHOCOLATE FONDANTS • FLOURLESS WALNUT
TORTE • HAZELNUT & SUMMER BERRY ROULADE •
MARBLED MOCHA CHEESECAKE • GINGER TUILE
SABAYON BASKETS • MARY'S TIRAMISU CAKE •
PAUL'S CHOCOLATE VOLCANOES • MARY'S
NEAPOLITAN BAKED ALASKA

PUDDINGS
& DESSERTS

HOT WHITE CHOCOLATE SPONGE PUDDINGS

A soft, rich sponge with a hot, slightly bitter, dark chocolate sauce – truly a gloomy day emergency treat! Buy the best white chocolate rather than a children's bar for this.

MAKES FOUR INDIVIDUAL PUDDINGS

For the sponge mixture

75g good-quality white chocolate, chopped
125g unsalted butter, softened
125g caster sugar
$\frac{1}{2}$ teaspoon vanilla paste
2 medium free-range eggs, at room temperature, beaten to mix
125g self-raising flour
1 teaspoon milk

For the chocolate sauce

125ml single or whipping cream
100g dark chocolate (about 70% cocoa solids), chopped or broken up
25g unsalted butter

4 small pudding tins OR moulds, 175–200ml capacity, 8cm across the top and 5cm base, greased with butter (see TIP); a baking sheet

1 Heat your oven to 180°C/350°F/gas 4. Put the white chocolate into a heatproof bowl and set over a pan of steaming hot water (make sure the water is not boiling and that it doesn't touch the base of the bowl – white chocolate melts at a lower temperature than dark chocolate, and quickly 'seizes' if it gets too hot). Heat until the chocolate is about three-quarters melted, stirring frequently, then remove the bowl from the pan and stir until smooth. Set aside.

2 Put the butter, sugar and vanilla paste into a mixing bowl (or the bowl of a free-standing electric mixer fitted with the whisk attachment). Whisk until the mixture is very light and creamy. Scrape down the sides of the bowl, then gradually whisk in the eggs a tablespoon at a time, adding a tablespoon of the weighed flour with each of the last 2 portions of egg.

3 Sift the remaining flour into the bowl and fold in with a large metal spoon. Add the melted white chocolate and the milk and fold in until thoroughly combined.

4 Spoon the mixture into the prepared tins until about two-thirds full. Tap the tins firmly on the worktop to settle the contents and dislodge any air bubbles, then set the tins on the baking sheet. Bake in the heated oven for about 35 minutes until the puddings are risen and golden brown and a wooden cocktail stick inserted into the centre comes out clean.

5 While the puds are in the oven, make the sauce. Put the cream, chocolate and butter into a small pan and stir gently over low heat until smooth. Pour into a jug and keep hot.

6 Unmould the puddings on to small warmed plates, pour over the hot sauce and serve.

TIP

Try this pastry chef's trick. Brush the inside of each tin with very soft butter, then put into the freezer for 5 minutes to set. Press a disc of baking paper into the base and brush the inside with butter a second time. For a special finish, dust the inside evenly with a coating of cocoa powder (fill the tins carefully so you don't dislodge the cocoa).

APPLE, CIDER & RAISIN CRUMBLE

Apple crumble is one of our national treasures, made with Bramley apples, full of tart flavour, that turn fluffy in the oven and release wonderful juice. The fruit is often mixed with orange or lemon zest and juice, or another fruit like blackberries. Reduced cider, raisins and just a touch of cinnamon is another perfect combination.

SERVES SIX

For the crumble topping
150g plain flour
50g porridge oats
125g unsalted butter, chilled and diced
100g caster OR demerara sugar

For the filling
200ml cider
45g light brown muscovado sugar
$1/2$ teaspoon ground cinnamon
45g jumbo raisins
1kg Bramley apples (about 5)

1 baking dish, about 1.5-2 litre capacity
  (such as a pie dish)

1 Start by making the topping so it has time to firm up in the fridge. Mix the flour with the oats in a mixing bowl using your hand. Add the chunks of butter and rub into the flour mixture using just the tips of your fingers until the mixture looks like coarse breadcrumbs. Add the sugar to the bowl and mix in with your hand, then gently work the mixture, pressing it together with your fingertips rather than rubbing this time, to make a few pea-sized clumps in the coarse crumbly mixture. Cover the bowl with clingfilm and chill while you make the filling (the crumble topping mix will keep well in the fridge – for up to 4 days – as long as it's tightly covered).

2 Heat your oven to 180°C/350°F/gas 4. While the oven is warming up, put the cider, sugar, cinnamon and raisins into a small pan and bring to the boil. Stir and adjust the heat so the liquid boils gently (a bit faster than a simmer). Leave to cook until it is reduced by half, then remove from the heat and cool slightly.

3 Meanwhile, peel and quarter the apples. Cut out the cores, then cut into slices about 5mm thick – they don't have to be neat or precise. Put them into a bowl, add the slightly cooled cider mixture and mix thoroughly.

4 Transfer the apple mixture to the baking dish and spread evenly, making sure the apples are quite packed in – they will cook down. Scatter the topping over the apples to make an even layer, but don't press or compact it or you won't get a light crumbly finish.

5 Bake in the heated oven for 35-40 minutes until the top is a good golden brown and the juices are bubbling around the edges. Leave to cool for a few minutes before serving, with plenty of hot custard.

BITTER CHOCOLATE & STEM GINGER PUDS

Very dark and rich, these little baked sponge puddings have a melting centre. The inclusion of stem ginger cuts the richness perfectly. Serve with ice cream or crème fraîche.

MAKES SIX INDIVIDUAL PUDDINGS

250g dark chocolate (about 70% cocoa solids), chopped or broken up

75g unsalted butter, softened

125g dark brown muscovado sugar

1 tablespoon ginger syrup (from the jar of stem ginger)

4 medium free-range eggs, at room temperature, beaten to mix

5 lumps stem ginger (about 80g in total), drained of syrup

50g self-raising flour

1 tablespoon cocoa powder

good pinch of salt

3 tablespoons milk, at room temperature

icing sugar, for dusting

1 baking sheet; 6 small pudding tins or moulds, 175–200ml capacity, 8cm across the top and 5cm base, greased with butter, base-lined* and dusted with flour (see TIP page 268)

1 Heat your oven to 200°C/400°F/gas 6. Put the baking sheet in the oven to heat up.

2 Put the chopped chocolate into a heatproof bowl and set over a pan of steaming-hot but not boiling water (don't let the base of the bowl touch the water). Melt gently, stirring occasionally. Remove the bowl from the pan and leave to cool while making the sponge mix.

3 Put the soft butter, sugar and ginger syrup into a mixing bowl (or the bowl of a free-standing electric mixer fitted with the whisk attachment). Beat well for about 3 minutes until very smooth and fluffy in texture. Scrape down the side of the bowl, then gradually beat in the eggs, a tablespoon at a time – the mixture will look rather sloppy.

4 Chop the ginger into medium-fine pieces and stir into the mixture. Sift the flour, cocoa and salt into the bowl and fold in with a large metal spoon or plastic spatula. Fold in the melted chocolate followed by the milk – work quickly as the mixture will stiffen up.

5 Divide the mixture among the prepared tins and level the surface. Tap the tins on the worktop to dislodge any air pockets, then set them on the heated baking sheet in the oven. Bake for about 13 minutes until puffed and the top feels firm when pressed in the centre – the middles will still be soft. Turn out immediately on to little plates, dust with icing sugar and serve.

TIP

The little puddings can be kept, tightly wrapped, in the fridge for up to 4 hours before baking; add an extra 2 minutes to the baking time.

NANCY

Where do you live?
Barton on Humber, North Lincolnshire.

What do you get up to when you are not baking?
When I am not baking I enjoy growing my own fruit and veg, walking and cycling, and through the winter months I learn French.

How would you define yourself as a baker?
I have baked for many years but have taken a keen interest and improved my skills over the past 7 or 8 years. I would have to describe myself as a classic baker with a modern approach.

Why do you enjoy baking?
I enjoy baking because above all home-baked food is much better tasting, better for you and much cheaper than anything you can buy.

How did you get into baking?
My first baking teacher was my grandmother. As a little girl I would help with the Christmas baking – she taught me to never throw pastry away and would use every last pastry trimming to make her jam pastie!

What are your favourite 3 items of kitchen equipment?
My grandmother's kitchen scales, which take pride of place but do have to step aside sometimes to make way for digital ones.
An electric hand blender because it can do so much and saves on washing-up!
A small angled palette knife – it has so many uses (spreading, levering, lifting) – I wouldn't be without it.

SHOWSTOPPER NANCY'S
SUMMER PUDDING ALASKA

A glorious, impressive and wonderful summer dessert made of three different ice creams set on an almond sponge, with home-made jam and finished with a piped Italian meringue.

For the forest berry ice cream

400g frozen mixed forest berries, thawed but still chilled
100g caster sugar
1½ tablespoons crème de cassis (blackcurrant liqueur)
225ml double cream, well chilled

For the strawberry and mint ice cream

250g fresh ripe strawberries, hulled and halved
1–2 mint leaves (to taste)
50g icing sugar
juice of ½ lemon
1 tablespoon crème de framboises (raspberry liqueur)
½ x 410g can evaporated milk, chilled overnight

For the vanilla parfait

2 large free-range egg yolks, at room temperature
50g caster sugar
½ teaspoon vanilla paste
150ml double cream, well chilled

For the sponge base

2 large free-range eggs, at room temperature
50g caster sugar
50g plain flour
20g ground almonds
few drops of almond extract

1 Make the 3 ice cream mixtures first, so they have plenty of time to freeze (do this the day before if possible). Line the largest freezer-proof bowl with clingfilm – this will hold and shape the forest berry ice cream. Cover the outsides of the other 2 bowls with clingfilm – these will be used to form the shapes that will eventually be filled with the other 2 mixtures. Clear space in the freezer.

2 To make the forest berry ice cream, put the berries and sugar into a food processor and blitz to make a purée. Press through a sieve into a bowl. Stir in the crème de cassis and cream. Taste and add more sugar or cassis as needed. Pour the mixture into the ice-cream maker and churn until firm. Spoon the ice cream into the largest freezer-proof bowl and make a hollow for the middle-sized bowl. Fit in this clingfilm-covered bowl. Cover and freeze for 4 hours until very firm.

3 Now make the strawberry ice cream. Put the strawberries, mint, sugar and lemon juice into a food processor and blitz to make a smooth purée. Press through a sieve into a bowl and stir in the crème de framboises. Pour the chilled evaporated milk into a chilled bowl and whisk with an electric mixer or rotary whisk until very thick and mousse-like. Stir in the strawberry mixture, then taste – you may want to add a little more sugar, lemon juice or crème de framboises. Pour into the (cleaned) ice-cream maker and churn until firm.

4 Using the clingfilm to help you, lift out the bowl set in the middle of the forest berry ice cream. Spoon the strawberry ice cream into the hollow, then make a hollow in the middle big enough to fit in the smallest freezer-proof bowl. Carefully place the clingfilm-covered small bowl into the hollow. You want the levels of both ice creams to match up, so they will make a flat surface when they are all fitted together. Cover with clingfilm and return to the freezer. Freeze for about 3 hours until firm.

5 For the vanilla parfait, put the yolks, sugar and vanilla paste into a heatproof bowl set over a pan of simmering water (don't let the base of the bowl touch the water). Whisk with an electric mixer or a rotary whisk until the mixture is very thick and will leave a ribbon-like trail when the whisk is

For the berry jam
200g frozen mixed berries, thawed
100g caster sugar

For the Italian meringue
525g caster sugar
150ml water
6 large free-range egg whites,
   at room temperature

To decorate
100g each fresh strawberries,
   raspberries, blackberries and
   redcurrant sprigs
fresh mint and strawberry leaves
30g toasted flaked almonds

3 freezer-proof bowls (1 x 300ml
   capacity and 11.5cm across the top;
   1 x 900ml capacity and 17cm across
   the top; and 1 x 1.5 litre capacity and
   20cm across the top); an ice-cream
   maker; a 20cm sandwich tin, greased
   with butter and base-lined*; a large
   disposable piping bag and a star
   tube; a thin card cake board; a sugar
   thermometer; a kitchen blowtorch

lifted from the bowl (see the Baker's Guide page 9 for more information). Remove the bowl from the pan and whisk until the mixture cools to room temperature.

6 In another, larger bowl, whip the cream until it will form soft peaks. Add the yolk mixture and whisk on the slowest speed just to combine. Lift out the small bowl (with its clingfilm) set inside the strawberry ice cream and completely fill the hollow with the vanilla parfait mixture. Level the surface, cover with clingfilm and freeze.

7 Meanwhile, make the sponge base. Heat your oven to 180°C/350°F/gas 4. Put the eggs and sugar into a mixing bowl and whisk with an electric mixer until the mixture is very thick and mousse-like, and will make a ribbon-like trail when the whisk is lifted (see the Baker's Guide page 9). Sift the flour and ground almonds into the bowl, add the almond extract and gently fold in. Transfer the mixture to the prepared sandwich tin and spread evenly. Bake in the heated oven for about 12 minutes until the sponge is golden and will spring back when gently pressed in the centre. Turn out on to a wire rack and leave to cool.

8 To make the jam, put the berries in the food processor and blitz to make a smooth purée. Press through a sieve into a small pan. Stir in the sugar, then set over low heat and stir until the sugar has dissolved. Turn up the heat and boil gently for 7–10 minutes until the mixture is thick and jammy. Pour into a heatproof bowl and leave to cool, then cover and keep in the fridge until needed.

9 Once the ice cream bombe is frozen you can assemble the dessert. Set the large piping bag fitted with the large star tube into the neck of an empty bottle (one with a fairly wide neck, like a milk bottle), then pull down the sides of the bag so it is inside out (apart from the very end stuck in the bottle neck). With a pastry brush or paintbrush, paint 3 good stripes of berry jam down the inside of the piping bag. Turn the bag up the right way and leave it on one side until you've made the meringue.

10 Set the sponge base on a card cake board. Spread the rest of the jam over the sponge. Invert the bowl of ice cream on to the sponge and lift off the bowl and the clingfilm. Return the ice cream on its sponge base, uncovered, to the freezer.

11 To make the meringue, put the sugar and water into a saucepan and heat gently, stirring frequently, until the sugar has dissolved. Meanwhile, put the egg whites into a large heatproof bowl (or a free-standing electric mixer fitted with the whisk attachment) and whisk with an electric mixer (or in the free-standing mixer) until just frothy.

12 Once the sugar has dissolved, turn up the heat, put the sugar thermometer into the syrup and boil until it reaches 120°C. Now carry on whisking the whites until they are stiff. When the syrup has reached 129°C, remove the pan from the heat. Carefully pour the hot syrup on to the whites in a thin steady stream while whisking at full speed (take care not to splash yourself or the sides of the bowl). After all the syrup has been added, continue whisking until the meringue has cooled down to room temperature.

13 Using an off-set palette knife, quickly cover the whole dessert – ice cream and sponge – with a thin covering of meringue. Put it back in the freezer for 5 minutes while you fill the piping bag with the remaining meringue. Now quickly cover the whole thing with small piped 'kisses' – the flashes of jam will suggest a leaking of juice.

14 Use a kitchen blowtorch to tinge the top of each meringue kiss a golden brown. Return the dessert, uncovered, to the freezer and keep it there until ready to serve.

15 To finish, set the Alaska on a cake stand and decorate with fresh berries, mint and strawberry leaves, and flaked almonds. Serve immediately.

ESPRESSO CRÈME CARAMEL

For the best results, slow-cook the little custards in a roasting tin filled with hot water (a bain-marie), making frequent checks so the result is perfectly creamy.

MAKES SIX INDIVIDUAL PUDDINGS

For the caramel
100g caster sugar (white, not golden)
50ml water

For the custard
350ml milk
300ml double cream
4 tablespoons ground espresso coffee
75g caster sugar
pinch of salt
2 medium free-range eggs plus 3 yolks, at room temperature

6 x 150ml ramekins OR heatproof baking dishes; a roasting tin

1 To make the caramel, put the sugar and water into a small, heavy-based saucepan. Set over the lowest heat and leave until the sugar has completely dissolved, tilting the pan gently now and then. Turn up the heat so the syrup boils, then let it boil furiously until it turns a deep caramel colour – gently tilt and rotate the pan frequently so it colours evenly.

2 Immediately pour the caramel into the ramekins, dividing it equally. Quickly swirl each dish so the base is evenly coated. Set the dishes in the roasting tin and set aside.

3 Pour the milk and cream into a medium-sized saucepan. Add the coffee and bring to the boil, stirring constantly with a wooden spoon. Remove from the heat and leave to infuse for 15 minutes. Meanwhile, heat your oven to 150°C/300°F/gas 2.

4 Strain the coffee cream through a paper coffee filter or a fine tea strainer into a jug. Rinse out the saucepan, then pour the strained cream back in. Add the sugar and salt and stir over medium heat until the sugar has dissolved and the cream is steaming hot, but not boiling. Remove from the heat.

5 Put the whole eggs and the yolks into a bowl with a lip (or a wide-necked jug) and mix well with a wooden spoon. Pour on the hot coffee cream, stirring constantly. When thoroughly combined, pour into the ramekins to fill equally.

6 Place the ramekins (in the tin) in the heated oven. Pour hot water into the tin so it is half filled. Lay a sheet of foil loosely over the top to make a tent (don't let the foil touch the surface of the custards). Allow a baking time of 30–40 minutes but after 25 minutes check the custards at 5-minute intervals: they are ready if they wobble like jelly when you gently jiggle them – they shouldn't seem sloppy, but take care not to overcook.

7 Remove the tin from the oven. Leave the ramekins in the hot water for 5 minutes, then carefully lift out. Leave to cool before covering and chilling overnight (this allows the custard to firm up and for the caramel layer to turn into a thick sauce).

8 To serve, gently pull the custard away from the side of each ramekin with your fingertip, to loosen the custard and break the vacuum. To turn out, set an upturned small, deep plate on top of each ramekin, then hold them tightly together and turn over. Lift off the ramekin and serve immediately.

STICKY APPLE SPONGE PUDDING

This combination of caramelised apples, maple syrup and a light cinnamon sponge, layered and baked, is easy to make but hard to resist. Serve with extra maple syrup and/or some hot vanilla custard.

For the apple mixture
2 large Braeburn or other tart
    eating apples
25g unsalted butter
25g demerara OR golden
    granulated sugar
115g maple syrup

For the sponge mixture
115g unsalted butter, softened
115g caster sugar
2 medium free-range eggs, at room
    temperature, beaten to mix
115g self-raising flour
2 teaspoons ground cinnamon
75g pecan pieces (optional)

1 deep ovenproof pudding basin,
    1.25–1.5 litre capacity, greased
    with butter

1 Heat your oven to 180°C/350°F/gas 4. Peel and quarter the apples. Cut out the core, then cut into slices about as thick as a pound coin. Put the butter and sugar into a frying pan (preferably non-stick) and set over medium heat. Stir until the butter has melted, then turn up the heat and add the apples. Fry, stirring frequently, for 3–5 minutes until the apples are golden brown. Leave to cool for 5 minutes.

2 Measure the maple syrup into the prepared basin or dish and tilt to cover the bottom. Arrange half the apple mixture on top. Set aside while you make the sponge mixture.

3 Put the soft butter into a mixing bowl and beat until creamy with an electric mixer or wooden spoon. Add the sugar and beat until light and fluffy. Gradually add the eggs, a tablespoon at a time, beating well after each addition. Sift the flour and cinnamon into the bowl and gently fold in with a large metal spoon or plastic spatula. Fold in the pecans now if you are adding them.

4 Spoon half the sponge mixture into the baking dish on top of the apples. Cover with the remaining apples, then spread the rest of the sponge mixture evenly over the top.

5 Bake in the heated oven for 50–60 minutes until the sponge is golden and just firm when gently pressed in the centre. Serve hot with extra maple syrup and/or a jug of custard.

BLUEBERRY & LEMON BREAD PUDDING

Comfort food at its very best: fresh berries and plenty of lemon flavour added to a creamy yet light bread pudding with a crunchy topping. A pudding like this is a good way to use up slightly stale bread – like The Perfect Soft White Sandwich Bread on page 58 or the Hot Cross Bun Loaf on page 104, but also brioche, panettone or even baguette.

(like The Perfect Soft White Sandwich Bread on page 58 or the Hot Cross Bun Loaf on page 104)

SERVES SIX

4–6 thick slices slightly stale bread
200g blueberries
250ml double cream
250ml milk
finely grated zest of 1 large
    unwaxed lemon
5 tablespoons caster sugar
4 medium free-range eggs
icing sugar, for dusting

1 deep, 1-litre capacity baking dish;
    a roasting tin

1 If the bread crusts are hard and dry, trim them off; with softer breads (like brioche, Hot Cross Bun Loaf, panettone or white sandwich loaf) you may not need to do this. Cut the bread into 1.5cm cubes and put them into the baking dish to be sure you have enough to almost fill it. Tip the cubes out of the dish into a mixing bowl, then grease the dish with butter.

2 Add the blueberries to the bread cubes and mix well. Tip into the prepared baking dish.

3 Put the cream, milk, lemon zest, sugar and eggs into a wide-necked jug, or a bowl with a lip, and mix thoroughly with a hand whisk or plastic spatula. Pour the mixture over the bread and blueberries to almost fill the dish. Gently push the bread cubes under the surface of the liquid (they will bob up again but will become moistened). Leave to stand, at room temperature, for 2 hours so the bread can soak up liquid.

4 Towards the end of this time, heat your oven to 180°C/350°F/gas 4. Half-fill a roasting tin with cold water and set the baking dish in it. Carefully transfer to the heated oven and bake for about 1 hour until the top of the pudding is golden and crisp and the centre feels set when gently pressed.

5 Remove the baking dish from the roasting tin and leave to cool on a heatproof surface for about 15 minutes before dusting with icing sugar and serving.

TIP
If you don't have an immediate use for slightly stale bread, cut off the crusts and cut into thick cubes, then freeze. When you want to make a bread pudding, or need crumbs for stuffings and crumb coatings, you can remove as many cubes as you need; they thaw in minutes.

CELEBRATION RUM TORTE

Perfect for a summer party, this is a rather deceptive dessert – it looks like a substantial four-layer iced cake, but it's very light indeed, and slightly tipsy as it's subtly flavoured with rum. There is quite a lot of work here, but all the elements can be made in stages, well in advance, and the assembled cake benefits from a few hours in the fridge.

For the sponge layers
6 medium free-range eggs,
  at room temperature
good pinch of salt
200g caster sugar
2 medium navel oranges (see recipe)
185g plain flour

For the crème pâtissière
250ml creamy milk
3 medium free-range egg yolks,
  at room temperature
50g caster sugar
1½ tablespoons cornflour
1 teaspoon finely grated orange
  zest (see recipe)
150ml whipping cream, well chilled
1 tablespoon dark rum

For the rum syrup
100g caster sugar
2 tablespoons orange juice
  (see recipe)
100ml water
2 tablespoons dark rum

For the rum cream
250ml whipping cream, chilled
3 tablespoons caster sugar
1 tablespoon rum

2 x 20.5cm round, deep sandwich tins,
  greased with butter and base-lined*

1 Heat your oven to 180°C/350°F/gas 4. Start by making the sponges. Separate the eggs, putting the whites into a large, spotlessly clean, grease-free mixing bowl, and the yolks into another bowl. Add a pinch of salt to the whites and whisk with an electric mixer until they stand in soft peaks when the whisk is lifted out of the bowl. Gradually whisk in half the sugar to make a light meringue. Set the bowl to one side.

2 Add the rest of the sugar to the egg yolks. Finely grate the zest from both oranges into a small bowl. Halve one orange and squeeze the juice. Keep the second orange whole for now. Add a rounded teaspoon of the grated zest and 6 tablespoons of the juice to the yolks (save the rest of the zest and juice for the other elements of the torte). Starting on low speed – to avoid splashes – and then increasing speed as the mixture thickens, whisk until it becomes very thick, light and mousse-like, and will fall in thick ribbons from the whisk when it is lifted from the bowl (see the Baker's Guide page 9 for more information about whisking to the 'ribbon stage').

3 Fold in the meringue in 3 batches using a large metal spoon or plastic spatula. Sift the flour on top and delicately but thoroughly fold into the mixture. Divide the mixture equally between the prepared tins and spread evenly. Bake in the heated oven for about 25 minutes until the sponge is golden brown and springs back when gently pressed in the centre.

4 Remove the tins from the oven and set on a heatproof surface. Run a round-bladed knife around the inside of each tin to loosen the sponge. Leave to cool and firm up for 5 minutes, then turn out on to a wire rack and peel off the lining paper discs. Leave the sponges until cold. (If you are not using the sponges right away they can be kept in an airtight container for a day.)

5 While the sponges are baking and cooling, make the crème pâtissière. Heat the milk in a heavy-based saucepan until steaming hot but not boiling. Remove from the heat. Put the yolks, sugar, cornflour and a rounded teaspoon of the saved grated orange zest into a heatproof bowl and beat well with a wooden spoon for a couple of minutes until lighter in colour and very smooth. Stir in the hot milk until thoroughly combined.

6 Pour the mixture back into the pan (no need to rinse it) and set over medium heat. Stir constantly until the custard thickens and boils. Remove from the heat. Wash and dry the heatproof bowl, then pour the hot crème pâtissière into it. Press a piece of clingfilm on to the surface (to prevent a skin from forming). Leave to cool, then chill thoroughly for at least 2 hours (the crème can be kept in the fridge for up to a day).

7 Whip the chilled cream until it is thick and will stand in soft peaks. Whisk the chilled crème pâtissière until smooth. Whisk the rum into the crème, then fold in the whipped cream using a metal spoon. Cover and chill for 2 hours (it can be kept in the fridge for up to 12 hours).

8 For the rum syrup, put the sugar, 2 tablespoons of the saved orange juice and water into a small pan. Heat gently, stirring, until the sugar has dissolved, then bring to the boil. Simmer for 3 minutes. Remove from the heat and stir in the rum. Leave to cool. Cover and chill until needed (the syrup can be kept in a clean jam jar in the fridge for up to 2 days).

9 When ready to assemble, cut each sponge into 2 equal layers (see the Baker's Guide page 10 for how to do this). Brush all the cut surfaces with rum syrup.

10 Set one sponge layer, crust-side down, on a cake board or flat platter. Cover with a third of the crème pâtissière, then top with a second sponge layer, crust-side up, using the nick to line up the layers. Brush the top of the sandwiched sponge with rum syrup, then spread over half of the remaining crème pâtissiere. Add another sponge layer, crust-side down, and spread with the rest of the crème pâtissière. Top with the last sponge layer, crust-side up as before, and brush with any remaining rum syrup. Don't worry about the sides,

however messy they look now. Cover loosely, or put into a covered cake container, and chill for 4 hours (at this point the cake can be kept in the fridge overnight).

11 When you are ready to cover the cake, whip the chilled cream until it stands in soft peaks. Add the sugar and rum and whip for a further 2–3 seconds until thick enough to spread. Spread the rum cream evenly over the top and sides of the cake. Spend a few minutes making the sides as smooth as possible – leave the top slightly 'textured'. Cover as before and chill for at least an hour, and up to 12 hours.

12 Cut off the peel and all the white pith from the second orange using a very sharp knife, then cut the orange into the thinnest possible round slices. Cover and chill.

13 To serve, drain the orange slices on kitchen paper, then use to decorate the top of the cake. Sprinkle over any remaining grated orange zest and serve immediately.

TIP
Rather than decorating the torte with fresh orange slices, you could serve it with caramelised oranges.

LITTLE ORANGE SOUFFLÉ PUDS

These are the lightest and fluffiest of baked puddings. The whisked mixture is transformed in the heat of the oven to a just-set soufflé with a sauce underneath.

MAKES SIX INDIVIDUAL PUDDINGS

4 medium free-range eggs, at room
    temperature
good pinch of salt
90g unsalted butter, softened
150g caster sugar
grated zest of 1 large navel orange
60g plain flour
225ml freshly squeezed orange juice
    (from 1–2 large navel oranges)
225ml milk, at room temperature
500ml carton lemon or vanilla
    ice cream
icing sugar, for dusting

6 individual 250ml soufflé dishes OR
    deep ramekins, greased with butter;
    a roasting tin; a baking sheet, lined
    with baking paper

1 Heat your oven to 190°C/375°F/gas 5. Separate the eggs, putting the whites into a large mixing bowl and the yolks into another; set the yolks aside. Add the salt to the whites and whisk with an electric mixer until they stand in stiff peaks when the whisk is lifted from the bowl. Set on one side.

2 Add the butter, sugar and orange zest to the egg yolks, then add the flour and whisk (no need to wash the electric mixer beaters first) for about 2 minutes until the mixture is thoroughly combined and lighter in colour and texture.

3 Whisk in the orange juice on low speed – the mixture will look a curdled mess, but don't worry. Scrape down the sides of the bowl, then gradually whisk in the milk. The mixture will look even more curdled – again don't worry. Pour the yolk mixture on to the whisked whites and gently but thoroughly fold in with a large metal spoon or plastic spatula.

4 Divide the mixture evenly among the 6 prepared dishes. Set them in the roasting tin and put it into the oven. Pour very hot water (from the tap) into the roasting tin to half-fill it, then close the oven door. Bake for about 40 minutes until the puddings are well risen, golden and just firm (with a slight wobble) when you press the centre.

5 While the puds are baking, remove the tub of ice cream from the freezer and let it 'come to' on the worktop for a few minutes. Then, using a pair of kitchen spoons (the sort you use for eating dessert or cereal), scoop the ice cream into 6 small neat ovals and set them on the lined baking sheet. Return these, and the remaining ice cream, to the freezer.

6 When the puds are ready, quickly remove the dishes from the roasting tin, dust the top of each pud with icing sugar, drop a scoop of ice cream into the centre and serve immediately. Serve the rest of the ice cream separately.

GINGER & PEAR PUDDING

Here's a new, dramatic-looking twist on an old favourite – whole pears, stuffed
with walnuts, baked upright in a dark ginger sponge pudding. The sponge is made
by the melting method, like gingerbread, and quickly mixed. Choose just-ripe
pears that are short and squat (rather than tall and thin) for the best results.
The walnuts can be replaced with chopped stem ginger if you like.

SERVES SIX

225g plain flour
1 tablespoon ground ginger
1 teaspoon ground cinnamon
80g dark brown muscovado sugar
125g golden syrup
125g black treacle
125g unsalted butter, diced
150ml milk
1 teaspoon bicarbonate of soda
5 small pears (see above)
30g walnut pieces
1 medium free-range egg, at room
    temperature, beaten to mix
icing sugar, for dusting

For the butterscotch sauce
200g dark brown muscovado sugar
100g unsalted butter
150ml double cream
good pinch of sea salt

1 x 23cm springclip tin, greased with
    butter and base-lined*

1 Heat your oven to 180°C/350°F/gas 4. Sift the flour, ground
ginger, cinnamon and sugar into a mixing bowl. Make a well in
the centre.

2 Measure the golden syrup, black treacle and butter into a
small pan. Set over low heat and leave to melt gently, stirring
now and then. Meanwhile, heat the milk in another small pan
until it is warm but still feels just comfortable when you dip
your little finger in. Stir in the bicarbonate of soda and set
aside for now. Remove the melted syrup mixture from the heat
and leave to cool to lukewarm.

3 While the melted mix is cooling, peel the pears, leaving the
stalks attached. Using the tip of a small knife, the end of a
peeler or a grapefruit knife, carefully remove the core from
each pear, working from the base end. Trim the base so the
pear stands upright without wobbling, then stuff the hollow
with walnuts (making sure the pear still stands upright).

4 Now make up the sponge mixture. Pour the melted syrup
mixture into the well in the flour. Add the just-warm milk
mixture and the beaten egg. Working quickly, mix everything
together with a whisk or wooden spoon to make a smooth,
thick batter. Pour it into the prepared tin.

5 Place the pears in the sponge mix, arranging them so they
stand upright, stalks up, and are evenly spaced. Bake in the
heated oven for 50–60 minutes until the sponge is risen and
firm, and a skewer inserted in the centre comes out clean.

6 Meanwhile, make the sauce. Put the sugar, butter and cream
into a medium-sized non-stick saucepan and heat gently until
the butter melts. Bring the mixture to the boil, then simmer
gently, stirring now and then, for about 5 minutes until thick
and toffee-coloured. Remove from the heat, stir in the salt and
keep hot.

7 Run a round-bladed knife around the inside of the tin to
loosen the sponge, then unclip the side. Serve the pudding
warm, dusted with icing sugar and with the sauce. Any
leftovers can be eaten like a cake, cut in thick slices.

RICHARD

....

Where do you live?
North West London.

What do you get up to when you are not baking?
I'm a builder by day. In my spare time, I like fly-fishing, sea-fishing, gardening, walking the dog and most of all spending time with my family.

How would you define yourself as a baker?
I have been baking all my life, pretty much, but much more since becoming a dad. I am fairly traditional, but I do like to cook with things I've grown myself.

Why do you enjoy baking?
I enjoy it because I can lose myself in it. I find it really relaxing.

What is the trickiest bake you've ever mastered?
Filo pastry – in fact I am still trying to master it!

What are your favourite 3 items of kitchen equipment?
Stand mixer.
Mini off-set palette knife.
Silicone spoon.

RICHARD'S
BLACK FOREST CHOCOLATE FONDANTS

▼▼▼▼▼▼▼▼▼▼▼▼▼▼▼▼▼▼▼▼▼▼▼▼▼▼▼▼▼▼▼▼▼▼▼▼▼

Very dark and very rich! Tart fresh cherries are an excellent complement to the intense chocolate fondant: they are added to the little puddings, filled and dipped in chocolate for the decoration, and used to flavour the whipped cream accompaniment.

MAKES SIX INDIVIDUAL PUDDINGS

For the cherry coulis
250g fresh, dark red or black cherries, pitted and halved
1½ tablespoons granulated sugar
2 teaspoons lemon juice

For the fondant mixture
12 fresh, dark red or black cherries, pitted
1 tablespoon cherry brandy
300g dark chocolate (about 75% cocoa solids), chopped
200g unsalted butter, diced
4 large free-range eggs, at room temperature
4 large free-range egg yolks, at room temperature
110g caster sugar
75g plain flour
2 tablespoons cherry coulis (see above)

For the chocolate cherries
12 fresh, dark red or black cherries, with stems
75g dark chocolate (about 75% cocoa solids)
1½ tablespoons double cream, at room temperature

1 Start by making the coulis. Put the cherries into a medium-sized pan and add the sugar, lemon juice and 1½ tablespoons water. Stir over low heat until the sugar has dissolved, then turn up the heat so the mixture is boiling gently. Cook, stirring occasionally, for 5–10 minutes until the cherries are very soft. Tip into a food processor and blitz to make a smooth purée. Press through a sieve into a bowl, then cover and keep in the fridge until needed.

2 To make the chocolate fondant mixture, put the cherries into a small bowl and add the cherry brandy. Leave to macerate until needed. Put the chopped chocolate and butter into a heatproof bowl, set over a pan of steaming hot water (don't let the base of the bowl touch the water) and melt gently, stirring occasionally. Remove the bowl from the pan and set aside to cool until needed.

3 Put the whole eggs and yolks into a large mixing bowl (or a free-standing electric mixer fitted with the whisk attachment). Add the sugar and whisk with an electric mixer (or in the free-standing mixer) for about 4 minutes until the mixture is very thick and mousse-like and will make a ribbon-like trail when the whisk is lifted from the bowl (see the Baker's Guide page 9 for more information). Slowly whisk in the melted chocolate mixture. Sift the flour on to the mixture and carefully fold in with a large metal spoon or plastic spatula.

4 Spoon enough of the chocolate mixture into the prepared pudding moulds to half fill them. Drain the macerated cherries (save the liquid for the chocolate cherry filling) and add 2 cherries to each pudding mould. Stir the chilled cherry coulis, then spoon a teaspoon of coulis over the cherries in each mould (cover the remaining coulis and return it to the fridge). Spoon the rest of the chocolate mixture on top and spread evenly – the mixture should be about 1cm below the rim of the mould. Cover with clingfilm, then set the moulds on the baking sheet and chill for at least 30 minutes or until ready to bake (the moulds can be prepared up to 4 hours ahead).

For the cherry cream

200ml double cream, well chilled
cherry coulis (see page 293), well
  chilled
icing sugar, for dusting

6 small pudding moulds, 175–200ml
  capacity, about 8cm across the top
  and 5cm across the base, greased
  with butter, base-lined and dusted
  with cocoa powder (see TIP page
  268 for how to do this); a baking
  sheet; a small disposable piping bag

▼▼▼▼▼▼▼▼▼▼▼▼▼▼▼

5 Meanwhile, prepare the chocolate cherries. With the tip of a small sharp knife, carefully slit open each cherry at the side and remove the pit – keep the cherry as intact as possible; set aside. Chop up 25g of the dark chocolate and melt gently in a small heatproof bowl, as on page 293. Remove the bowl from the pan and, using a hand wire whisk, whisk in the cream and the reserved cherry brandy (from macerating the cherries for the fondant mixture).

6 Set the piping bag in a mug or small jug (don't snip off the tip) and pour the chocolate mixture into it. Leave until the chocolate has thickened up enough to pipe and to hold a shape without running, then snip off the end of the bag. Pipe the mixture into each cherry, through the slit in the side, to fill the cavity and to 'glue' the cherry back into shape. Set the cherries on a plate lined with baking paper and chill for about 20 minutes until firm.

7 Meanwhile, chop up and melt the remaining chocolate in a small heatproof bowl, as on page 293. Remove the bowl from the pan. Holding each cherry by its stalk, dip it in the melted chocolate to coat thoroughly. Put back on the lined plate and chill for about 30 minutes until set.

8 To make the cherry cream, whip the cream in a mixing bowl just until it stands in soft peaks. Gently fold in the rest of the chilled cherry coulis. Spoon the cream into a serving bowl, cover and keep in the fridge until ready to serve.

9 When ready to bake, heat your oven to 180°C/350°F/gas 4. Uncover the moulds and bake in the heated oven for 11–15 minutes until slightly risen and the top no longer looks raw and damp – the mixture in the middle of the surface will still be slightly soft. Quickly turn out on to serving plates and dust with icing sugar. Decorate each plate with 2 chocolate cherries and serve immediately, with the cherry cream.

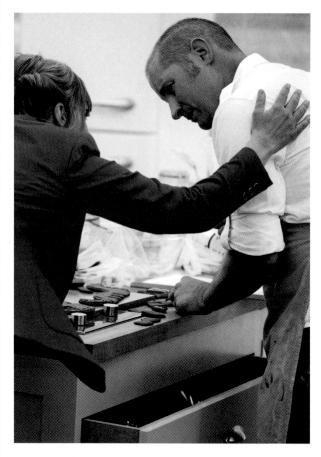

FLOURLESS WALNUT TORTE

There's plenty of flavour in this lovely summery dessert. Ground toasted walnuts make a moist, rich sponge that is filled with fresh apricots and whipped cream.

> MAKES ONE MEDIUM CAKE

For the sponge

350g walnut pieces
130g caster sugar
1 teaspoon baking powder
6 medium free-range eggs,
  at room temperature
good pinch of salt

For the sauce

225g raspberries
3 tablespoons icing sugar

For the filling

125g apricot conserve
2 teaspoons almond liqueur
150ml whipping or double cream,
  well chilled
2 large, ripe apricots
icing sugar, for dusting

2 x 20.5cm round, deep sandwich tins,
  greased with butter and base-lined*

1 Heat your oven to 180°C/350°F/gas 4. Tip the walnuts into an ovenproof dish and toast in the oven for 6–8 minutes until lightly browned. Leave to cool. Reduce the oven temperature to 170°C/325°F/gas 3.

2 Put the cold nuts into a food processor. Add 1 tablespoon of the weighed sugar and the baking powder, and 'pulse' to make a fine powder. Set aside.

3 Separate the eggs, putting the whites into a large, spotlessly clean and grease-free bowl and the yolks into another mixing bowl. Set the yolks aside. Add the salt to the whites and whisk with an electric mixer until they stand in stiff peaks. Set aside.

4 Add the remaining sugar to the yolks and whisk for 3–4 minutes until the mixture is very thick and mousse-like and leaves a distinct ribbon-like trail when the whisk is lifted (see the Baker's Guide page 9). Sprinkle the ground nuts over the yolk mixture and gently fold in with a large metal spoon or plastic spatula. Fold in the whisked whites in 3 batches.

5 Divide the mixture between the prepared tins and spread evenly. Bake in the heated oven for 25 minutes until the sponges are golden and have started to shrink away from the side of the tin; they should spring back when gently pressed in the centre.

6 Transfer the tins to a heatproof surface. Run a round-bladed knife around the inside to loosen each sponge, then leave to cool and firm up for 5 minutes. Turn the sponges out on to a wire rack and peel off the lining paper. Leave until cold.

7 To make the sauce, purée the berries with the icing sugar in a food processor. Press through a sieve to remove the seeds, then transfer to a jug.

8 To finish, set one sponge crust-side down on a serving platter. Mix the conserve with the liqueur and spread over the sponge. Whip the cream until it stands in soft peaks, then spread on top of the conserve. Halve the apricots, discard the stones and cut into thin slices. Arrange evenly over the cream. Top with the second sponge, crust-side up. Finish with a dusting of icing sugar. (If not serving immediately the torte can be kept in an airtight container in the fridge for up to 3 hours.)

HAZELNUT & SUMMER BERRY ROULADE

Sweet and crunchy meringue, perfectly ripe berries and thick cream make for the perfect summertime dessert. Ground toasted hazelnuts, which you'll find on supermarket shelves, really boost the flavour of the meringue to complement the fruit. For a glamorous finish the roulade is decorated with dipped strawberries: half covered in a glossy raspberry coulis, the rest in melted chocolate – tempered for a glossy sheen.

SERVES EIGHT

For the meringue
4 medium free-range egg whites,
    at room temperature
1 teaspoon lemon juice
225g caster sugar
1 teaspoon cornflour
100g ground toasted hazelnuts

For the filling
250ml whipping cream OR crème
    fraîche, well chilled
250g mixed berries (your choice
    of raspberries, ripe strawberries,
    dessert blackberries)

For the coulis
250g raspberries
65g caster sugar

To decorate
200g strawberries with stalks attached
50g dark chocolate (about 70% cocoa
    solids) OR white chocolate, melted
    or tempered (see page 9)

1 Swiss roll tin, 20 x 30cm, greased
    with oil; baking paper

1 Heat your oven to 150°C/300°F/gas 2. Cut a sheet of baking paper (NOT greaseproof) 24 x 34cm and press it into the oiled tin so it sticks to the bottom and sides. Smooth out any creases and press the paper firmly and neatly into the corners.

2 Put the egg whites and lemon juice into a spotlessly clean mixing bowl – any spots of grease will prevent the meringue from gaining its full volume. Whisk with an electric mixer until the whites form stiff peaks when the whisk is lifted out of the bowl.

3 Mix the sugar with the cornflour. Gradually whisk into the whites, a heaped tablespoon at a time, to make a stiff and glossy meringue. Sprinkle the ground nuts over the meringue and very gently and delicately fold in with a large metal spoon or plastic spatula, using as few strokes as possible. When just combined, spoon the meringue mixture into the prepared tin and gently spread evenly, right into the corners.

4 Bake in the heated oven for about 45 minutes until the meringue is risen, golden and firm to the touch – it will still be slightly soft in the centre. To make sure the meringue bakes evenly it's a good idea to rotate the tin after 30 minutes.

5 Set a sheet of baking paper on the worktop and turn out the meringue on to it. Lift off the tin, then leave the meringue to cool for about 5 minutes before carefully peeling off the lining paper. Leave until thoroughly cold.

6 While the meringue is cooling, whip the whipping cream until very thick – thick enough to spread but not quite at the stiff peak stage. (You don't need to whip the crème fraîche.) Remove the stalks from the strawberries, and quarter or halve so they are roughly the same size as the raspberries. Gently mix the berries together.

7 Spread the cream evenly over the meringue to within 2cm of one long edge. Scatter the berries on top, then roll up the roulade from the other long side: guide the roll into shape with

one hand and with the other pull up the paper to support the meringue. Once the meringue has become a roulade, wrap the paper firmly around it to hold it in shape. Set on a baking sheet or board and chill for at least an hour – up to 4 hours if possible – to firm up.

8 Meanwhile, make the raspberry coulis. Put the berries and sugar into a food processor and blitz to make a thick purée. Press through a fine sieve into a bowl to remove the seeds.

9 Wipe the strawberries for decoration, leaving the stalks attached. Set a sheet of baking paper on the worktop. Holding each berry by the stalk, dip half of them in the coulis to lightly coat, then set on the baking paper; they will remain glossy (and tacky) for up to 4 hours. Dip the rest of the strawberries in the melted chocolate, letting the excess chocolate drip off, and leave to set on the baking paper. Pour the rest of the coulis into a serving jug, cover and chill.

10 When ready to serve, unwrap the roulade and set it on a serving plate. Decorate the top and sides with the dipped strawberries and serve with the raspberry coulis.

TIP
If you don't have a Swiss roll tin you can make your own case for the meringue from a 24 x 34cm sheet of parchment-lined foil. Set this foil-side down on a baking sheet, then fold in the edges to make a base 20 x 30cm. Raise the edges so they stand vertically, pinching them together at the corners, to resemble a Swiss roll tin.

TIP
To make your own ground toasted hazelnuts, heat your oven to 180°C/350°F/gas 4, then toast 100g unblanched (unskinned) hazelnuts in a baking dish or tin for 6–8 minutes until golden. Leave to cool before grinding in a food processor with the teaspoon of cornflour (rather than adding this to the sugar as in the recipe above).

MARBLED MOCHA CHEESECAKE

A heavenly smooth and creamy chocolate cheesecake, this is spiked with coffee to offset the richness. The mixture is easy to make in a food processor. For the best results, leave the baked cheesecake to chill overnight – the flavours will develop and it will slice neatly.

MAKES ONE LARGE CHEESECAKE

For the base
75g unsalted butter
180g dark chocolate digestive biscuits (11 or 12)

For the filling
2 teaspoons instant coffee (powder or granules)
2 teaspoons boiling water
1 tablespoon coffee liqueur (e.g. Kahlua)
200g dark chocolate (about 70% cocoa solids), finely chopped or broken up
700g full-fat cream cheese, at room temperature
275g caster sugar
125ml soured cream, at room temperature
1½ teaspoons vanilla extract
3 medium free-range eggs, at room temperature

1 x 23cm springclip tin, greased with butter; a baking sheet

1 Heat your oven to 150°C/300°F/gas 2. Start with the base. Melt the butter, pour into a mixing bowl and leave until cool but still liquid. Crush the biscuits in a food processor (or by putting them in a plastic bag and bashing with a rolling pin). Tip the biscuit crumbs into the butter and mix well, then tip them into the prepared tin. With the back of a spoon, press the crumbs, fairly firmly, on to the base and about 1.5cm up the side of the tin to make an even layer. Chill for 10 minutes.

2 Set the tin on the baking sheet and bake for 10 minutes. Remove from the oven and leave to cool while you make the topping. Leave the oven on.

3 Dissolve the coffee in the boiling water in a small heatproof bowl, stirring well. Stir in the coffee liqueur. Leave on one side until needed.

4 Put the chopped chocolate into a heatproof bowl and set it over a pan of steaming-hot but not boiling water (don't let the base of the bowl touch the water). Melt gently, stirring now and then until smooth. Remove the bowl from the pan and leave to cool.

5 Meanwhile, put the cream cheese, sugar, soured cream, vanilla and eggs into the bowl of a food processor and process until smooth, scraping down the sides of the bowl from time to time. (The ingredients can also be mixed in a large bowl with a wooden spoon or plastic spatula, or electric mixer on low speed.)

6 Remove the processor bowl and pour 450ml of the mix into a measuring jug. Add the coffee mixture to the jug and stir well. Set aside.

7 Set the processor bowl back in place and add the cool but still liquid chocolate mixture. Process just until combined – the mixture will stiffen fairly rapidly (it will be much, much thicker than the coffee mixture).

MARBLED MOCHA CHEESECAKE CONTINUED...

8 Spoon half the chocolate mixture on to the biscuit base in the tin and spread evenly. Pour the coffee mix on top. Using a tablespoon measuring spoon, or a large kitchen teaspoon, drop the rest of the chocolate mixture into the tin in a random fashion. With the tip of a small sharp knife or a chopstick, gently swirl the 2 mixtures to marble them – don't over-mix or the effect will be spoiled. Gently tap the tin on the worktop to dislodge any air bubbles.

9 Place the tin, still on the baking sheet, in the heated oven and bake for about 1 hour until the cheesecake is just set with a slight wobble. Turn off the oven, open the door so it is just ajar and leave the cheesecake inside to cool for 15 minutes.

10 Remove from the oven. Run a round-bladed knife around the inside of the tin to loosen the cheesecake, then leave until cold. Cover with clingfilm and chill overnight before unclipping the tin and serving.

GINGER TUILE SABAYON BASKETS

You need to work quickly to shape these thin biscuits into cups, because they firm up after only a few seconds out of the oven. The result is impressive though. The delicate tuile baskets are filled with a light and foamy ginger sabayon, finished with summer berries.

MAKES EIGHT

For the tuiles
1 medium free-range egg white,
  at room temperature
60g caster sugar
30g unsalted butter, melted
  and cooled
30g plain flour
$\frac{1}{2}$ teaspoon ground ginger

For the sabayon
4 medium free-range egg yolks
4 tablespoons caster sugar
5 tablespoons white wine
  (or leftover sparkling wine)
1 tablespoon ginger syrup
  (from the jar of stem ginger in syrup)
1 lump stem ginger, finely chopped

For the topping
350g mixed berries (raspberries,
  small strawberries, blueberries,
  loganberries, dessert blackberries)
icing sugar, for dusting

1 baking sheet, lined with baking paper

1 Heat your oven to 180°C/350°F/gas 4. To make the tuile mixture, put the egg white into a clean, grease-free bowl and whisk with an electric mixer or rotary hand whisk until the egg white stands in stiff peaks when the whisk is lifted. On low speed whisk in the sugar, a tablespoon at a time. Fold in the butter with a plastic spatula or metal spoon. Sift the flour and ginger into the bowl and gently stir in.

2 Spoon a flat tablespoon of the mixture on to the lined baking sheet and spread to a thin, even disc about 11cm across. Bake for about 5 minutes until pale gold with darker edges – start checking after 4 minutes as the biscuit will be hard to shape if it gets too dark.

3 Set the baking sheet on a heatproof surface and immediately start to loosen the biscuit with a palette knife. As soon as you can, slip the knife under the biscuit, lift it off the sheet and drape it over a small inverted brioche mould or small orange. Gently press the biscuit over the mould to shape it into a bowl. The biscuit will harden in seconds. Carefully remove it from the mould and turn it upright.

4 Repeat with the rest of the mixture – once you've got the knack you can bake 2 biscuits at a time. If a biscuit becomes too firm to shape, return it on the sheet to the oven for a few seconds to soften. Store the shaped tuiles in an airtight container in a dry spot so they stay crisp. The mixture will make 10 tuiles, to allow for breakages.

5 You need to make the sabayon just before serving, so have everything ready and to hand. Put the yolks, caster sugar, wine and ginger syrup into a large heatproof bowl. Set over a pan of gently simmering water (don't let the base of the bowl touch the water) and whisk with an electric mixer or hand whisk for about 7 minutes until the mixture is very thick and mousse-like and will make a ribbon-like trail on its surface when the whisk is lifted out of the bowl.

6 Remove the bowl from the pan and continue whisking until the sabayon is barely warm, then stir in the ginger. Set 8 tuile baskets on a serving platter and spoon the sabayon into them. Quickly top with the berries, dust with icing sugar and serve.

MARY'S TIRAMISU CAKE

SERVES NINE

For the sponge
4 large free-range eggs
100g caster sugar
100g self-raising flour

For the filling
1 tablespoon instant coffee
150ml boiling water
100ml brandy
3 x 250g tubs full-fat mascarpone
   cheese
300ml double cream
3 tablespoons icing sugar, sifted
75g dark chocolate
   (36% cocoa solids), grated

To decorate
100g dark chocolate
   (70% cocoa solids), broken up
2 tablespoons cocoa powder

1 Swiss roll tin, 35 x 25cm, lined with
   baking paper; an 18cm square
   loose-based cake tin; a small
   paper piping bag; thermometer

1 Heat your oven to 180°C/350°F/gas 4.

2 To make the sponge, put the eggs and sugar in a large bowl and whisk together with an electric mixer until the mixture is very pale and thick and will leave a light trail on the surface when the whisk is lifted. This will take about 5 minutes. Sift the flour over the whisked mixture and fold in gently using a metal spoon or plastic spatula, taking care not to over-mix.

3 Pour the mixture into the prepared Swiss roll tin and tilt the tin to level the surface. Bake in the heated oven for 20 minutes until risen, golden and springy to the touch. Cool in the tin for 5 minutes before turning out on to a wire rack to cool completely.

4 For the filling, dissolve the coffee in the boiling water and add the brandy. Set aside to cool.

5 Put the mascarpone cheese in a large bowl and beat until smooth. Gradually beat in the cream and icing sugar to make a spreadable frosting.

6 When the sponge is cold, carefully slice it horizontally in half, so you have 2 thin sponges of equal height. Using the loose base of the square cake tin as a guide, cut 2 squares from each thin sponge. Discard the sponge trimmings.

7 Line the base and sides of the square tin with baking paper. Set one sponge square in the base. Spoon a quarter of the coffee mixture evenly over the sponge to moisten, then spread a quarter of the frosting over the sponge. Scatter a third of the grated chocolate over the frosting. Lay a second sponge square on top, moisten with coffee mixture and cover with frosting as before. Scatter over another third of the grated chocolate. Repeat with the third sponge, coffee mixture and frosting and scatter over the remaining grated chocolate.

8 Place the fourth sponge on top and spoon over the remaining coffee mixture. Using a palette knife, spread a very thin layer of the remaining frosting over the top of the cake – this is called a 'crumb coat' and will seal in any loose crumbs of sponge. Then wipe the palette knife and spread the rest of the frosting over the cake in a thicker layer. Chill for at least 1 hour in the fridge.

9 Meanwhile, melt 50g of the broken-up chocolate in a small heatproof bowl set over a pan of gently simmering water.

Gently stir the chocolate until it reaches a melting temperature of 53°C. Remove the bowl from the pan. Add the remaining 50g broken-up chocolate and continue stirring gently until the chocolate cools to 31°C or lower and is thick enough to pipe.

10 Spoon the melted chocolate into the small paper piping bag. Snip off the end. Pipe 9 – or more, just in case some break – decorative shapes (fleur de lys, for example) on to a sheet of baking paper or a silicone mat. Leave to set until required.

11 Dust the top of the chilled cake with the cocoa powder before turning out on to a serving plate – use the lining paper to help lift the cake out of the tin. Decorate with the chocolate shapes.

SIGNATURE BAKE

PAUL'S CHOCOLATE VOLCANOES

unsalted butter and cocoa powder for the moulds
165g dark chocolate (70% cocoa solids), chopped into small pieces
165g unsalted butter, cut into small pieces
3 medium eggs
3 medium egg yolks
85g caster sugar
2 tablespoons plain flour

6 small pudding moulds

1 Grease the pudding moulds with butter and dust the insides with cocoa powder. Chill for 30 minutes.

2 Gently melt the chocolate and butter in a heatproof bowl set over a pan of simmering water. Remove the bowl from the pan and stir until the chocolate mixture is smooth.

3 Combine the eggs, egg yolks and caster sugar in a bowl. Using an electric mixer, whisk together for several minutes until thick, pale and mousse-like in consistency. Carefully fold in the chocolate mixture, then fold in the flour, trying not to knock any air out of the mix.

4 Divide the chocolate mix equally among the 6 prepared moulds. Place in the fridge and chill until firm. (You can make the puddings up to 24 hours in advance and leave them in the fridge until you are ready to cook them.)

5 Heat your oven to 200°C/400°F/gas 6. Place the moulds on a baking sheet and bake for 8 minutes until the puddings are risen but not cracked.

6 Turn out the puddings on to individual plates and serve, with pouring cream.

SHOWSTOPPER
MARY'S NEAPOLITAN BAKED ALASKA

1 litre vanilla ice cream
1 litre strawberry ice cream
1 litre chocolate ice cream
mixed berries, to decorate

For the sponge base
2 large eggs
50g caster sugar
30g self-raising flour
20g cocoa powder
20g butter, melted

For the meringue
225g caster sugar
90ml water
4 large egg whites
pink gel paste colouring
yellow gel paste colouring

1 x 3-litre freezer-proof pudding bowl, lined with clingfilm; a 20cm sandwich tin, base-lined*; a large disposable piping bag fitted with a 2D star tube

1 In a large bowl or free-standing electric mixer, beat the vanilla ice cream to soften it a little, then spoon into the base of the pudding bowl. Level with a spatula. Freeze for 1 hour until firm.

2 Next, beat the strawberry ice cream to soften a little, then spoon it over the vanilla ice cream in the pudding bowl. Level with a spatula and freeze for 1 hour until firm.

3 Meanwhile, make the sponge. Heat your oven to 190°C/375°F/gas 5. Put the eggs and sugar in a large bowl and beat at full speed with an electric mixer until the mixture is pale in colour and thick enough to just leave a trail when the whisk is lifted.

4 Sift the flour and cocoa powder over the surface of the mixture and gently fold in with a metal spoon or plastic spatula. Pour the butter down the side of the bowl and gently fold in.

5 Turn the mixture into the prepared sandwich tin and tilt the tin so the mixture spreads evenly to the sides. Bake in the heated oven for 10–12 minutes until springy to the touch and beginning to shrink from the side of the tin. Turn out the sponge on to a wire rack and leave to cool.

6 Now beat the chocolate ice cream to soften a little. Spread it over the strawberry ice cream in the pudding bowl. Level with a spatula and freeze for 1 hour until firm.

7 Place the now cold sponge on an ovenproof serving dish. Turn out the layered ice cream (still wrapped in clingfilm) on to the sponge, then return it to the freezer while you make the meringue.

8 Heat your oven to 240°C/475°F/gas 9. Put the sugar and water in a heavy-based saucepan. Stir over medium heat until the sugar dissolves, then bring to a fast boil and boil until the sugar syrup reaches 110°C.

9 Now whisk the egg whites in a free-standing electric mixer until stiff. When the syrup temperature reaches 115°C, slowly and carefully pour the syrup over the whisked whites in a thin stream, taking care not to let the syrup run on to the whisk. Continue whisking for about 15 minutes until the meringue is completely cold.

10 Take the cake and ice cream from the freezer and remove the clingfilm. Using a palette knife, spread a thin layer of meringue over the ice cream and sponge to form a coating.

11 Using a paintbrush or small pastry brush, paint a line of pink gel paste up the inside of the piping bag, in a line from the tube to the top. Repeat on the opposite side of the bag with the yellow gel paste. Spoon the meringue into the piping bag.

12 Starting from the top of the dome of ice cream and working quickly, pipe small rosettes of meringue over the ice cream dome until it is completely covered.

13 Bake in the heated oven for 4–5 minutes until the meringue is tinged golden brown. Decorate with mixed berries and serve immediately.

INDEX

ACKNOWLEDGEMENTS

BBC Books and Love Productions would like to thank the following people for their invaluable contribution to this book.

Linda Collister, Norma Macmillan, Susanna Cook, Maeve Bargman and Allies Design, Andrew Barron and Thextension, Kristin Perers (and Ben, Emma and Ben), Annie Rigg (and Kathryn and Laura), Annie Hudson (and Olivia), Lizzie Kamenetkzy, Jo Harris, Juliet Sear, Clare Sayer, Kathy Steer, Hilary Bird, Anna Beattie, Samantha Beddoes, Andy Devonshire, Chloe Avery, Jake Senior, Hannah Griffiths, Helen Cawley, Mark Drake, Becca Watson, Georgia May, Faenia Moore, Rupert Frisby, Emma Willis, Jamie McIntosh, Simon Antoniw, Jonathan Scrafton, Jules Richardson, Jo Penford, Mark Bourdillon and Debby and James Puxley and all at Welford Park.

Thank you to Mary Berry and Paul Hollywood for contributing their recipes and also to the amateur bakers: Chetna, Claire, Diana, Enwezor, Iain, Jordan, Kate, Luis, Martha, Nancy, Norman and Richard.